Praise for *Young Leaders 3.0*

"It's trite to say that our future depends on the education of our next generation. But Jason Ma's *Young Leaders 3.0* demonstrates how youngsters striving to make a difference can help their peers become the leaders of the next generation, and there's not a trite lesson or suggestion in any of the stimulating chapters. As the chair of a university board, I'm always impressed by the motivation, idealism, and potential of the many student leaders whom I meet. Jason's stories of the young leaders rendered and his concluding advice in this book provide invaluable guidance, example, and direction for any ambitious youngster who aspires to lead and have a disproportionate impact in the decades ahead."

—**Paul Tagliabue**, chairman of the Board of
Directors, Georgetown University, and commissioner,
National Football League (NFL) 1989-2006

"Jason L. Ma's book, *Young Leaders 3.0*, is a tour de force. This book is not only extremely helpful in guiding young people but also advantageous for parents and any adults, both young and old. A classic in the making."

—**Narayana Murthy**, founder and former chairman
and CEO, Infosys, listed as one of "The 12
Greatest Entrepreneurs of Our Time" by *Fortune*
Magazine in 2012

"Jason Ma's *Young Leaders 3.0* is a must-read for aspiring teenagers and young adults. Period. By bringing to light first-hand stories of leading students and budding entrepreneurs, and reflective advice from them, he offers hard-won guidance for the big decisions that high school kids, college students, and young professionals and entrepreneurs face today. Highly recommended!"

—**Heidi Roizen**, operating partner, Draper Fisher
Jurvetson (DFJ), and lecturer, Stanford University

"*Young Leaders 3.0* by Jason L. Ma should be informally required reading for all students. As one of the top-rated public high schools in the United States, Lowell High gets what it means to be achievers. This extraordinary and unparalleled book teaches students on how to reflect on their own successes, failures, mistakes made, and lessons learned, and to realize their own potential beyond the transcript, the SAT, the résumé. Students must take advantage of this practical and inspirational resource!"

—**Andrew W. Ishibashi**, principal, Lowell High School, San Francisco, California

"Jason Ma's new book, *Young Leaders 3.0*, exemplifies the most basic principles of great teaching and management. Simply put, narrative is how we learn, and great writers and leaders are great storytellers. Bridging gaps between generations requires telling stories that tease out causes and effects, so that readers can identify with and understand the players. While this is certainly a great book for aspiring young leaders, it also offers senior managers delightful insight into the thinking of the next generation. Global success in the 21st century will require both the new and enlightened thinking of young professionals and entrepreneurs as well as the guidance and wisdom of seasoned leaders. This book serves to get the synapses firing between both generations and acts as a catalyst for a future that starts with passion, education, entrepreneurship, and an informed passing of the torch to a new generation of leadership."

—**Jonathan Rosenberg**, former senior vice president of products, Google, and author of *How Google Works*

"Inspirational and authentic! Different from so many other books that focus on getting into college or starting a career, *Young Leaders 3.0* covers the most transformational years in a young adult's life—that pressurized, stressful, intimidating, confusing, and uncertain time before, during, and immediately following college. How refreshing it is to experience and learn from and with an exciting group of promising young adults as they navigate this transition from teenagers into young adults. It is a journey Jason Ma helps numerous individuals successfully navigate, including my own son, through his personal mentorship. Now his experience and the personal stories of these remarkable young women and men will help guide and inform others."

—**Don Levy**, president and cultivator, Smith Brook Farm and former senior vice president of marketing and communications, Sony Pictures

"Whether you are a high school student, university student, young professional, parent, or senior executive, you shouldn't wait to pick up this exceptional and enriching leadership book. This masterpiece will inspire and benefit you. The real stories told are heartwarming and thought-provoking. Author Jason Ma's observations on success patterns and habits and his concluding actionable advice can be applied by just about anyone from early teens to middle-aged adults. My very strong recommendation for *Young Leaders 3.0*!"

—**Peter Liu**, founder and chairman of WI Harper Group
and member of the Committee of 100

"In all my years as a large public high school principal, I have never seen any other nonfiction book that is as inspiring and practical for high school students as *Young Leaders 3.0*. Jason Ma takes readers on a highly engaging and exciting journey through the minds and spirits of interesting youth leaders as they reflect on childhood, high school extracurriculars and achievements, college admissions, the transition into college, college life, and beyond. This exceptional book is a must-read for all young achievers as well as parents and educators."

—**Grettel Castro-Stanley**, principal, Independence High
School, San Jose, California

"What a great book for young people about to venture out on their own. With such thoughtful and generous advice from peers to guide them through the high school, college, and early career years, *Young Leaders 3.0* is a critical resource for future leaders. I wish I'd had such a resource when I was first starting out."

—**Keith Ferrazzi**, author of the NY Times Best Sellers
Never Eat Alone and *Who's Got Your Back*

"The strength of this book comes from students and young professionals speaking from the heart as they convey their own personal and often painful experiences growing up, navigating the awkward adolescent years, and striving to achieve in college and afterward. Through their life experiences and personal growth, many have been inspired to take positive steps to give back. I can imagine that young people (and parents) reading this book would benefit from and be inspired by the stories of hardship, the importance of failure as a motivator and life lesson, and the general message to not give up. A great resource!"

—**Muhammed Chaudhry**, president and CEO, Silicon
Valley Education Foundation

"Not since Amy Chua's *Battle Hymn of the Tiger Mother* landed on bookshelves has there been a global mentoring book more certain to become a major best seller for years to come than Jason L. Ma's *Young Leaders 3.0*. While equally thought-provoking as Chua, Ma focuses on education and careers. Eschewing irony and remaining in the background, Ma shines a light on the young women and men striving to become tomorrow's leaders, allowing them to tell their own stories, which are authentic, engaging, and entertaining all at once. Each account shimmers with extraordinary insights and accomplishments. This book is a must-read for ambitious high school and college students, young professionals and entrepreneurs, and their parents."

—**Clark Kepler**, owner and former CEO of Kepler's
Books for 33 years

"*Young Leaders 3.0* is a groundbreaking repository of insight and life advice from an impressive cohort of young visionaries and change makers. The inspiring storytelling contained in this work instills actionable advice that is accessible to a wide range of readers, especially those who face many unanswered questions about college, career choice, and their impact on the world. I wish I had this book as a resource to better align my inner résumé of core values with my paper résumé earlier in my personal and professional growth. Mr. Ma's incredibly useful insights derive from his rich experience mentoring students and from his ability to leverage what distinguishes each student to help navigate his or her personal success story."

—**Carolyn Yang**, senior at Princeton University's
Woodrow Wilson School of Public and
International Affairs

"*Young Leaders 3.0* is a groundbreaking book that focuses on the ground floor of how leaders emerge. The millennial generation is filled with inspiring individuals who are tackling real challenges, but they rarely get the recognition and exposure to share their stories with the world. Jason Ma's work is especially important in guiding and directing attention to young leaders who are actually solving problems. This book establishes these young leaders as role models who will inspire generations to come."

—**Alex Fiance**, CEO, Kairos Society

"Very rarely are we exposed to transformative and transparent guidance from young adults and students. Jason L. Ma's *Young Leaders 3.0* explodes on the scene, sharing the advice and voices of the next generation. This book profiles some of the best and brightest minds through an unfiltered and unbiased lens, illustrating the great lengths young people are taking to create their own desired paths. Jason Ma continues to connect the proverbial dots of education, entrepreneurship, and youth leadership through cutting-edge messaging that transports us around the globe and to the kitchen tables of cultures far and wide."

—**Dr. Rod Berger**, education media personality and
thought leader

"Jason Ma's *Young Leaders 3.0* is an outstanding treasure trove that showcases inspiring success stories among young people. It is a book about hope, dreams, dedication, courage, ingenuity, and conviction. The collection of real life stories highlights essential traits of leadership that are required to think through and implement change in a meaningful way. It is a book about young leaders, but the insights and teachings are applicable and relevant for all ages. *Young Leaders 3.0* is a truly inspiring must-read for anyone who wants to develop or enhance leadership capabilities!"

—**Martin Roll**, business and brand strategist at Martin
Roll Company, advisor to Fortune 100, lecturer at
leading global business schools, and author of *Asian
Brand Strategy*

"To all teenagers and twentysomethings out there: YOU are the next generation of leaders. Let Jason Ma and the inspirational stories in *Young Leaders 3.0* give you the tools to navigate these transitional years, to identify your passions, to set lofty goals, and to chase them successfully. This enlightening and fun-to-read book can change your life positively and powerfully."

—**Abbe Wright**, contributing editor at *Glamour*
Magazine, in charge of the 2015 Top Ten College
Women competition

"Jason Ma is a visionary in the education industry, and his new book, *Young Leaders 3.0*, provides the best guide available to help the next generation of young leaders plan their strategies for success in life. Jason not only provides his unique perspective and guidance on how to access prestigious colleges and jobs but also has tapped some of the best examples of millennial students to share their own experiences in defining their customized paths to realize their dreams. These students from across the globe share their unique insights in each chapter, yet by combining these stories into one unique book, Jason ultimately defines the "DNA" needed to be successful in a complex world. I strongly recommend this book to all students looking to define their own paths as future leaders!"

—**Paul W. Bradley**, chairman and CEO of Caprica
International, vice chairman of Supply Chain Asia,
and one of the 40 "New Asian Leaders" of the World
Economic Forum in 2004

"Every once in a while a book is published that can dramatically alter the course of a person's life. *Young Leaders 3.0* is such a book. It provides rare insight into what it takes to lead and succeed in this world. From getting into an Ivy League school, to landing that first great job, to starting a business, to making a positive and significant impact in the world we live in, the inspiring stories and pragmatic information in this book will become a treasured resource that you will refer to time and time again."

—**Howard VanEs**, president, Let's Write Books, Inc., and
author of 19 books

"*Young Leaders 3.0* is the definitive global guidebook to early career success—either professional or entrepreneurial. An original and invaluable resource for the coming-of-age generation and their parents alike, Jason Ma's book is a wellspring of encouragement, example, insight, and phronesis (practical wisdom). Any student or parent who takes this anthology's advice to heart is bound to prosper, both in exercising laudable virtues and in attaining worthy aspirations."

—**Lou Marinoff**, PhD, professor of Philosophy at the
City College of New York, founding president of the
American Philosophical Practitioners Association, and
author of *The Power of Tao, Plato Not Prozac*, among
other books

YOUNG LEADERS

3.0

Stories, Insights, and Tips for Next-Generation Achievers

JASON L. MA

YOUNG LEADERS 3.0 PRESS

Young Leaders 3.0
Stories, Insights, and Tips for Next-Generation Achievers

Jason L. Ma

Published by Young Leaders 3.0 Press

ISBN: 978-0-9909734-7-8

Library of Congress Control Number: 2014919955

Cover design by Irving Torres, Young And CEO
Interior design by Let's Write Books, Inc.

Version 1.1
www.youngleaders3.com/#updates

To Lydia, Sabrina,
all you teenagers,
twentysomethings,
and parents

Contents

Act I: Freshmen, Sophomores, and Juniors

Act II: Seniors on the Threshold

Act III: Seniors Stepping into the World

Act IV: Graduated and Making Their Way

Act V: One to Two Years in the World and Advancing

Introduction

Why and How Does This Book Help You?

Becoming a leader and rising as one require pragmatic EQ–
emotional, social, and leadership intelligence. The good news is that
you can raise yours and keep honing it.

—Jason L. Ma

Welcome to *Young Leaders 3.0: Stories, Insights, and Tips for Next-Generation Achievers!* You are about to embark on a journey through the minds and transformations of a diverse group of twenty-three exemplary young leaders. This book tells their personal stories, including their successes, failures, and lessons learned along the way.

Their reflections, pieces of advice, and personal visions are combined with my own analysis and nuggets of wisdom. For more than eight years, I have served as a mentor to numerous high-achieving students and young adults, a confidant to parents, and a business and education thought leader.

These young adults have shown me the extent of what is possible and have challenged my own outlook on life. I hope that they will inspire and challenge you as well, and encourage you to apply some of the lessons they learned to your own life. Happy reading!

WHAT IS THIS BOOK ABOUT? HOW DOES IT BENEFIT YOU?

This book is the culmination of years of my focus—learning from a wide array of amazing people, mentoring talented individuals, and reflecting on my own successes and lessons learned. In my work mentoring students and young leaders over the past eight years, I have recognized patterns in their approach to life, school, and work that have inspired me. This book identifies and suggests new models and paths that these young leaders have paved.

I have been privileged to see what inspired these people to become leaders in their fields, and I would like to share with you how they think, act, and wish to change the world. Their stories go beyond standardized test scores such as the SAT and the GRE, academic performance, and résumés, to reveal a more human and multifaceted view of individuals. I have designed this book to be especially helpful to teenagers and young adults in school or venturing into the world.

Teenagers and young adults: Learn from these young leaders' experiences, advice on high school and college activities and achievements, and definitions of success. They also reflect on college admissions, the transition into college, college life, summer activities, internships, and leadership development. Gain a rare look into their secrets for career planning and, just as importantly, their valuable insights into managing failure.

Parents and business executives: Discover what the next generation of leaders is thinking and how they wish to change our future. Learn how you can support them. Take parenting for success to the next level. Understand what leadership education is really all about.

The majority of these twenty-three featured young leaders have been (formally or informally) my mentees. I have helped them develop successful habits, skills, and strategies, and guided many of them through the college admissions process. I have also shared insightful information with the other featured individuals from afar. In addition to this introductory chapter and the epilogue, elements of my teachings and advice are (subtly) communicated through many of these chapters.

Please note that this book is but a small sampling of thought-provoking high achievers; it is not a definitive list. I realize that countless other people worldwide with various experiences would also be worthy of inclusion in this book, but it would be impossible for me to embark on such an inclusive endeavor. I nonetheless hope that this small group of young adults will enable you to learn from their—and my—experiences.

HOW TO READ THIS BOOK

I have set aside one chapter for each of the twenty-three contributing young leaders. In each of these twenty-three chapters, the first page displays the contributor's name, chapter title, degree, school, and short biography; the second page is where her/his story begins. In each chapter, I intentionally keep my observations, lightly shaded in the background, to a minimum so that the individual's authentic voice fully comes through. Each chapter concludes with a perfectly imperfect (perfectly fine being imperfect!) takeaway on the person.

Here is the good news: you don't have to read this entire book to gain a lot from it. If I were you, I would (1) finish this introductory chapter, (2) select from the featured young leaders who tickle your fancy (see tips below) and read their chapters, and (3) read the epilogue chapter on success patterns seen and concluding advice.

Or, if you love learning and find it adventurous (like me), then read all twenty-three!

If you feel time-pressed and want to read only chapters of the select young leaders who interest you, there are two methods that I'd suggest:

Method 1: Select by chapter title, life stage, and/or school
Read about the young leaders by chapter title, life stage, and/or school that interests you. The following table shows the following about each of the twenty-three young leaders:
- Name—one chapter per individual
- Chapter title (slogan)—a core part of her/his identity and passions
- Life stage—college freshman, sophomore, junior, senior on the threshold ("Senior I"), senior stepping into the world or working already ("Senior II"), graduated this year and making their way ("Graduate"), and one to two years in the world and advancing ("1–2 Years Out")
- School—currently attending or graduated from this college

	Name	Chapter Title (Slogan)	Life Stage	School
1	Sabrina Ma	Kindness Kid from Silicon Valley	Freshman	Georgetown
2	Danny Levy	Outdoor Educator and Environmental Ambassador	Sophomore	Colgate
3	Felipe da Paz	Brazilian Golfer Turned Entrepreneur	Junior	USC

	Name	Chapter Title (Slogan)	Life Stage	School
4	Shreya Indukuri	Sustainability Designer	Junior	Dartmouth
5	Erica Ma	Diplomat Building Bridges of Peace	Senior I	Penn
6	Ivy Xing	Lonely Child to Geeky Girl	Senior I	Bowdoin
7	Kimberly Han	Filmmaker Dreaming of the Oscars	Senior I	UChicago
8	Youyang Gu	Wall Street Hacker	Senior I	MIT
9	Jeremy Fiance	Relentlessly Resourceful Master of None	Senior II	UC Berkeley
10	Max Song	Gritty Data Scientist	Senior II	Brown
11	Sophie Mann	Strategic Planner from NYC	Senior II	Columbia
12	Angela Wang	Long Mohawk	Graduate	UCLA
13	Enrico Bonatti	Citizen of the World	Graduate	Cornell
14	Leila Pirbay	Anthropologist from Madagascar	Graduate	Harvard
15	Ngan Pham	Happily Depressed Two-Time Dropout	Graduate	UC Berkeley
16	Ryan Mango	Midwest Wrestler Chasing Olympic Hopes	Graduate	Stanford
17	Sally Zhang	Truth-Seeking Journalist	Graduate	Northwestern
18	Tim Hwang	Government Innovator	Graduate	Princeton
19	Timothy Lee	Unconventional Engineer	Graduate	UC Berkeley; Georgia Tech
20	Chris Pruijsen	Nomadic Entrepreneur	1–2 Years Out	Oxford
21	Kemaya Kidwai	Wildlife Buff and Consulting Newbie	1–2 Years Out	Yale
22	Patrick Ip	Digital Entrepreneur	1–2 Years Out	UChicago
23	Sonia Agarwal	Gandhian Innovator	1–2 Years Out	Babson

The perfectly imperfect, diverse mix of my contributors can be summed up as follows. I am being sincere and am using the words they use to describe themselves:

- 17-to-24-year-olds
- All four college undergraduate grade levels, recent grads, and well into the real world

- 17 Americans, both US-born and immigrant (African, Caucasian, Chinese, Indian, Korean)
- 1 Brazilian, 2 Europeans, 1 Italian-Indo-Malagasy, 2 South Asians now back in India
- Faiths (or lack thereof): Buddhist, Catholic, Christian, Hindu, Jewish, Muslim, secular
- Fields and industries of interest (past, present, and aspirational): athletics; banking and finance; business; consulting; education; entrepreneurship and innovation; environment and nature; fashion; international; law; medicine; media and entertainment; NGO; politics; professional sports; public service; science, technology, engineering, and math (STEM); social engineering; venture capital
- 20 top universities and colleges in the United States, public and private, plus Oxford in the United Kingdom.
- Languages: English, Arabic, Chinese, Dutch, French, German, Gujarati, Hebrew, Hindi, Italian, Korean, Malagasy, Portuguese, Spanish, Telugu, Vietnamese
- Hair colors: Black, dark blond, brown/brunette (I'm kidding here!)
- 12 women, 11 men

Method 2: Select by fields or industries, or type of learning environment

Read about the young leaders by the fields, industries, or school types that interest you. Some of these achievers fall into multiple categories because of their varied involvements in and outside of class. The names in each category are listed from the youngest to the eldest, not in alphabetical order. Here it goes:

Athletics	Danny, Felipe, Jeremy, Angela, Ryan, Sally, Kemaya, and Sonia
Banking and Finance	Youyang and Enrico
Business	Sabrina, Felipe, Shreya, Jeremy, Kimberly, Max, Sophie, Enrico, Leila, Ngan, Ryan, Sally, Tim, Chris, Kemaya, Patrick, and Sonia
Consulting	Sophie and Kemaya
Education	Angela, Ngan, Leila, Tim, and Kemaya
Entrepreneurship and Innovation	Sabrina, Felipe, Shreya, Jeremy, Kimberly, Max, Ngan, Leila, Tim, Timothy, Chris, Patrick, and Sonia
Environment and Nature	Danny, Felipe, Shreya, Kemaya, and Sonia
Fashion	Sonia

International	Sabrina, Felipe, Erica, Ivy, Jeremy, Kimberly, Max, Enrico, Leila, Ngan, Ryan, Sally, Tim, Chris, Kemaya, Patrick, and Sonia
Law	Erica, Sally, and Tim
Medicine	Danny and Ngan
Media and Entertainment	Kimberly and Sally
NGO	Sabrina, Danny, Shreya, Angela, Enrico, Leila, Ngan, Chris, Kemaya, Patrick, and Sonia
Politics	Erica, Tim, and Patrick
Professional Sports	Felipe and Ryan
Public Service	Sabrina, Felipe, Shreya, Erica, Angela, Ngan, Leila, Tim, and Patrick
Science, Technology, Engineering, and Math (STEM)	Sabrina, Danny, Felipe, Shreya, Ivy, Jeremy, Kimberly, Max, Sophie, Youyang, Enrico, Leila, Ngan, Ryan, Tim, Timothy, Chris, Patrick, and Sonia
Social Engineering	Sabrina, Danny, Felipe, Shreya, Erica, Leila, Ngan, Tim, Chris, Patrick, and Sonia
Venture Capital	Sabrina, Jeremy, and Tim
Public universities—Georgia Tech, Oxford, UC Berkeley, and UCLA	Jeremy, Angela, Ngan, Timothy, and Chris
Ivy League universities—Brown, Columbia, Cornell, Dartmouth, Harvard, Princeton, UPenn, and Yale	Shreya, Erica, Max, Sophie, Enrico, Leila, Tim, and Kemaya (This book covers young leaders from all eight Ivies)
Private universities and colleges other than Ivies—Babson, Bowdoin, Colgate, Georgetown, MIT, Northwestern, Stanford, UChicago, and USC	Sabrina, Felipe, Danny, Ivy, Kimberly, Youyang, Ryan, Sally, Chris, Patrick, and Sonia

WHAT FURTHER DROVE ME TO WRITE THIS BOOK?

In today's society, we all more or less enjoy our share of pleasures from achievements, wins, great relationships, certainty, finding our voice and applying it constructively, boosts in confidence and identity, growth, and a variety of goodies personal to each of us.

But, we oftentimes experience the pains of being uncertain and fearful, feeling beleaguered or overwhelmed, having poor connections/relationships, experiencing insignificance, disempowerment, drift, purposelessness, entropy, and other limiting emotions or states of mind. These come from all the pressures, stresses, information overload, bad (in)decisions from false assumptions or limiting beliefs, miscommunications, misdirection, tangible losses, opportunity costs, subpar skills, poor strategies, ineffective execution, lack of guidance or preparation, mistakes made, and/or failures in our daily lives.

As a parent, mentor, and entrepreneur who senses a higher purpose, I want to help uplift and inspire people—especially young people, who have far more choices these days than they can imagine but who often lack direction—to significantly reduce time/energy-sapping pains and add meaningful gains and pleasures. An efficient and convenient way to achieve this goal is through this book.

My mission is to enhance and perhaps even transform the minds of young people around the world. I hope to see an exciting world in which a dynamic global network of my mentees, students, and readers will shine as value-added, good-hearted leaders and citizens around the world.

WHY DID I TITLE THE BOOK *YOUNG LEADERS 3.0?*

I wanted to refresh, reset, or redefine what becoming and serving as a young leader really means today and in the foreseeable future. While many "2.0" phenomena and ideas (for example, Web 2.0) have added value to the world, it may be time for 3.0, including youth leadership. I believe that *Young Leaders 3.0* reflects an innovative way of thinking and doing while being mindful of our basic human needs and wants.

"Movie making is about character, story, and production," says Don Levy, my friend and former senior vice president of marketing and communications at Sony Pictures. "A catchy title is also important." Imagine this book as a movie. It radiates the character and story of each of the twenty-three wonderful souls with varied backgrounds, interests, dreams, and aspirations, combined with my occasional perspective. We are all passionate about living, connecting, learning, giving, growing, and playing. In this book, vivid storytelling abounds.

"I love you more than the biggest number in the whole wide universe and more than that! Go, Dad . . . go work on *Young Leaders 3.0!*" my younger daughter said to me as her big brownish-black, beautiful eyes pierced my soul. Now a high school freshman, she influenced me and helped me decide on the book's title.

May your journey through this book be meaningful, adventurous, and fulfilling!

Cheers and Godspeed,

JASON L. MA
Author and Founder
YOUNG LEADERS 3.0
www.YoungLeaders3.com

Act I
Freshmen, Sophomores, and Juniors

1

Sabrina Ma

Kindness Kid from Silicon Valley

BS in Foreign Service with major in Science, Technology, and
International Affairs and minor in Computer Science, Class of
2018, Georgetown University School of Foreign Service

Sabrina Ma is an enthusiast of underground hip-hop, iPhone photography, and social entrepreneurship. To help alleviate her peers' and her own stresses and angst, Sabrina founded the Acts of Random Kindness Club (ARK) when she was a fourteen-year-old high school sophomore. She led building ARK to 250+ members, one of the largest clubs at her school, and inspired the formation of ARK clubs at more than thirty high schools across California and beyond. In recognition of her work's influence, the Random Acts of Kindness Foundation, a nonprofit that is the US delegate to the World Kindness Movement, made and released a video documentary about ARK.

While interning at the Singapore Kindness Movement in the summer before her high school senior year, Sabrina spoke to 6,000 Singaporean secondary school students about her "crusade for kindness" and helped initiate "social media for social good" campaigns. This past summer, Sabrina held two internships, one at Back to the Roots, a start-up, and another at Stanford University School of Medicine's Center for Compassion and Altruism Research and Education (CCARE). She is currently a freshman at Georgetown University.

> *Human beings are complex, multifaceted entities who simply cannot be described in 500 words or less.*
>
> —Sabrina Ma

Yes! Sabrina Ma is my eldest daughter, now seventeen. I must admit that my wife and I at times wondered whether we had made the right decision to let Sabrina skip fourth grade and miss out on one year of childhood. Luckily, she turned out OK and has become a valued contributor to society. As the youngest member of my book's contributor team, Sabrina has begun her college freshman year and is humbled and tickled to share her story here. I am very proud of her and all of my teammates for this book.

FAMILY

I am in the MAfia. No, not the mafia. The MAfia. Weaving together filial piety, liberal creativity, dark humor, unending love, and intellectual curiosity, the Ma family is beautifully dysfunctional.

My family rarely eats dinner together. The exceptions are Saturday nights, when my family resynchronizes, whether at a sushi bar, Italian restaurant, or California Pizza Kitchen. At my ever-changing dinner tables, playful knife-twisting is a norm. My parents' open-mindedness has allowed for brutal honesty and complete openness to brew during dinner conversations. Our weekly, humor-filled communion symbolizes that, in spite of my parents' workaholic schedules and the mounds of homework I must combat, the MAfia will always make time for one another.

As a teenager, when change seems to be constant, I cherish that my family has provided me with both the towering expectations and the unconditional support I have needed to thrive. From holding my dainty, four-year-old hands in the operating room as I got stitches to letting go of my manicured sixteen-year-old hands so I could independently venture to foreign countries, the MAfia may not be a criminal syndicate, but we do possess the mafia's strongest weapon: family-oriented faith, trust, and alliance.

HIGH SCHOOL

I've undergone a complete metamorphosis over the course of my high school career, evolving from an under-the-radar, raccoon-eyed girl to a social butterfly with a generally positive disposition. So many ingredients contributed to my transformation, but I owe it to especially my extracurricular activities. The following are the Common Application essay prompt and my response about the Acts of Random Kindness Club, the student organization I founded, during the college application season:

Some students have a background or story that is so central to their identity that they believe their application would be incomplete without it. If this sounds like you, then please share your story.

Inhaling the crisp morning breeze, I walk past the graffiti sprawled across the walls and etched into the windows. At my high school, ambition is scarce and gang activity abundant. Yet, in the midst of all the fights, litter, and vandalism, I have found an elixir: kindness.

"Join ARK!" I shout weakly, handing out ads I had made using Microsoft Paint. As Jade approaches me, I grin, handing her an ad. She scans the paper and grimaces: "You're in ARK? Why? That club is so stupid . . ." She walks away, carrying my pride with her.

My crusade for kindness began when I, an overstressed and mildly depressed sophomore, yearned to escape the doldrums. I noticed that many of my friends were undergoing similar adversities, from family problems to self-consciousness. Simply to lift my and other students' spirits, I established the Acts of Random Kindness (ARK) Club as a student organization at my large public high school.

But initially, ARK had the opposite effect. During meetings, I tried to compensate for my limited leadership skills by barking orders at my small, indifferent team of ten. The year droned on, and I frequented failure often, seeing ARK crafts littered on the ground and hearing remarks that ARK was a "stupid" or "dumb" club. My sinking feeling lingered—until I met someone who had actually reached the bottom.

"Here," he murmurs, shoving the pocketknife in my hands, his eyes darting to the ground. At that moment, myriad emotions dashed through my mind. Relief. Elation. Gratitude. My friend gave me the knife he had used to cut himself, a gesture indicating that his despondent days were over. The night before, I had offered him my shoulders to lean on and had listened to his concerns. Clutching the knife in my hand, I finally understood the potent power of small gestures. It was at that moment when I swore that I would not only be a true beacon of kindness, but also reform ARK and myself.

Starting my junior year, I completely changed the club's infrastructure. I stepped off my pedestal and elected board members, who would help plan and lead our activities every week. Facilitating debate and creative thoughts, ARK's leadership became a collaborative team effort. We also utilized social media to publicize activities and to share our updates with the general public. We collaborated with other student organizations and local businesses, magnifying our impact. By conducting an assortment of activities that catered to a target audience of the week (e.g., rainbow bracelets for LGBTQ club) or to the general student body (e.g., Finals Week Care Packages, Kindness Flash Mobs), we changed students' negative perception of ARK.

Today, ARK strives to make high school more pleasant for everyone. ARK has also massively changed me as a person. I was once an insecure teenager who lacked sleep, friends, and purpose. Through ARK, I have found happiness in making others happy and fulfillment by advocating for a cause that transcends age, race, and social hierarchy.

Through determination, resilience, and synergy, I have led ARK's growth to 250+ members. It is now a sprawling movement blossoming at over 30 high schools across California. Although simply a grassroots movement, ARK has nonetheless sparked a smile—or two.

I dream of founding a visionary venture to create products and services that will massively benefit communities worldwide. Whether my creations enhance the lives of individuals, families, enterprises, or governing bodies, I aspire to be a global leader who radiates compassion in all of my endeavors.

ARK's first meeting was in half a detention hall. Then we moved to a classroom. And then to an auditorium. And then, we seeped into schools across the State. Today, ARK is *my* world. But tomorrow and beyond, I will continue spreading the message of kindness across the *world* as a college student and ultimately global entrepreneur. Today, I may be recognized as the "Kindness Kid." But tomorrow, the "Compassionate CEO."

High school students: To start a club at a public school, you typically need to form an initial (founding) team, fill out a club constitution, find an advisor, and get the student government to approve the club idea.

One of Sabrina's college application essays also reflected on her travel and internship experiences in other countries, which sharpened her humility and oratory skills. The following is this essay.

"Come up with me during the Q&A and help me answer a few questions," says Dr. Wan, the General Secretary of Singapore Kindness Movement, in the taxi. "Okay!" I reply, feigning excitement but feeling terrified.

Last summer, I was the youngest-ever intern for an acclaimed NPO in a nation where the cost of living looms as high as the high-rises. With the Singapore Kindness Movement, I explored Singapore's secondary schools, enriching my global perspective at magnitudes beyond textbook-based learning.

Dr. Wan and I arrive at Raffles Girls' School (RGS), an elite Singaporean secondary school, to speak about our endeavors in kindness. On stage, tempests of anxiety rack my mind as I gaze at the sea of teenage girls, hundreds of pairs of eyes staring back at me. *Breathe, Sabrina, breathe.*

Then, a voice soars above the crowd: "There are so many looming global problems today. So, of all things, why did you choose to pursue kindness?" My passion enflamed, my courage bolstered, I respond, "I met a young girl who showed me the importance of giving despite not having."

I time traveled from Singapore to Ningxia, an underdeveloped province in China (where I had visited the previous summer). Sunrays licking my face, corn crop stroking my legs, I wandered through the field alongside the village girl. "For you," she whispers in Mandarin, handing me a handmade grass bracelet. "T-thank you so much," I stutter, my eyes welling with tears.

While interning for a microcredit platform the previous summer, I met the village girl. Despite her destitution, she was rich in generosity. She insisted that I eat first, gave me hand-woven gifts, and always wore a contagious crescent-moon-eyed smile. A quintessential friend and sparkling role model, the village girl emerged to the surface of my consciousness as I spoke onstage. I was determined to inspire the RGS girls as she had affected me.

After the talk, I spewed jubilance when students initiated kindness-related movements, read heartfelt thank-you messages with bleary eyes, and even received a few requests for my autograph. But, it was not the attention that made me happy. My true slivers of pride were from transcending ethnic barriers, disregarding the school's elite status, and unearthing a deep-rooted sense of empathy. The audience comprised driven teenage girls who were juggling teenage angst, rigorous academics, demanding extracurriculars, and towering expectations—but not always successfully. Just like *me*.

I have had role models (village girl from Yanchi included) who have helped me bloom throughout high school. So to hear shocked gasps flood the auditorium after mentioning I was sixteen years old and to be called "inspirational" and a "role model" by both Singaporean and American peers felt absolutely surreal. During my internship, I realized that it was my turn to play a role in the continuum of inspiration, not as some glorified goddess on a pedestal, but as a trustworthy friend, big sister, and humble leader.

From this tale of two regions, I have added a dash of Singaporean ambition, a spoonful of Yanchi-grown graciousness, and a cup of insatiable curiosity to my own recipe for cross-cultural understanding. Onstage, I revisited the Ningxia cornfield in my mind for a few seconds. Little did I know that I was actually in a field of my own, sowing seeds of oratory and maturity that would last me a lifetime.

Sabrina graduated from high school summa cum laude as a valedictorian. In high school, she was honored as a keynote speaker and/or panelist at multiple events, including a social media conference in Singapore, a women empowerment summit in Silicon Valley, and a TED-like event at UC Berkeley. She participated at the Yale Young Global Scholars Program during the summer before her senior year. She also founded her school's online Admiration Wall, which has enhanced school spirit in a different way, and inspired other schools to create their own Walls.

Sabrina applied to a range of private and public universities and received her share of acceptances and rejections. Why did she choose Georgetown?

Deciding where to spend the next four years of my life was a difficult struggle between name brand and fit. I was slightly skeptical about Georgetown, for it was a smidge less "prestigious" than some of the Ivy League schools to which I was accepted.

However, all my false assumptions vanished when I stepped onto campus. As a West Coast native and suburban girl, I yearned for a metropolitan, East Coast experience. I could see that living in Washington, DC, the nation's political hub and a corporate cluster, would be a fantastic experience because of foreseeable opportunities to seize invaluable internships and to build key relationships.

I loved Georgetown's Jesuit values—in particular, their deep adherence to service and advocacy of "men and women for others." These values were clearly reflected in the students I met. I also loved the campus culture and adored the alumni, faculty, and administrators whom I met. Finally, Georgetown's wealth of student organizations, including Girls Who Code and Startup Hoyas, and its brand-new Social Innovation and Impact Center (just erected a few months ago), left me in awe of the resources related to my passions, all within hand's reach.

Today, Sabrina has begun her freshman year in college. I've asked her to reflect on the following question:

To what extent has your post–high school experience met your expectations? In what ways did your experience cause you to change your perspective on your academic career, your dreams and aspirations, and your life?

I had a phenomenal, work-hard/play-hard summer. I served in two internships, one at the Stanford University School of Medicine's Center for Compassion and Altruism Research and Education (CCARE), and the other at Back to the Roots (BTTR), a start-up. BTTR's business incorporates social, environmental, and economic impact.

As an intern at these organizations, I was the youngest and least experienced person in the room, a circumstance that gave me a phenomenal learning environment. At CCARE, I had the opportunity to learn about the myriad psychological and physiological benefits of kindness, ranging from decreasing stress to fostering favorable gene-expression profiles in immune cells. Interning at BTTR allowed me not only to pick up professional skills, specifically business operations and marketing, but also to analyze my coworkers' synergy, problem-solving skills, and grit. While contributing, I also learned a great deal about myself; I find excitement in the dynamic days and constant innovation present in the start-up culture and I prefer team-based projects.

Now in college, I can safely say that my post-high school experience has been exhilarating. I have experienced my share of failures, rejections, breakdowns, inferiority complexes, and long caffeine-fueled nights. Yet, at the end of the day, I always fall asleep happy. I am grateful to serve on the Student Leadership Team at Startup Hoyas, the hub of entrepreneurship at Georgetown, and as communications co-chair of the Inaugural Student Impact Board at the Beeck Center for Social Impact and Innovation. I am also a Compass Fellow, part of a selected group of fifteen students who, with guidance from upperclassmen mentors, will learn the skills necessary to launch a social business by the end of the year.

In addition, I plan to major in science, technology, and international affairs (STIA) at the School of Foreign Service and minor in computer science because these programs align with my aspirations in technology, business leadership, and entrepreneurship.

Through my extracurriculars, social groups, and classes, I have met friends and mentors whom I do not deserve. With content, I look back on memories like discussing the "meaning of life" with my theology professor, running to the Washington Monument at midnight, and haphazardly searching up financial jargon on Investopedia during Georgetown's Venture Capitalist Investment Competition. Although I still have "what-am-I-doing-with-my-life" moments often, college has tested my limits in the best way possible, and I am excited to continue growing academically, socially, and spiritually.

Given what you know now, if you could redo high school, what would you do differently, and why?

STUDY LESS

The road to summa cum laude was arduous, requiring lots of trial and error, failure, and stress. During my sophomore year, I remember declining offers to hang out with friends, choosing to spend hours reading my textbooks for hours on end. It was inefficient and, frankly, miserable. What I mean by "study less" is "study more efficiently, thereby decreasing net time spent studying." Once I ditched rote memorization for more effective strategies, I rose out of my funk. There is no correct way to study, but I have personally found success through these strategies:

- During transition times, such as in waiting line or car rides, use Quizlet's smartphone app to review vocab.
- While taking notes, write the main topic in question format. For example, instead of the title being "The three branches of government," write "What are the 3 branches of government?" This way, while you review, you can quiz yourself by covering your notes and seeing if you can answer the question.
- While reviewing notes, pretend you are teaching a class. If you can articulate it, you have mastered it.

- Study in places with minimal distractions (distractions such as electronic devices, social networks, wailing younger siblings). My oasis was the public library.
- Study during your peak hours. For me, I did the work that required complete focus right after school, and random busywork late at night, so I could blast music.

I highly recommend the book *How to Be a High School Superstar* by Cal Newport for more insight on productivity and overall success in high school.

GO OUT MORE

From crashing tech entrepreneurship summits to attending microfinance conferences to vibing at EDM concerts, I now find excitement in flinging myself into the unknown. Experiential learning not only bolsters your interpersonal skills and street smarts but also opens opportunities. On several college applications, for example, I wrote an essay about a hip-hop festival I attended (please see * below). At TiEcon, a large technology entrepreneurship conference, I serendipitously bumped into a co-founder of Back to the Roots—and I ended up interning at his start-up this past summer.

In life, things are usually not handed to you. But sometimes, when you cast your fishing pole into uncertain waters, you'll get a bite. So go on late-night excursions. Find a cool hobby or learn a new skill. Go to interesting places and meet interesting people. In a decade, you won't be reminiscing about the nights you spent cramming for that midterm, but the crazy things you've done with the people you love or enjoy. Just never forget what your priorities—and, sometimes, moral code—are.

* The following is Sabrina's college application essay on hip-hop and its influence on her:

Wafts of cigarette smoke filling my lungs, rhythmic beats pulsing through my body, I negotiated through the lively crowd at Hiero Day, a festival commemorating the hip-hop group "Hieroglyphics." Among clusters of young adults, I saw elderly couples, scantily clad women, and rambunctious toddlers of every color and size. Oakland sunshine complementing the happy crowd, a common force transcended the concertgoers' differences in age, race, and socioeconomic background: hip-hop.

Delve beneath the "sex, money, and drugs" scene sprawled across MTV and one will discover underground hip-hop, the crossroad of folk culture and globalization. Hip-hop songs often include allusions to artists' local inner cities, yet, due to online marketing and the Internet's time-space compression, hip-hop has diffused across the world, uniting individuals from Nigeria to Brazil.

I find it meaningful that, instead of succumbing to gang violence or substance abuse, artists transpose their internal strife into mellifluous beats and meaningful lyrics. For example, one of my favorite songs, "Fly (Song of Liberation)" by Blu, provides commentary on the American Dream, human trafficking, drug addiction, and religious skepticism—in four minutes. Emanating resilience, hip-hop's creative cultivation has inspired me to pursue innovation thorough many mediums, including entrepreneurship.

A musically inept teenager whose #1 fan is her showerhead, I don't aspire to be a hip-hop artist. But, from delivering a rhythmic poem during my middle school valedictorian speech to rapping about Penicillin in my AP Biology class, I have surreptitiously expressed my love for this genre. Shown during the Hiero Day festival, amid the violence, poverty, and crime that taint cities like Oakland, hip-hop has served as stronghold against geopolitical turmoil for many—and as a beacon of inspiration for me.

What else would you like to share with or suggest to high school students and college students, and why?

ON PUBLIC SPEAKING

Early in high school, I was a terrible public speaker. When I spoke in front of audiences, my voice would tremble and my hands were fidgety. Nonetheless, I seized every opportunity to speak: in front of my classes, my church group, my family, my mirror. I watched historical speeches and TED talks alike, analyzing the orators' appearances and usage of rhetoric. After lots of practice, my public speaking skills improved, creating a multiplicity of benefits. Communication skills helped me mobilize hundreds of high school students every week during ARK meetings, as well as got me invited to be a speaker at conferences on social media and women's empowerment. But most important, communicating effectively has helped me gain some of my most valued friendships. Being able to articulate your thoughts may be just a soft skill, but it is extremely useful.

COLLEGE APPS

Some rapid-fire tips: Keeping journals, blogs, and other concrete mementos throughout your life helps you remember who you once were, who you are today, and who you want to be. While writing essays, sprinkling in vivid anecdotes helps illustrate stories. Avoid stuffing ornate SAT words into every sentence, thereby saving very busy and probably stressed admissions readers' time in looking them up in the dictionary. Explaining *why* something is important to you is often more important than *what* you actually did and *how* you did it because *why* reveals more about your values, beliefs, character, or motivations.

Above all, *don't procrastinate!* College planning should start early in high school. Start your college app process early, during the summer before the start of your senior year, if possible. It will take you dozens to more than 100 hours—over months, not weeks—to brainstorm, draft, and revise dozens of long and short college app personal essays (plus short takes), and your résumé, when applying to ten or more schools. This also includes asking for and getting input from friends, teachers, mentors, and parents (while keeping your voice intact)! Through this intense but interesting process, you will discover and learn a lot about yourself and maybe even improve your reflective thinking and writing skills.

Budget additionally more than 100 hours in purposefully researching colleges, preparing for the SAT or ACT with Writing and SAT IIs (if still not done by junior year), working with teachers, your school counselor, and any other non-school recommenders, attending college-related events, preparing for interviews, and taking care of whatever else is necessary to ensure you're submitting high-quality applications on time—all on top of your busy schoolwork and extracurricular activities.

Try not to take admissions rejections personally as I did. Admissions decisions can be a mysterious crapshoot. For example, I was rejected by Columbia, waitlisted at Harvard, and accepted at Dartmouth. Human beings are complex, multifaceted entities who simply cannot be described in 500 words or less. Acceptances or rejections—in regards to college admissions and life as a whole—should not and do not define you or your self-worth. Just try your absolute best and be yourself. If colleges can't see how awesome you are, they don't deserve you anyway.

A perfectly imperfect takeaway on Sabrina:

Having begun her freshman year at Georgetown, Sabrina says, "I am still a slightly melodramatic, super klutzy seventeen-year-old with a mild case of imposter's syndrome and an unhealthy obsession with milk tea. I no longer use test scores or acceptance letters or awards as metrics of success. Now, success means doing what I love, loving what I do, and significantly benefiting society. I have passed down the torch for the ARK Club and the other social ventures I started in high school, and am grateful the experiences and lessons learned there have strengthened my values and belief system. I aspire to be a globally influential business leader and/or entrepreneur who radiates compassion in all my endeavors . . . but after I survive my first year of college!"

1: SABRINA MA

2

Danny Levy

Outdoor Educator and Environmental Ambassador

BA in Biology or Geology (TBD), Class of 2017,
Colgate University

Surfer, diver, hiker, and skater Danny Levy grew up in Southern California, fascinated by the oceans and sea life. He developed his passion for the environment as a child and spent six summers between the ages of twelve and seventeen at the Catalina Island Marine Institute (CIMI) studying marine biology and meeting individuals who share his passion. His attraction to the deep blue pushed him to become a NAUI-certified scuba diver when he was only thirteen years old.

At Colgate University, he leads various trips through the Outdoor Education Program and helps his peers discover and experience nature. He is also a certified Wilderness First Responder, ready to aid people on trips and in the streets when needed. Danny brings his passion for the outdoors to the classroom and labs, where he studies biology and geology in Colgate's liberal arts setting. In his free time, he loves to witness beautiful sights with his friends. From mountaintops to the ocean floor, he is determined to understand, respect, protect, and preserve his true love: Mother Nature.

Among the distractions of life I always tend to forget what I truly want. But the minute I step into the woods I remember exactly who I am, what I want, and who I want to become.
—Danny Levy

Much of a young man's value system, which is core to his character, is shaped by his parents or family. Born and bred as a Southern Californian, Danny Levy reflects on his family and Jewish upbringing, and how they helped to shape him:

Neither my family nor I are particularly religious, in the regular go-to-services or strictly observant way. But my Jewish upbringing, however casual and Californian, shapes who I am and how I think. I was raised with certain morals, values, historical awareness, and traditions.

Be good, be honest, and work hard. The rest will come. These are words I heard, saw, and lived at home. I interpret "good" to encompass kindness, consideration, and respect. Honesty is integrity and being true to myself and others. Hard work is not so much about strain, struggle, and difficulty as it is about simply putting in the necessary time and effort to get things done.

When I was twelve years old and studying for my bar mitzvah, a Jewish coming-of-age ritual, I did not fully appreciate the significance of those preparations. Some view the event solely as a party—and I won't deny that we celebrated—but today I see that the words I studied helped me build my set of values.

I did not choose the Torah portion I read during my bar mitzvah: it was predetermined according to the calendar and the date on which my bar mitzvah took place. At first, the portion I read seemed pretty strange: it was about skin diseases and the removal of people from a community. But I learned much more about health, cleanliness, community, acceptance, ostracism, and restoration. It was not only about what it means to be part of a community—or removed from one—but what it means to *participate.*

This idea of participation has resonated with me since the day I became a bar mitzvah. At the time, I decided that I was going to invest my effort in helping the community by working with a charity that gave carts to homeless people. When I attended camp at Catalina I became a part of an amazing community by participating in countless scuba classes that taught each of my fellow divers and me the importance of the ocean. To become the best person I wanted to be, I've learned that I have to participate and become an active member of my community.

We've always been encouraged to keep our minds and eyes open and to be ourselves. For instance, one day during my junior year of high school I decided I was bored with my hair and shaved the sides off, causing my hair to resemble a golden pineapple. I wanted to do something that I felt would add to my personality, so I went for it.

I have always been encouraged to pursue my interests. As I grew more appreciative of the outdoors, my family and I would go on trail walks and spend time at the beach checking out tide pools. We'd go to the Aquarium of the Pacific in Long Beach, the Monterey Bay Aquarium, the Boston Aquarium . . . Then we learned from a family friend about the Catalina Island Marine Institute and my involvement in the Institute sealed my passion.

I follow the examples both my parents and older brother set. I see the effort and care they put into what they do, as well as their curiosity and love of learning. I've also seen them take some risks, deal with change, and follow their own interests. My mom just started a new career in her fifties and my dad is starting a new business. My brother has the guts to do stand-up comedy. We've lived relatively simply. They stress quality over quantity.

From my bar mitzvah, to my friends, to CIMI, and to my family, all these aspects of my life contribute to who I am today.

Danny cares about meaningful relationships, is loyal to close friends, and believes that his decisions reflect his value system. He reflected on an intense experience in which he tried hard to help a best friend to move away from a drug addiction and how that in turn affected him, on a personal statement when applying to college in his high school senior year:

Recollections of better days penetrate my consciousness as my car decelerates to a halt. The front door of the house is always unlocked, beckoning me to come inside and rescue him. I walk up familiar steps into a room that I have slept in a hundred times over. I am now a stranger here. Inside he sits—staring. What is next to him cuts my heart. Crushed up Xanax, a medication used to treat anxiety and panic disorders, and a rolled-up dollar bill stare at me. Pure disgust consumes me. I hate them. They are the cause of this. They have stolen my best friend.

I ask my friend how he is doing. He lies. I've known him for too long to fall for it. But I look at him and am hopeful. What else can I be? What our friendship meant to me cannot be justly defined through writing. He was the first person to express truthful empathy towards anything we talked about. He was the most genuinely good person I had ever met.

I lie restless in bed. It's 5 AM, and I haven't slept a minute. Thoughts race around my brain. Meaningless propositions cause me to give in to the demons of my subconscious. The world is collapsing in front of me, and I am helpless. The panic attacks have begun. They continue for the coming year. I need help.

Therapy was the next step. Dr. Lin was surprised to hear that the same anxiety that haunted my mother and grandfather was affecting me. After diagnosing me, Dr. Lin wrote a prescription for Xanax. I sat there and began to cry tears of anguish. I would not let the culprit that ruined my friend's life solve my problems. I would solve my problems in my own way.

I could only look at my friend's addiction created from his own anxiety and see it as the antithesis of how I was to control my own anxiety. I would maintain self-control and remain a positive person. I petitioned into honors classes, built my organizational skills, continued to play lacrosse, and used the beach as my place of peace. I focused on dealing with my problems head-on instead of looking for an escape. I felt that through my empathy and knowledge of the emotions he faced, I could inspire change in him.

I dedicated myself to end his pill addiction. For two years, I told him to stop, threw away his "medication," cried for him, prayed for him, talked to his parents, and talked to counselors and therapists. But everything was futile. He didn't want to change. I had to accept this eventually because I wasn't going to follow in his failure. I never gave up on him, but I learned a valuable lesson: change cannot be forced upon anyone—you have to want it.

He is doing better now but needs time. I love him and always will. I refuse to fail for the sake of our lifelong bond. I will succeed—for myself and for him.

Danny has always been passionate about uniting people and communities. He discussed this passion on a Colgate University application supplement short essay:

I am a uniter. I bring communities and people together through my personality and my passion for people. My skills as a uniter expand far beyond mere social interaction. Every year, upon returning from three-week sessions at the Catalina Island Marine Institute (CIMI), I would be motivated to share with my peers the amazing lessons, experiences, and knowledge that I had gained on the island. As an active member of the Surf Rider Foundation, I have brought together friends and acquaintances to clean beaches all along the northern Los Angeles coastline. As avid divers, my friend from CIMI and I engage in various shore dives to explore and clean the undersea kelp expanses of California.

At Colgate, I hope to share my passion for the ocean, the environment, and the earth's inhabitants with all whom I meet. I hope to unite a community of individuals who share my passion for the world around us through my studies, events, clubs, and by contributing to the Colgate community as a whole. In response, I hope that in my willingness to promote communal growth, others will follow suit and appreciate the compassion that I bring to the community I hope to gain insight on regions of the world that I am not familiar with and carry some of their values along with me on my path into adulthood.

In high school, Danny focused largely on his schoolwork, taking nine AP classes and achieving a 4.4 weighted GPA while playing lacrosse and water polo. He also participated in Mock Trial during his junior and senior years, which helped him become an effective public speaker. Through the Advancement Via Individual Determination (AVID) student leadership program, a program that allows high school students to mentor younger kids in the community, during his senior year, Danny spent much of his leisure time tutoring seventh- and eighth-graders at a nearby middle school.

Today, Danny is a sophomore at Colgate. I've asked him to reflect on the following question:

To what extent did your college experience—on and off campus—meet your expectations? In what ways did your experience cause you to change your perspective on your academic career, your dreams and aspirations, and your life?

TOOK A DETOUR (PRE-MED) BUT DETOURED BACK TO WHAT MAKES ME HAPPY (NATURE AND BIOLOGY)

No shirt, no shoes, plenty of sunblock. The sun is sweltering, but a cool breeze lifts my spirit. I hiked seven miles along my favorite trail for some solitude. Outdoors is where my free spirit lives, where anything is possible. On this day, I needed a place to think, to make sense of all that had passed and what might follow. "Now what?" I kept asking myself.

I was a senior just about to graduate from high school, accepted and committed to attend Colgate University in the fall, with the added freedom of a day off from rolling burritos at Chipotle. Atop Sandstone Peak, the pinnacle of the Santa Monica Mountains, I could look west to the horizon across the Pacific. To the north, the wilderness of the Channel Islands, and southward was Catalina Island, where I spent six incredible summers unlocking the mysteries of life underwater and making friends afield from high school. The suburbs of northwestern Los Angeles and eastern Ventura County fan out behind me in quilted geometric patterns of development across what was once farm and range. It's a place where houses look similar, where cars are new, and where almost everyone is on track for college and careers. Life seems as planned as the communities where we live. I'm a little less on track.

Atop Sandstone that day, I wasn't sure what to expect at Colgate. The Common App made it easy to apply to twenty schools. Only after acceptance letters arrived did my family and I invest in whittling the list and visiting the most interesting. Colgate was the second to last place we visited. I was exhausted from traveling cross-country and the pressure of having to make a big decision. But inside of an afternoon I felt "the fit." I could sense that it was a learning environment where I could explore.

I didn't plan to be a good student. I didn't calculate my high school résumé. I just liked to read and I'm curious. I'm interested in people, places, and things. I love to laugh. I like to do things and have fun. I went to class. I did my work. I got good grades—not valedictorian good, but solid. It's not that it was easy; I just knew how much I needed to work in order to succeed.

Colgate welcomed me with a wild social atmosphere and a competitive classroom setting. This definitely was not going to be like high school. I decided on Colgate because I wanted to be challenged on every level: intellectually, socially, and physically.

Those summers on Catalina sensitized me to nature. I've loved nature and the very idea of protecting it all my life. I left for Colgate ready to take on the world's problems and do my best to be a steward of the planet. I was up to the challenge, whatever it might be!

Colgate has an incredible outdoor education program, which I immediately joined. As I picked my classes for the first semester, I considered broadening my knowledge of science and its application from marine biology and environmental science to medicine. I remembered how Colgate structures its pre-med studies to encompass more than health science and has an outstanding track record for getting students into top graduate programs. I was starting to consider aspiring to be a doctor, something I'd never previously considered. Medicine actually seemed like a safe and sensible choice, a way to constantly be challenging myself and also do incredibly rewarding work. And being a doctor pays well.

College is an adjustment. Many of my classmates came better guided and prepared academically and in life skills from private boarding schools, so maybe the transition was a little less of an issue for them. But for me, coming from a public high school environment with limited resources (even though it was a fine one), I had a lot to learn about balancing academics, high expectations from top-notch faculty, athletics, social activities, extra-curricular activities, and the freedom of being on my own.

Calculus and chemistry were the only enemies I made first semester. I was stressed, overworked, and miserable. However well placed my intentions were, I was doing poorly during that semester. Then I asked myself: "How could I endure four years of very demanding math and science courses through a pre-med track, four more years of graduate school, residency, and then finally finding a hospital to work at?" In this new pursuit of medicine, I realized that I was taking classes for the wrong reasons, and was unhappy. And so I decided the pre-med track was not a sensible choice for me, a first-year who still had much to learn about himself.

It also bothered me that I was surprisingly alone in appreciating the urgency of protecting nature and our natural resources. An incantation began in my head: "If no one is willing to dedicate themselves to this need, let me be one who will."

After a rough first semester academically I decided that my second semester would be a time of exploration. I chose to go back to being the person I was just before I came to Colgate—that stress-free, confident individual who did what made him happy. I want to build on these traits because I know I lost them during my first semester. Thankfully, I don't need to declare a major until the end of my sophomore year, allowing a large amount of flexibility to decide what is right for me. I decided to take a class on the Crusades, Introduction to Psychology, Intro to Studio Art, and a core class titled Legacies of the Ancient World. I even took piano lessons just because I was interested in it.

None of these may have a single thing to do with nature, but that's OK. I chose to attend a liberal arts school because I thought it was appropriate for me to explore a wide range of subjects in order to find myself. I applied to and entered college a free and independent thinker.

I need to remember that as long as I'm happy, I cannot ask for anything else. As freshman year has passed, I reflect and think, Why would I stress myself trying to be something I'm not? I am now back on track to being a biology major because I love the discipline itself. In all honesty, I don't really know what I'm going to do with my education, but chances are I may do many things and pursue a variety of interests over the course of my lifetime. I'm happier not knowing than stressing myself out in order to become something of which I am not sure.

Today, I am immersed in the Colgate community. I have my classes, my Outdoor Education, my choir, my friends, and my faculty members that all help build my character.

If I leave you with one key concept from my experience, it's be true to yourself. If you don't love something and you aren't in it for the long haul, explore something else, discover, and find what you really love to do.

Given what you know now, if you could redo high school, what would you do differently, and why?

EMBRACE BEING ECCENTRIC, WEIRD, OR GOOFY (IN GOOD WAYS) IF THAT'S YOU

High school is such a mixed bag of judgment, emotions, and people being too timid to show their true personalities, but you have to be willing to accept that you are who you are.

I remember the title of a book we had at home called *What Do You Care What Other People Think?* While I might not have lived that idea during high school, I look back and see the value of this philosophy. I spent way too much time caring what others, especially my friends, thought about my ideas and me.

I became who I am because I learned to accept my eccentric, outgoing personality. I'm different. Some might even say weird. And that is one of the most important things that I have figured out. I've learned that "weird" in this day and age is just a negative spin on "different." Everybody is weird, at least in his or her own way. What you have to do is channel that inner eccentricity and own it.

In a high school do-over, I would have accepted that I had interests that my friends did not and I would have pursued those interests vigorously. I would have been less reluctant to do things and I would have cared much less about always being locked into one group of friends. My friends' apathy, especially toward my passions and interests such as marine biology, held me back from fully committing myself to the cause.

As much as I loved my friends, there were times when I felt torn. I wanted to make them happy, so I refrained from joining certain social groups in order to continuously hang out with them. By the end of high school, I became weary of my closest friends, which probably would not have happened if I had given myself some time for my other interests.

I decided I needed a change. The last months of high school was not necessarily the ideal time to remove myself entirely from my friend group but I compensated by getting a job and spending more time with my musician friends whom I'd never really spent time with before. I spent time alone, too, hiking almost every day and doing yoga at the top of local mountains. It might sound weird to you, but truth be told I never felt better. That wandering through the Santa Monica Mountains led me to join Outdoor Ed at Colgate, and from that I've met some truly great people and gained skills that I will cherish for the rest of my life.

Readers, it's a powerful thing to wake up every day and be who you are and do exactly what you want. You feel good; you feel free. If you pursue a sport or hobby because it actually interests you, that is one thousand times more valuable to you than something that feels like a monotonous grind.

Schoolwork, however, is always essential. You need to get that done and stay on top of things. If nothing else, it makes classes more interesting when you are prepared. Focused hard work pays off, especially if you are working toward what makes you happy.

Let your hobbies and interests exemplify your true personality, but be sure to prioritize academics as well.

I would rather give 100 percent and get something out of it than give only half and merely get through the process.

What else would you like to share with or suggest to high school students and college students, and why?

MY LESSON LEARNED FROM HAVING A GIRLFRIEND IN HIGH SCHOOL

Relationships and balance are complicated, especially in high school. I learned the hard way that you can dedicate way too much of your time and money to love when you could be doing amazing things for your community. I'm not saying don't have a girlfriend or boyfriend in high school. But I am admitting that I committed so much emotion, care, energy, and love into a relationship that, at times, I could not handle the pressure during my junior year.

I simultaneously played lacrosse, did mock trial, committed my heart to my high school sweetheart, and kept getting straight A's, but not many people knew that I gave up sleep most of the time. My parents trusted that I was handling everything well because I seemed to somehow manage to get my priorities straight most of the time.

My girlfriend and I did not know if we were going to stay together during college, and in retrospect I really had no idea if I was going to marry this girl. I was always aware that our future had not begun and I was not going to let emotions bog me down—too much.

"School comes before girlfriend," I often reminded myself. And she was similarly focused on her school career. It's a sad, utilitarian approach to how I saw our relationship, but please bear with me. We both had very demanding school schedules accompanied by a multitude of extracurriculars, so together we understood that school was going to have to come first.

I realize now that I was personally driven to do well in school. It wasn't pressure from home. Instead, I saw school as my responsibility, like a job, at this time. So I wanted to do it well. That's what we do. So I put school before everything. I put it before sleep. I put it before sports. I put it before meals at times. This crazy-person mentality was what allowed me to do so well, but I needed more balance.

I burned out early in my senior year. I drove myself crazy trying to do everything. My college applications made me think and also made me question: "What have I accomplished? Did I do enough? Where do I stand? What do I stand for?" I started to worry that it was too late to do more. As a result, I drifted for a period, which is not to say I didn't work hard. My focus was different.

Fortunately, things turned out well, with support from family, mentors, and friends. My earlier focus and interests did come through on my college applications. I got to know myself better, and that helped in deciding where to go to school and what interests to pursue. Colgate welcomed me and I could not be happier.

The moral of the story is that school performance and your overall involvement in activities and community are what will ultimately lead you to your future dream college. It did for me. Remember that life exists after high school, and the future is full of amazing opportunities. So don't over-commit your time to just a girlfriend/boyfriend relationship in high school, especially if you see it as a demand on your time and energy, bringing you down at times, and disrupting your balance and important priorities that affect your future.

A perfectly imperfect takeaway on Danny:

Danny is an eccentric nineteen-year-old who loves nature and the people close to him. In the years to come Danny will spend as much time as he can in the wilds of the United States and try to take in all of the beauty that the land has to offer. He will continue to be the goofy, outlandish, and ridiculous human being that he already is and spread joy in the hearts of those he loves. He will graduate from Colgate with a major that pertains to biology or geology and use the Colgate community as a resource to make the world that he already influences a better place. But most of all Danny will forever be Danny.

3

Felipe da Paz

Brazilian Golfer Turned Entrepreneur

BA in Business Administration
with a focus on Entrepreneurship, Class of 2016,
University of Southern California

Originally from Brazil and the son of hotel executives, Felipe da Paz has lived in ten different countries. At age thirteen, Felipe started competing in golf and reached top Brazilian national rankings in just three years, earning him a golf scholarship in the United States. While spending most of his time practicing, Felipe still found the time and the funds to co-found Forpax Solutions, a Brazilian nonprofit organization that turned paper waste from large schools into recycled notebooks. Forpax donated notebooks to more than 150 underprivileged children who couldn't afford them.

Felipe eventually gave up competitive golf to focus on his next start-up, a cultural-immersion travel company that allows students to live in a family home in Brazil for two months, learning the language, sports, and even cooking. After helping hundreds of kids embark on new cultural experiences, Felipe decided to move into the tech world and is now working in marketing for a tech start-up in Los Angeles. He is also part of Conquest Capital Ventures, a student-run impact venture capital fund at the University of Southern California, and is on the executive team of Startup Equinox, the largest student-run event on campus.

When you take a deep look into your goals, make sure they align with the path you are taking—be that in sports or anything else you do in life.

—Felipe da Paz

How many young entrepreneurs have grown up in ten countries across five continents and have played semiprofessional golf in their teen years? Felipe da Paz reflects on his upbringing into his late teens.

Making eight international trips takes most people a lifetime, but for me, it took only until my first birthday. With hotel-executive parents, my childhood was marked by constant relocations and learning new languages. My mix of broad cultural awareness, ease of adapting, friends around the world, and fluency in four languages has deeply affected my values and molded my life's path.

When I boarded the 11:00 p.m. American Airlines flight from São Paulo to LAX to start my junior year of college, I couldn't help but wonder about my dad's concern for me. About a year prior to that day, I had told him about my decision to quit competitive golf in North Carolina to pursue an entrepreneurial route in California. Although my parents have been nothing but supportive of every decision I have made, my dad was concerned that I would never learn to settle down—that I was consumed by new beginnings. As the large 747 took off to my new destination, I could not determine whether his concern was valid or not.

For virtually the first half of my life, I was forced to move to a new country every ten months or so. In my eyes, this constantly moving and changing environment was normal, and I learned to embrace it. My mom tells me that when I was eleven and we finally had settled in a coastal town for more than a year, I would eagerly question her about when we were going to move again.

Four years later, at age fourteen, I found myself spending more time at the golf course than in my own home. At that time my parents had decided to branch out and build a golf course exactly two minutes away from our home. With the full support of my parents and the fortune to have a golf course as my backyard, I began pursuing my dream to play professional golf at a golf academy in Orlando, Florida. I played and improved so much during the final years of high school that I was able to get a scholarship to a top Division II (NCAA) small university in North Carolina—one of the greatest things that has ever happened to me. Once in college, I was surrounded by a pool of new interests that led me to once again switch gears and focus my energies into what I believe is the culmination of my diverse upbringing: entrepreneurship.

Throughout high school, Felipe was more concerned about maintaining his position atop the Brazilian national golf rankings than about his grades. This dedication earned him a sports scholarship at Wingate University, a small school in North Carolina. Once plunged into the university ecosystem, Felipe gained additional interests and ended up becoming the president of the Environmental Club, vice president of the International and Multicultural Club, and a researcher for the Economics Department.

While Felipe was doing well at Wingate, he wanted to realize his potential in a new university environment with greater resources and educational values that aligned with his emerging entrepreneurial aspirations. During his sophomore year, he applied to select universities, including USC, as an international transfer applicant.

His Common Application and Supplement essay prompts and responses for USC are as follows:

Common App essay prompt #1: Please provide a statement of 250–500 words that addresses your reasons for transferring and the objectives you hope to achieve, and attach it to your application before submission.

As an aspiring serial entrepreneur and global networker, I desire a dynamic and lively academic environment like USC's, in which I can explore my passions and interact with a diverse group of people. Although my current college provides an intimate environment in which I can cultivate lifelong friendships and personal relationships with my professors, it lacks the dynamism and opportunities that will enable me to fully pursue my entrepreneurial ambitions. I look forward to tackling a challenging course load at the Marshall School of Business and exploring my eclectic academic interests through the numerous trailblazing departments at USC.

My diverse upbringing, which includes having lived in ten countries on five continents, has fueled my desire for constant personal challenges. However, given the few resources available at my current school and the small range of classes available, I find a lack of exciting opportunities, and feel under-challenged. USC has the essential resources to challenge me both inside and outside the classroom. I plan to be actively involved in organizations such as the USC e-Club and on participating in events such as the West Coast Research Symposium on Technology Entrepreneurship to further challenge myself.

Although my current school has all the benefits of a small college, its 18 units of electives do not offer enough flexibility to pursue a well-rounded education. I deeply believe that along with a strong business foundation, which the Business Administration major provides, an extensive knowledge of the social sciences is crucial to becoming the successful serial entrepreneur that I aspire to be. Marshall's 32 units of electives will give me the necessary array of options to acquire those much-needed skills in global-minded classes such as "Multinational Enterprises" and "International Negotiations."

USC's global perspective, resources, and network greatly attract me. Adaptability and cultural pluralism are just two of the biggest traits that define me. Because of my global travels, I consider myself a citizen of the world, with an indubitable responsibility to create a better future for my generation. I deeply believe that USC has the best resources and opportunities to make me a prolific entrepreneur and an active leader in tomorrow's society.

Prompt #2: Please briefly elaborate on one of your extracurricular activities or work experiences in the space below.

After college freshman year, two friends and I started a small non-profit organization that collected and recycled paper waste from schools to make notebooks for disadvantaged children at local schools. This project aimed to help hundreds of underprivileged children looking for a better education in Brazil's countryside. Our vision was to not only be of significance to poverty-stricken children but to also have an impact in our communities and encourage thousands of other students to boldly take on projects of the same nature.

Finding reliable funders and recruiting volunteers demanded the best of our skills and uncountable hours of work, but the journey was incredibly rewarding. Forpax Solutions succeeded after many failed meetings with local companies and government officers. Once we had the necessary funds and support, we quickly initiated the program and immediately saw results. Initially only an entrepreneurial dream, Forpax made a positive change not only in the community but also in the lives of three young aspiring entrepreneurs.

The above is a slightly expanded version of Felipe's essay for this particular Common Application short prompt. Felipe's Additional Information on the Common Application included the following:

Competing in golf since I was thirteen also helped shape who I am. Focusing my energy to playing golf for 6 straight years, I gained lifelong skills and values that will accompany me in my college career and in business. While in Brazil, I received the Best Young Player of the Year award, led the Sao Paulo state under 18 rankings, and was regularly in the top 10 under 18 national rankings. All those accomplishments allowed me to pursue my dreams in an American university. However, life took its turns and I ended up following a different path.

While my dream was to become a professional golfer, my involvement in student organizations and groups has led me to think differently. Being in leadership positions with very limited time, I was able to see that if I wanted to become a successful entrepreneur I would have to prioritize my life. This is when I realized that the academic and entrepreneurial sides of me spoke louder. Although I loved golf, it would have to become a lifelong hobby instead of a career.

It was an extremely hard decision at the time, but I don't regret one second of it. I am able to effectively use and focus the extra time gained on academics, extracurriculars, and new ventures. Following my passions with purpose and determination has opened various opportunities. This will be vital in reaching my dream of becoming a serial entrepreneur.

Describe your academic interests and how you plan to pursue them at USC. Please feel free to address your first- and second-choice major selections.

I don't want to build and own just one business; instead, I want to own an array of innovative ventures that can shape the future of my generation. Building my own non-profit organization as well as a student travel company has ignited my passion for entrepreneurship. International recognitions, such as being a fellow of the Kairos Society—a fellowship that works to find and empower young pioneers who are pushing the world forward through entrepreneurship and innovation—have only strengthened my entrepreneurial ambitions. I want to keep pushing my limits, broadening my business skills, and breaking the parameters of what students can do. I deeply believe that USC's Marshall School of Business and the thriving Lloyd Greif Center have all the necessary tools to help me achieve those goals.

I look forward to not only the remarkable in-class experience but also engaging organizations like the Trojan Start-ups and the Global Brigades clubs. The extracurricular activities, along with the advanced classes in the Business Administration or Global Studies major will uniquely shape my future as a serial entrepreneur.

Today, Felipe is a junior at USC. I've asked him to reflect on the following question:

To what extent did your college experience meet your expectations? In what ways did your experience cause you to change your perspective on your academic career, your dreams and aspirations, and your life?

"The Tourist." This was my nickname in high school. I spent so many days traveling to golf tournaments that out of the sixteen weeks in my last semester of high school I was only present for twelve of them. The only reason I didn't flunk for absences was because of my spot on the junior national team. This sport was what I breathed, ate, and lived for those four years. Although it brought lifelong values, the wholehearted commitment to golf deprived me from the experimentation with and discovery of academic interests, passions, and tastes that most teenagers go through. While my peers were participating in clubs, events, and trying out classes, I was taking the minimal course load and spending all my extra time hitting golf balls. Needless to say, the path I was following gave me no breathing room to advance in a career of knowledge, and no academic and professional pursuits in any other areas but sports.

Noting my confusion during registration period, Mrs. Blythe, my freshman academic advisor in college, instructed me to experiment for a while until I could decide which major to pick. And so this is what I did. With a vague impression that I would enjoy economics and business, I enrolled in a few classes such as one on the economics of environmental damages and another one on consumer behaviors in global markets. These classes were utterly distinct from what I was used to in my small Brazilian high school and a newfound appetite for knowledge stirred up in me.

My involvement in extracurricular organizations such as the Multicultural Committee, the Economics Research Team, and the Environmental Club, which I came to lead in the following months, began to help me spread my wings. Without even noticing, I was already following a path of academic and professional pursuits, and my desire to pursue a career in professional golf started to dwindle.

The months following that year of many trials, countless errors, and extensive self-discovery were perhaps the most defining ones of my life. With a renewed sense of what interested me and the change I wished to see in the world, two good friends and I founded the nonprofit Forpax. Although the results generated by our venture was merely in the hundreds, the ensuing joy it gave me marked the assurance I needed to decide to leave the golf team during my second year of college. Coupled with my restless personality and broad cultural awareness, I came to realize that the joy in helping others and in building influential ventures was much more fulfilling than trying my luck in golf.

Without golf, I started my sophomore year with much more free time and a strong sense of direction, and I wanted to make up for time "lost" in high school. I worked and became president of the Environmental Club and vice president of the International and Multicultural Committee, and began to do research on the monetary costs of deforestation in the Amazon. New accomplishments on and off campus gave me the courage to ask some entrepreneurial friends in different countries to introduce me to the Kairos Society, a global organization of young entrepreneurs tackling the big problems of the future.

Immersed in Kairos' environment of high-achieving students, I realized that my ambitions and quest for challenges would be much better met at a larger school. With the help of my peers and mentors, I applied to a few universities and I decided to enroll at the University of Southern California, which seemed to offer the best entrepreneurial business program of all the schools I was admitted to. At USC, I continue growing my interests and pursuing new ones.

After countless twists and turns, mistakes, and accomplishments, I can only now see how significant it was to embrace my interests wholeheartedly and let them guide my path. Nietzsche stated it perfectly: "Freedom is the will to be responsible for ourselves." Just as I started taking responsibility for my future, it began to open up in front of me.

I've asked Felipe to further reflect on this question:

Given what you know now, if you could redo high school and earlier years in college, what would you do differently, and why?

Looking back at the past three years, I wish I could tell my younger self only one thing: do not procrastinate and do not hesitate to pursue truly constructive interests. Even though I was always very involved with golf, I still had an itch for starting new activities. During high school, I had an idea about nonprofits, I deeply wanted to learn an instrument, and I would have loved to improve my French. At the time, though, I was so caught up in golf that I kept telling myself that I would find a better time to do them. The truth, which I discovered a couple years later, is that I would never find a better time to get involved in true interests than in high school. Once you get to college, you will be infinitely busier and exponentially more interested in learning new things, so whatever you want to do, do it as soon as possible.

I started my nonprofit at the end of my college freshman year. The experience taught me a great deal about myself and what makes me happy. I also learned that I could have saved myself a ton of stress and several dozen college credits that I lost when I transferred schools if I'd known these things about myself sooner.

When I look back now, I realize that if I had decided sooner to take the challenge to start my company or simply pursued my interests, I could have been much farther down the path I desire. Discovering yourself can be the basis for a successful and passionate life, as I see now, but it also requires the ability and courage to pursue your interests. The reality is that, as you grow older, trying new things becomes harder and more costly, so the sooner you do it, the better. High school students, I urge you not to procrastinate.

What else would you like to share with or suggest to high school students and college students, and why?

HAVE YOUR OWN VOICE

Always strive to find your own voice. This is not another one of those "be yourself" speeches but rather a personal strategy to stand out in a world where competition dominates every field. Coming to college, you will immerse yourself in a jungle where everyone around you is really good at something, and it will seem to you that everyone else has figured life out. It becomes really easy to mirror the expectations of others—but nothing except frustration will result.

As I explained earlier, during the end of my college freshman year, I started Forpax, and building and growing this venture gave me incredible joy. I thought I had finally found my purpose in life. For months straight, I worked incessantly to keep these young students supplied with school materials. However, the distance between Brazil and the United States and a budget shortfall in Forpax's sponsor organization took a big toll on its effectiveness. So, when I decided to shut down operations in the middle of my college sophomore year, I suddenly found myself looking for the next project to get involved in, as if I were starting from scratch.

While I was too distracted to realize it, most of my friends were getting into finance or investment banking. They all had great internships and were already making way too much money for a college student. As I saw them enjoy the perks of making a good deal of money, I began to question myself. Why wasn't I doing the same? I started feeling guilty for not taking advantage of such a career and its long-term benefits. I was so plagued with doubts that I forgot how much joy actually helping others had given me. It was not until I hit the bottom of self-loathing that I realized I was truly happy and most effective while doing work that directly affected others in a positive way. I had started to judge myself and my ambitions through the eyes of others, and this self-doubt was only hurting me.

This is the reason why I urge you to search within yourself and find your own voice, to discover what you want to tell the world, what you want to be remembered for. It doesn't matter what it is, and no one can judge its true value but you. As long as your voice and identity are authentic, the money, success, and happiness will take care of themselves.

INVEST TIME IN YOURSELF

Your greatest asset is you. Regardless of your career path or years in business, you should never stop growing. Technology and business are evolving faster than ever, and new trends are emerging and disappearing more quickly than we can grasp them. Big data, 3-D printing, growth hacking, robotics, the cloud . . . it seems as if every day the media tells us a new buzzword that we "must know." This swarm of impending must-knows can easily overwhelm and paralyze us.

After Jorge Paulo Lehman, Brazil's investing tycoon and the world's twenty-eighth richest man, spoke in 2011 at one of Latin America's best universities, Insper, I boldly approached him and asked what would be the one piece of advice he would give me. This man, who had graduated from Harvard in three years while on a tennis scholarship, looked at me and said, "Above all else, invest in yourself." I had heard this numerous times before, but I had never paid too much attention to it. That day, I finally grasped what it meant, and this piece of advice has stuck with me ever since.

I found a certain beauty in constantly working to better myself, whether in the personal or professional realm. Although a bit vague, the idea that I can work to become a better person every day resonated with me more than any other quantifiable metric. I found this advice especially useful given my ever-changing wants and interests. Regardless of what career path I ultimately choose, such assets as technical know-how, interpersonal skills, emotional intelligence, leadership abilities, and cultural knowledge will always prove useful in my future; therefore, I make a conscious decision to reserve time daily to work on at least one of my goals.

LEARN TO SAY NO

I found a funny thing about the process of achieving great things. Before you achieve something, anything at all, you will have only a very limited number of opportunities knocking at your door. Most of what you want to achieve will be done through your own hard work, and your success will be directly related to your will to create opportunities for yourself; moreover, the more you achieve, the more "opportunities" life will hand you. The funny thing is that your future success depends greatly on how you handle those opportunities that do appear.

In the beginning of my sophomore year of college, I was accepted into the Kairos Society. At the Kairos Global Summit at the New York Stock Exchange, I met hundreds of absolutely brilliant peers with a deep desire and will to change the world. During those few, heady days of brainstorming and networking, many of these young pioneers became good friends, with whom I would stay in close contact in the future. As we all shared a passion for large-impact ventures, many of these friends invited me to join them to work on different ideas. Plagued with the fear that I was passing up a great opportunity, I decided to accept most of the offers. As people say, you should not do things halfheartedly. I would eventually understand this lesson the hard way.

Juggling student life and founding a company are already hard enough. In my sophomore year I was trying to do just that: help my friends' ventures, lead two organizations, and transfer schools. It became impossible to perform anywhere near well enough in all these endeavors. So, I had to learn the hard way that in order to make success sustainable, I must choose wisely how I spend my time. Saying no is often the best answer. Therefore, I urge others in my position to think about what they want to tell the world and use that as a basis for assuming responsibilities, all while being mindful that you only have twenty-four hours in a day.

A QUICK NOTE ON SPORTS

Even though I am overjoyed by the path I have decided to take on and do not regret my decisions one bit, I still often wonder where I would be if I had decided to stick with golf and pursue a life of professional athletics. Most days I come to the conclusion that I would not be as happy as I am now, but conjuring up in my head a different scenario where I see myself as a professional golfer allows me to see how much the sport has shaped me into who I am. From the dedication of waking up before dawn to hit balls in the driving range to the tenacity to endure months of bad results and keep going to the patience of knowing one day all the hard work will pay off. And finally, the mental strength to stand the pressure on the eighteenth hole knowing all your teammates need you.

For others in a similar situation, I will warn you now that it will be extremely hard to decide whether to quit your sport or not. Some days it will be clear that it is the right choice, on others, like the biggest mistake of your life. Think deeply about how you feel when playing the sport you love and how it matches your goals and aspirations. For me, playing golf made me feel great, but there was a big part missing—with a life of professional athletics I would never be able to achieve my vision for the future. When you take a deep look into your goals, make sure they align with the path you are taking—be that in sports or anything else you do in life.

A perfectly imperfect takeaway about Felipe:

After years of trial and error, Felipe finally listened to his own advice and decided to stop living through other people's expectations. His decision to pivot from becoming a professional golfer to aspiring to be a serial entrepreneur led him to become involved in many amazing organizations, such as the first impact venture capital fund at USC. He looks forward to the next exciting challenge as he strives to be a change maker. Felipe adds, "I sincerely hope my advice will save you from making some of the mistakes I made. Good luck on your journey in becoming whoever you want to be!"

3: FELIPE DA PAZ

4

Shreya Indukuri

Sustainability Designer

BA in Cognitive Science with double minors in Digital Arts
and Human-Centered Design, Class of 2016,
Dartmouth College

Shreya Indukuri grew up in the Bay Area. Her passion in high school was bringing energy-efficient initiatives to high school campuses to reduce the schools' carbon footprint, save money, and teach students about energy. At Dartmouth, she served as a freshman EcoRep to bring sustainable initiatives to campus, and she took an engineering class that inspired her to pursue her newfound passion—design. Designing ergonomic products and programs fascinates Shreya because its essential goal is to make people's lives easier. She currently serves as a teaching assistant for an engineering class, Design Thinking; is a member of the Digital Arts Leadership & Innovation (DALI) Lab; and serves as the Class of 2016 Council Secretary. Shreya believes that sustainable design can be applied to everything in life and that everyone has the potential to be creative and innovative if they have the courage and confidence to pursue their ideas.

Try something different, give it 100 percent dedication, and don't be afraid to fail! Every time you work hard and fail, you will be one step closer to success.

—Shreya Indukuri

Growing up in Silicon Valley, Shreya Indukuri was exposed to the high-tech world from a young age.

Both of my parents were working in the tech field, so I was used to seeing several computers, floppy disks (yes, I'm that old!), hard drives, and routers scattered around the house. Though I thought that technology was really cool, I never developed a true interest in my math and science classes, and I just assumed that I would not be an engineer.

After learning about all the possibilities of integrating environmentally conscious behavior into my lifestyle in high school, I realized there was huge crossover between sustainability and technology. I thus decided to co-found SmartPowerEd, an organization that brought smart energy projects to high schools. I also contributed my artistic skills, honed in middle and high school, to founding SmartPowerEd by providing feedback to the design of the Online Energy Dashboard. This software program presented information about energy use to high school students in an engaging fashion, encouraging them to reduce their dependence on electric use (chargers, lights, and so on) whenever possible.

Shreya reflected on why she co-founded SmartPowerEd and how the experience and contributions strengthened her identity, as a topic of her choice on the Common Application personal essay during the college application season:

ENVIRONMENTAL ACTIONIST

I would like to label myself as an eloquent and articulate teenager, but for a long time, one question would stump me:

"When did you decide that you wanted to be a climate activist?"

I never knew how to answer this because, frankly, I don't want to be a climate activist. Yes, I believe that educating the public on global warming is immensely important, but it's simply *not* enough. For years, I've heard about climate change and how such minimal activities as recycling or turning off the lights can cumulatively make a substantial difference. There had to be something *more* that I could do.

Alliance for Climate Education sparked that passion within me when it funded an environmental grant to reduce the carbon footprint of our school. My partner and I identified a "smart-energy" technology that reduced our school's energy consumption and saved thousands of dollars. The successful project at our school led me to co-found an organization, SmartPowerEd, that galvanizes students to transform their campus's energy usage.

The technology was astounding to me: identifying errors meant reducing our energy use, thus lessening our reliance on fossil fuels and saving money, which schools love! Our "simple" yet empowering project led to some incredible recognition from the Chief Technology Officer of the United States and the opportunity to speak at the White House on a panel alongside Secretary of Energy Steven Chu. Discussing revolutionizing energy usage in schools with White House officials, and saving thousands of dollars on energy bills made my climate "activism" more real than ever before.

Because of my sustainability work, people have often labeled me an environmental "activist and expert," someone who understands all of the complexities of global warming, fuel consumption, greenhouse gases, along with the intricacies of recycling every item on this planet. Not true. I'm still learning as I go, forging a path of activism and charging ahead on the road to tangible action. So, when I first stumbled on Jess Weiner's blog and came across an intriguing term called an "actionist," I knew I finally had my answer. Weiner, an entrepreneur, defined actionists as those who take action to make positive changes within their personal life, family, school, workplace, community or the world at large.

The term really resonated with me, as I have found a way to enact concrete change in my community and my world. Although my friends may tease me for not always knowing exactly how to recycle sometimes and may call me a pseudo-activist, I don't mind. My experiences have helped me to appreciate the effect that I, or any young student, driven by inspiration and passion, can have just by working towards a real, sustainable goal. I am an actionist, and very proud to call myself one.

Audacious and curious, Shreya delights in reaching out to others. She reflected on this trait in another college app personal essay:

"Hi, I'm Shreya! What's your name?"

Whether I'm sitting next to someone on a bus or a train, standing next to him or her in a long line at a store, or (this often happens to me) seated in the spacious middle seat between two passengers on a plane, my favorite thing to do is to introduce myself.

My friends and family often attest to the fact that, when I was a child, I was very outgoing and rambunctious. Whether it was an intimidating adult, an unsociable toddler, or anyone in between, I had zero inhibitions about striking up a conversation with a complete stranger. My theory is: why not seize the moment to learn about new people? It's often likely that I won't ever encounter this stranger again, but I have a number of fleeting moments or hours with which to trace their story, discover their passions, and maybe even make new friends.

Once, while on a train to Oakland, for example, I met an engineer with a passion for cooking, and was in San Francisco for the summer to attend an elite culinary program. On a flight with my family, I conversed for hours with a law student from New York who was headed to Hawaii to pursue a career as a professional surfer.

I even encountered a forgotten friend of my family on a plane once. After talking to him about school, the future, and our families, I discovered that he and my father had worked together twenty years ago, and once we landed, our families reconnected. I could have just as easily fallen asleep on that flight or watched movies and read mundane magazine articles, but I chose not to do so because I might never again have the opportunity to sit next to this unique person.

I even happened to meet Daniela Lapidous, the co-founder of my company SmartPowerEd, while sitting next to her at that the Alliance for Climate Education assembly during my freshman year. This chance meeting influenced my passion for sustainability and my entire high school career.

As Frederic Nietzsche says, "Is life not a thousand times too short for us to bore ourselves?" I still have much to learn, but here is the one piece of wisdom that I would give to anyone of any age: take a moment to introduce yourself, learn someone's story, and share your own. You could very well be sitting next to the person who will change your life in ways you never expected.

In high school, Shreya worked extensively on sustainability projects. Especially SmartPowerEd, which she co-founded to empower, educate, and assist local high school students in their efforts to bring more efficient energy sources to their campuses. She also served as a member of the Youth Advisory Board for the Alliance for Climate Education. Shreya and SmartPowerEd's co-founder, Daniela Lapidous, spoke at several major conferences, including the Clinton Global Initiative, PowerShift 2011, and the White House Grid Modernization event, sharing their story of giving students the tools and motivation to make their high school campuses more energy-efficient.

Shreya valued leading purposeful extracurricular activities that significantly affected the community more than studying to get perfect grades. During her college app season, she applied to a range of colleges and was admitted to Dartmouth College, the University of Southern California, Boston University, and the University of Illinois at Urbana-Champaign. I asked her to tell us why she chose Dartmouth:

I chose Dartmouth because I immediately felt a strong connection with several of the people I met on campus. When I visited, all the students I spoke with were so passionate about their interests and their deep, shared love for this college on a hill! I wanted to attend college with a student body who inspired and taught me something new every day. I almost chose a university in California, but after meeting people from all over the world when I visited Dartmouth, I decided that it was time for me to break out of my West Coast bubble and start a new chapter of my life.

Today, Shreya is a junior at Dartmouth College. I've asked her to reflect on the following question:

To what extent did your college experience—on and off campus—meet your expectations? In what ways did your experience cause you to change your perspective on your academic career, your dreams and aspirations, and your life?

Contrary to belief, I honestly feel that most college students can truly pursue whatever career they are passionate about. I do not throw the term "passion" around lightly. Many people have interests and may enjoy certain subjects but *passion* is an overwhelming force that drives me to get out of bed every morning with this optimism to make a tangible, positive difference in the world.

As a child from a fairly traditional South Indian immigrant family living and working in Silicon Valley, I was brought up to have an interest in

55

certain subjects and careers that guaranteed financial stability upon college graduation. And that meant I needed to major in engineering, computer science, economics, or something with a lot of "job potential." I had no natural talent in any of those areas, and, even though I took most of the intro classes, I found my true passion in a random engineering elective class called Design Thinking during my freshman year.

That term, I put in twice as much time as necessary for any projects related to my Design Thinking class and only did the required work for my other classes. I didn't know what to do because the college had no design major I could pursue, and I feared telling my parents that I was still "undecided" regarding my academic pursuits at the end of my freshman year.

Then I started to think seriously about my career. Did I want to struggle through a difficult major that I wasn't passionate about and endure a job I didn't care much for? Or did I want to put in all my efforts and take advantage of the opportunities around me to pursue design? I spent the majority of my freshman summer at an economics-related internship but secretly wished that I was working at a design firm. I spent a good deal of my free time, for hours each day after I came home from work, learning about HTML, CSS, Photoshop, and reading design blogs and books.

Conversations with my professors also encouraged me to reach out to the incredible alumni network at Dartmouth. I perused LinkedIn and looked for Dartmouth students who were doing valuable design internships at established design firms like IDEO and working at big brand-name companies like Apple, Facebook, and Google. I was surprised to learn how many successful professionals are willing to take thirty minutes or an hour out of their day to help an enthusiastic, *passionate* student. It turns out people interested in design could major in whatever they wanted! I met sociology, English, film, engineering, computer science, government, and history majors who were doing design-related internships and pursuing careers in the design field. What made them stand out was their *passion*— they constantly read about design news, learned how to use Photoshop, coding, art, and a number of different skill sets in their free time. READ: free time.

I came back to Dartmouth my sophomore fall and realized that I truly loved product design and I would pursue my passion through whatever platforms the college offered. I joined the Digital Arts Leadership and Innovation Lab, applied for several different social-media and web-design jobs, and worked as a teaching assistant for a Design Thinking class. I discovered cognitive science as an appealing and relevant major because it was the study of information processing from several different fields (linguistics, psychology, computer science, philosophy). I am also minoring in human-centered design and digital arts; both subjects have given me the opportunity to visualize and create products and build my portfolio.

Your undergraduate education is such a valuable time in your life and you should be spending it pursuing things that you love! My dream career would be to work at a sustainable design firm helping clients integrate environmentally conscious products, methods, and technologies into their lifestyle and work. Even if design isn't your calling, and something else is, and you should work at that *every day* if you want to end up with the internship or job or career of your dreams!

Given what you know now, if you could redo high school, what would you do differently, and why?

I definitely took a more unconventional path to college than most of my college friends did. I went to a rigorous private school in the Bay Area that produced some of the most intelligent math and science students in the country. I was, honestly, a pretty typical student in that environment: I wasn't the leader of the pack, but I did take a number of difficult classes that challenged me. I was very passionate about SmartPowerEd, which brought energy-efficiency projects to local high school students. My passion for sustainability was a major part of my high school career.

Between schoolwork and SmartPowerEd, I didn't have many hours to myself to read books (and I don't mean textbooks) and the news as much as I would've liked to. Since so many of my most interesting and intelligent friends were information junkies, constantly reading blogs, literature, and the news, they kept me well informed. If I could go back in time, I would read books and blogs and interesting news articles more.

Nowadays, I try to read the news and keep up with a few good books as pleasure reading whenever I get a chance. *FastCompany* has become my bible because I love the intersection between technology and design. I use Twitter, actually, to keep up with the news because I follow major news sources, interesting people, and new organizations. It's a really easy way to consolidate all the information I want to learn about! The Internet is very powerful and can be an incredible learning tool if you are productive with your time spent surfing the web!

And this is important—read books! Not textbooks, but novels and nonfiction books that fascinate you. I love reading books related to different sociological trends, like *Freakonomics* or *Outliers*. I wish I had read more when I was in high school. A habit I am trying to maintain is reading a book for a few minutes every night before bed. Whether I read one page or thirty depends on how tired I am, reading a little bit each day is a good habit to have. Young people do *not* read enough books nowadays, yet books can make you that much of a more intriguing, worthwhile, and magnetic person (and writer!) if you read something of substance daily.

What else would you like to share with or suggest to high school students and college students, and why?

Don't try to fit into a mold. Yes, if you have a 4.0 GPA and stellar scores, your chances of getting into a great college are higher, but did all the studying make you that much more of a fascinating person? Colleges want a diverse student body. Imagine how homogenous or boring a graduating class would be if every single person was valedictorian of their high school and got a perfect 2400 on their SAT. Essentially, you would just have a class full of people always huddled in the library. You will excel at what you love because you will put in the required time and effort. Be different!

Start a club or an organization that revolves around something you care deeply for. You don't necessarily have to do research in a lab or join the robotics club. You can do something entrepreneurial and fun and challenging like starting a company. And this is the secret to success that I didn't understand for a long time: Don't be afraid to fail.

There is no better time in your life to try something and fail, because you have your whole life ahead of you and because you don't have much to lose. Learning to be unsuccessful at a young age is so crucial because no matter how perfect you are, you will inevitably fail at something, so you need to know how to pick yourself up and start over. You can learn from your mistakes and succeed.

Many times I faced rejection in high school, but I slowly learned to cope with it and use it to my advantage. I learned how *not* to do things and what to avoid. When working for SmartPowerEd, my co-founder and I got our proposals rejected from the majority of schools we approached, but after several months of trying, we found success with two high schools! We helped the school district save thousands of dollars, and we got the chance to speak about our experiences at the Clinton Global Initiative and White House Grid Modernization Event in 2011.

So, my advice to high school students is to try something different, give it 100 percent dedication, and *don't be afraid to fail*! Every time you work hard and fail, you will be one step closer to success.

A perfectly imperfect takeaway about Shreya:

Shreya believes that she is really good at failing, learning, and becoming more determined as a result of failure. Her less-successful experiences have helped her over time to develop a strong sense of optimism and resilience. She adds, "Failure really is a state of mind and it can provide you with the inspiration and strength you need to succeed if you are willing to look beyond the past." Her Design Thinking class in college strengthened her creative confidence. Now, as a cognitive science major and a digital arts and human-centered design minor, she would love to move back to the Bay Area and do sustainable design work for an innovative technology company, challenging people to think about and improve lives in new sustainable ways.

Act II
Seniors on the Threshold

5

Erica Ma

Diplomat Building Bridges of Peace

BA in International Relations and Modern Middle Eastern
Studies, Class of 2015, University of Pennsylvania

Erica Ma grew up in a small town in the state of Washington. In high
school, Erica participated in speech and debate and presided over her
school's Model United Nations organization. In addition, Erica was politically active, volunteering in local political campaigns. She graduated high
school in 2011, just as uprisings began to spread throughout the Middle
East. She was then inspired to pursue Arabic and Middle Eastern studies in
college and subsequently studied abroad in Rabat, Morocco, for a semester
in her junior year.

At Penn, she is an active student leader in international development
and human-rights organizations. She has served as a US Department of
State Virtual Student Foreign Service eIntern for the International Visitor
Leadership Program, and has interned for the United Nations Relief and
Works Agency. Erica is the recipient of the 2014–15 Foreign Language and

Area Studies Fellowship for Arabic study. She plans to study international law in law school and pursue a PhD in international relations.

Immersing yourself in another culture highlights the commonalities among people and makes you a better global citizen.
—Erica Ma

After immigrating to the United States from China at age two, HongYu (Erica) Ma and her family lived in the states of California and Washington and eventually settled in a small town called Vaughn in Washington.

I was raised with the mind-set that if I worked hard, I could reach the same level of success as anyone else. My blue-collar parents were able to seize economic opportunities, provided for me, and supported my academic pursuits. They have exemplified a great work ethic, and I have inherited the same kind of mentality of setting goals and striving to achieve them. Although my parents had always encouraged me to be a high achiever, I realized in college that my strongest driving force was an intrinsic motivation to pursue my passions. I find fulfillment in seizing and leveraging the opportunities available to me to help empower others, and it's my desire to help change the world for the better that pushes me.

In high school, Erica started developing a desire to build bridges of understanding and peace between peoples, governments, and countries. After taking a course on world history and participating in Model United Nations (MUN), Erica became very interested in international affairs and global issue resolution. She reflected on this as a topic of her choice on her Common Application personal essay when applying to college in her senior year.

BRIDGES

"I didn't know you lived on the Key Peninsula . . . I thought the KP was full of druggies."

I glanced at my friend Shane. "Come on, just because houses on the KP aren't as nice as the ones in Canterwood doesn't mean they're all meth houses." I could picture Canterwood, with its gates, security guards, and ideal location near the heart of Gig Harbor.

In my small town, a concrete bridge connects the Key Peninsula (KP) to the rest of the world. I cross the Purdy Bridge every day as my bus rumbles to school in the adjacent city of Gig Harbor. On the KP, our houses share a lawn with the dandelions, but across the water lies Gig Harbor, where houses grow taller than the evergreens.

At Peninsula High School, KP kids assume that Gig Harbor kids are rich snobs; Gig Harbor kids assume that the KP is filled with hidden caches of marijuana. The first day of freshman year, I spotted a Gig Harbor girl sitting alone in English, but I didn't know if I should approach her. Ignoring inhibitions, I marched forward and chirped, "Hi! Can I sit here?" Fortunately, she needed a friend and enjoyed my chattering, and even today I continue to make friends with anyone, regardless of which side of the bridge they live on.

In the spring of 2010, I attended Berkeley's MUN conference as Switzerland, and eager to debate women's rights in Afghanistan, I created a nursing plan. I garnered the support of poorer nations but not developed nations, whose funding would make the resolution feasible. The US delegate agreed to sponsor my plan only if I supported his resolution on sending UN troops. As Switzerland, I blanched at the idea of militant action, but I offered to compromise and send NGOs instead. Bridging the gap between the developing nations and the developed nations, I achieved a realistic resolution.

Purdy Bridge is small, and it doesn't seem like much, really. But to me, it's simple, sturdy, and inspires me to become a global architect of peace. When I drive across, I think about how I can mediate the differences of my two towns. I think of how it influenced me to join MUN, and I think how more bridges remain to be built. One day, in North and South Korea, I will build a bridge across the most heavily guarded border in the world, and open a line for communication. In Somalia, I will build a bridge between people and government, and mend a land ravaged by anarchy. I will build bridges in Afghanistan, in China, and in all corners of Earth.

I may still be a student with building blocks in my hand, but in time I will be an ambassador with bridges around the world. These are ambitious dreams, but they're driven by a simple force. All I want is to do is bring people together, to make peace, and to make my bridges as sturdy as the one in my hometown.

Erica graduated high school as valedictorian, having taken twelve AP classes—the maximum number offered at her school. As part of her school's Model United Nations organization, she won awards at the Berkeley and Washington State Model United Nations conferences and eventually ran the club in her senior year. In addition to school-related extracurricular activities, Erica worked on political campaigns, won local piano competitions, and did volunteer work mentoring elementary school students, all while holding a Chinese language-tutoring job. The summer before her senior year of high school, Erica participated in the Yale Ivy Scholars Program (now the Yale Young Global Scholars Program), a highly selective leadership and global studies program.

Erica applied to a range of top-tier universities, and of all the schools to which she was admitted, she chose Penn. She reflects on why:

Since early on in high school I wanted to major in international relations (IR). I chose Penn because of its strong IR program, which structured course requirements around a variety of fields, including political science, history, and economics. Now that I am in my final year as an IR major, I appreciate the program even more for its emphasis on research and writing. The major's unique research methods course requirement and yearlong senior thesis expose students to social science research early, and first inspired my own interest in research.

The following were the "Why Penn" essay prompt and Erica's response when applying to Penn:

Considering both the specific undergraduate school or program to which you are applying and the broader University of Pennsylvania community, what academic, research, and/or extracurricular paths do you see yourself exploring at Penn?

When I think about International Relations, I think of Alexander the Great, Sun Tzu, Winston Churchill, and what they've taught me about leadership and history. I think of learning about collectivism versus individualism, the conflicts between the two philosophies, and how these conflicts have manifested in the present day. I think of my emerging understanding of economics, and how I've begun to notice patterns in the economic history of the world. When I think about all of these subjects, I think about Penn.

Penn is important to me because of its emphasis on interdisciplinary programs. Every school has some kind of interdisciplinary option, but for me, Penn's IR program has the ideal combination of political science, philosophy, and economics courses that will help me translate my education into real-world practicality. I have no doubt that a wealth of courses ranging from "Human Rights and History" to "Revolutions and Dictators" will satisfy my desire to possess a diverse range of knowledge.

During my time in Speech and Debate, I've had to research extensively to prepare to argue for or against bills in Student Congress. As I compiled research on bills ranging from prioritizing foster parents in cases of adoption to mandating drug testing of welfare recipients, I discovered only objective information and data. However, as a student Senator debating societal issues, I lacked insight on the human aspect. There's only so much I can learn from facts, figures, and impersonal information from the internet. I want to view a problem through differing opinions and from passionate instructors, and so I hope to explore Penn's double-major option and major in International Relations and History.

Besides academic programs, I also plan to spend my free time participating in a diverse combination of clubs and sports I intend to continue with activities I've done in high school and explore previously unavailable options. I can imagine myself contributing answers on the Academic Demolition Team, organizing campaigns with Amnesty International, or perhaps rediscovering my volleyball skills. Additionally, the Kelly Writers House, with its emphasis on creative writing and academic independence, might inspire a whole new interest. Exploring my creative voice could help me discover my own kind of eloquence, or aid my writing in academic papers, Speech and Debate, and more.

In the future, I intend to work for the United Nations, a job requiring a background in a wide range of social and academic skills. I can think of no better preparation than the career-related opportunities, experience in collaborating with other talented students, and personal maturation that Penn will provide me. I will bring with me an unstoppable eagerness to learn, and I hope that Penn's endless options help me craft myself into a dependable leader.

Today, Erica is a senior at Penn. I've asked her to reflect on the following:

To what extent did your college experience meet your expectations? In what ways did your experience cause you to change your perspective on your academic career, your dreams and aspirations, and your life?

As I was entering college, I was very idealistic and wished to explore many career options. Going through college has been a process of narrowing and focusing my aspirations and molding my dreams into realistic goals.

In high school, I excelled at and was most interested in my history and government classes. I participated in Model United Nations, so I had known since sophomore year of high school that I wanted to major in international relations. I originally wanted to double-major in international relations and history, but after entering college, with a growing interest in the Middle East, I decided to take Arabic language courses and eventually decided on modern Middle Eastern studies as my second major.

Through the first half of my college career, I narrowed my general interests in international affairs and history and focused on international relations and foreign policy. One internship in particular helped me realize that I wanted to work for the public sector. The summer after my freshman year at Penn, I interned for my congressman on his congressional campaign. I had worked for his office before, when I was in high school and he was a state senator. During my internship, I worked on a team of young, enthusiastic staffers and interns, and engaged with voters daily on issues impacting our community, from public education to job creation. This experience gave me a new perspective on domestic politics, and my broad, overarching interest in international affairs back in high school gradually shifted to a desire to work in the public sector.

I entered college without clear expectations for my next four years beyond knowing that I would major in international relations, with keen interests in international affairs. During my first two years of college, figuring out what I *didn't* want to do in the future was just as important as knowing what I did want to do. Although I greatly enjoyed my congressional campaign internship, I realized that I had no interest in working on political campaigns as a career option. And although my involvement in the Penn Society for International Development has sparked my interest in international development, I've also realized that I might not necessarily want to work for an NGO in the private sector.

Studying abroad the fall semester of my junior year in Rabat, the capital of Morocco, has been a pivotal moment of my college experience. Living in a foreign country and navigating daily life in a different culture has greatly broadened my global perspective. My most profound learning experiences occurred outside of the classroom: bargaining in street markets, interacting with my host family, and talking to everyday Moroccans about their lives and our shared interests.

The second half of my college experience has been a process of narrowing my interests and pinpointing specific goals. As an upperclassman, I took higher-level courses in my majors and engaged more closely with professors and peers in my classes. I became interested in social science research after taking a research methods course in preparation for writing my IR senior thesis. In my junior year, I took a class on public international law at Penn Law, which completely convinced me to study law. The current work on my thesis and my emerging interest in research, combined with my interest in international law, have fundamentally changed my academic goals. I now have a clearly defined goal of studying law and pursuing a PhD in international relations, with the hopes of practicing and researching international law in the future.

The most important outcome of my college experiences thus far has been achieving a sharper focus of my academic interests and career goals while discovering post-graduation options. My broad interest in international affairs gradually narrowed to a strong interest in research and international law. Inevitably, my high school idealism and optimism faded, but I have held onto my steadfast passion to better my community and the world. Along the way, I've learned that it is acceptable, even beneficial, to make mistakes. My biggest learning opportunities came when I evaluated my failures and identified what I could improve on and what was out of my control. My failures have taught me more than any of my achievements have.

Given what you know now, if you could redo high school, what would you do differently, and why?

CONTRIBUTE TO YOUR LOCAL COMMUNITY

Given the experiences I've gained and all I've learned since graduating from high school, the one thing I would have done differently would be to get *even more* involved in my local community.

Working on a political campaign while in high school was an excellent learning experience, and I realize now that I should have been even more involved in local politics and community engagement. Besides internships, there were youth political organizations, volunteer opportunities, and other resources available to me, and I believe that students should aim to engage actively in bettering their local communities.

Even if these resources had not been available to me in high school, I could have done more to reach out to my community on my own. Back then, I didn't realize I had the power to effect change, but now I realize that young people are a powerful source of change and that community engagement is an invaluable learning experience. For example, during my junior and senior years of high school, budget cuts in both primary and higher education posed a problem for administrators and students alike, and I wish I could have done more to petition local and state lawmakers to oppose budget cuts.

Back in high school, I never realized the extent to which I could have aided my community and helped solve the problems I saw. High school students can, in fact, effect significant change, and it's important for students to seize available opportunities to do so. Looking back, I would have no hesitation in becoming involved and helping to better my community.

What else would you like to share with or suggest to high school students and college students, and why?

STUDY ABROAD

My biggest piece of advice is to study, live, or work abroad. Immersing yourself in another culture highlights the commonalities among people and makes you a better citizen of the world. You gain incredible insight into a particular region while developing a better appreciation for diversity. Personally, having to be largely independent while abroad has helped me become better able to work in unfamiliar situations and communicate despite language barriers. If you are able to, studying abroad will immensely widen your perspective of the world.

Before I studied abroad in Morocco, I was aware of the economic and political issues of the Middle East and North Africa, but living in the country allowed me to experience firsthand what these issues meant for everyday Moroccans. Like many Arab countries, Morocco has a large youth population dealing with decreasing economic opportunities. Faced with dwindling employment prospects, an increasing number of youth in Morocco who finish university education struggle to find jobs of any kind. In rural communities, providing children, especially girls, with quality education is another struggle I witnessed when I volunteered to teach English for a few days in a village in the Atlas Mountains. On-the-ground experiences will always be more meaningful than simply reading about an issue.

Living abroad has also strengthened my adaptability and communication skills. Throughout my time in Morocco, I constantly made mistakes—

either through communication errors or cultural unawareness on my part. The first time I dined at my now-favorite shawarma shop in Rabat, I attempted to order my shawarma platter "to go," but knew neither the appropriate Arabic nor French word. The owner of the shop gave me a quizzical look the entire time I struggled to communicate the concept (turns out that dining on the fly is a very American mind-set). Eventually I got my idea across, and the next time I visited the shop, I came well equipped with the phrase for "to go" (FYI – it's *emporter*).

Shopping in the souqs, or open-air marketplaces, of Morocco allowed me to communicate with shopkeepers and develop an understanding of their lives while observing their perceptions of Americans. Shopkeepers hawked goods from brightly colored scarves to iPhone accessories. The stalls with leather handbags had a pungent, lamb-like smell, which hung in the air along with the scent of cumin and Argan oil—common products in the souq. The owners of these shops were often pleasantly surprised when I communicated with them in Darija, the Moroccan Arabic dialect, and they were especially excited that foreign students like me were interested in Arabic and Morocco.

From struggling to speak entirely in Arabic to insulting a shop vendor accidentally by offering too low of a price while haggling, I made plenty of mistakes, even after several months of living in Morocco. However, all of these errors turned into learning opportunities, and by the end of my stay I was better able to deal with my mistakes gracefully and with cultural sensitivity.

Through my time in Morocco, I gained better awareness of cultural differences and, indirectly, a sharper understanding of the unique aspects of American culture. I returned to the United States with a deeper sense of connection to the Middle East and North Africa and a stronger academic interest in the region.

A perfectly imperfect takeaway on Erica:

As the events of the Arab uprisings played out during her high school years, Erica felt compelled to learn more about the complex history and politics of the Middle East. Her studies in international relations and the Middle East, combined with her passion in research and international law, have inspired her goal of studying and researching international law in the future. She aspires to become an influencer in working toward peace in the Middle East and throughout the world.

6

Ivy Xing

Lonely Child to Geeky Girl

BA in Mathematics and Computer Science (double major),
Class of 2015, Bowdoin College

Despite an unusually difficult home environment, Ivy Xing developed a strong passion for math and excellence in high school. Ivy founded and led the Math Club at her school. After attending a competitive math camp at UC Davis the summer after junior year, University of California faculty selected her to present her cryptography project to UC board members, Nobel laureates, and professors, and so she did. She also led the percussion section and played the flute in the California Youth Chinese Symphony.

Today, Ivy's diligent efforts have placed her on the Dean's List every year at Bowdoin College, a prestigious liberal arts institution in Maine. While continuing her math pursuits, she discovered a passion for computer science. She is now a math and computer science tutor and TA, as well as a STEM program mentor. She has served as the president of International Club for three years, organizing small-scale and campus-wide events with a team of ten officers. In her spare time, she likes to hang out with friends, solve puzzles, draw, practice flute, code, and play games. She recently published her own game on the App Store, has been working on a website and an iOS application, and plans to pursue software engineering after graduation.

Life is nothing but an attitude.

—Ivy Xing

To say that Ivy experienced a difficult childhood would be to do it an injustice. She recounts:

Born and raised in Guilin, China, I was eight when my parents divorced. Mom then told me that she had to go on a long business trip to Beijing, so I stayed with Dad and a nanny. Every day, Dad would leave for work before I woke up, and when he came back, he would rush through dinner and then go gambling with neighbors. If Dad won some money, I wouldn't see him until the next day, as he would gamble away the rest of the night. If he lost money, he would come back in a sullen mood—another silent night in the house. Although he wasn't the most caring father, Dad was generally nice toward me, so I never held any grudge against him. I just wished that Mom would come back.

A year passed by, and Mom was still away. One day when she called home I vaguely heard people speaking English in the background. When I questioned her about it, she told me the truth: She had settled in the United States, not for some long business trip but for the rest of her life—and the rest of my life too, I had just found out. I felt lost and cheated.

At age twelve, I moved to the States against my will. Upon seeing mom at the airport, I felt like I was greeting a stranger. Although Mom had often called home, after four years the bond between us almost became unreal. While in the States, Mom married my stepdad, a wealthy Caucasian. Because I spoke only broken English and my stepdad was very introverted, we barely talked for a year or two. My stepdad was friendly with me most of the time, but sometimes he was arrogant and ill tempered. Because he paid for all the living expenses for Mom and me, Mom always hurled accusations at me for not trying hard enough to please him. Our big house in the hills always felt so cold and empty.

As I began to lose hope in life, I became depressed and my grades plummeted, leaving an F, a D, and a C on my transcript in my high school freshman year.

When she was a high school freshman, Ivy attempted to escape her painful family environment and took an undue risk by running away from home. She slept in the streets of San Francisco for a few nights.

She reflected on this intense experience and its effects when applying to college during her senior year. The corresponding Common Application personal essay prompt and her response are as follows:

Please write an essay on a topic of your choice. This personal essay helps us become acquainted with you as a person and student, apart from courses, grades, test scores, and other objective data. It will also demonstrate your ability to organize your thoughts and express yourself.

RAN AWAY FROM HOME

"I repeated myself a hundred times. Are you sillier than a bull?" Mom's curses pierced my heart after I inadvertently left a few strings of hair on the dresser. Obsessed with perfection, mom cleaned and re-cleaned every tiny spot. Whenever I left a trace of dirt, her rages would explode.

Much more complex than matters of perfectionism, my troubled relationship with mom traces back to childhood. After mom left for America, 8-year-old me was under the care of my dad, an addicted gambler. Then I immigrated to USA to live with mom in 2005, but found that my separation from her during my most important formative years had made mutual understanding between us almost impossible. Mom limited my social activities. She sometimes slapped and even whipped me when I did not meet her standards of obedience. Always the target of her severe scolding at the slightest excuse, I endorsed "Patience at the moment of anger eschews a hundred days of sorrow" as my teeth-biting motto.

But even my absolute silence could not stop mom's petulant outbursts. Conflicts at home deteriorated, imprisoning me in shock and depression. At school, I vacuously stared at the whiteboard while my mind teemed with tangled thoughts about my family. Language barriers and feelings of alienation from classmates kept me from seeking help. When I went home, I tossed away the cumbersome homework and dove into isolation.

In 2008, when I was in 9th grade and was no longer able to bear the mental trauma, I ran away from home. I bought my necessities with the spare change I earned from working as an art assistant teacher. The piercing gust penetrated my bones as I crawled into my sleeping bag in downtown San Francisco. This was the third day of my journey. I shut my eyes to end the daylong weariness in the pitch-dark night, but a series of nightmarish memories haunted me relentlessly: mom grabbing my hair while banging my head against the wall in hysteria, hurling my flute on the floor, and ripping apart my favorite math book; step-father yelling out domineering commands and indulging in incessant beer-drinking . . . As the scenes fretted my mind, raindrops engulfed the tears that dimmed my eyes.

I walked to Jack-in-the-Box to find shelter. An elderly lady with a disheveled appearance sat next to me. I noticed the pile of clothing beside her. A homeless person? I thought. Then I realized that I was now homeless too.

"Don't you eat?" she asked.

"I'm not hungry." I said, but my stomach growled.

The conversation carried on. She tried to persuade me to go home. But in desperate fear of mom, I thought I would never return. She ridiculed my naiveté and revealed to me her life stories: a broke clerk abandoned by her children and employer, she subsisted on the monthly two-hundred-dollar government aid, roamed about the streets, and slept in rags outside stores and houses. Yet it was this same woman who treated me to a nice dinner. Her generosity melted my heart. When even a feeble elderly could bravely bear the slings and arrows of outrageous fortune, what pathetic tears was I shedding? I understood that my mawkish sufferings were trivial comparing to hers. And I finally saw my folly and willfulness.

In a whirlpool of repentance, I came home with new strength in my heart. But when mom saw my report card, her frantic snarl exploded. Proclaiming (in Mandarin Chinese) that I was "incorrigible," she asked my stepdad to pay a friend of hers to be my guardian and transferred me to Redwood Christian School, a small private high school in her friend's neighborhood for 10th grade.

Free from the cage mom locked me in, I enjoyed an extensive social life with my friends in the new environment. I met many international students at the new school, whose families stayed on the other side of the Pacific Ocean. Realizing that I was much luckier than they, I grew empathetic to their situations. I have since helped them with academic and personal issues whenever I could. The gradually developed tie between us motivated me to adopt an optimistic view. I no longer blamed fate for my hardships. Grasping my future in my own hands, I pursued academic excellence and rebuilt my social network.

From a low-performing student despairing in conflicts to a high-achiever fighting for my future, I have transformed from a discontented child under mom's control into an independent individual. I have come to see myself as part of a community where I learn, give, and live from the heart, and I long to continue my academic and other pursuits in college with my invigorated energy.

Through her teenage years, Ivy not only worked on strengthening her writing skills, but also has fashioned a strong interest in math since her middle school years. Naturally, she wrote about her passion for math on college apps. The Bowdoin application supplement prompt and Ivy's essay are as follows:

Bowdoin students and alumni often cite world-class faculty and opportunities for intellectual engagement, the College's commitment to the Common Good, and the special quality of life on the coast of Maine as important aspects of the Bowdoin experience. Reflecting on your own interests and experiences, please comment on one of the following:

1. Intellectual engagement [this is what Ivy chose to write about]

"Caught you!" The night-watcher shone his flashlight on me as I stealthily trotted along the corridor in the dark. At the camp, time was an abstract concept for us in Cluster 6: Math. After dinner I went to my friend's dorm room to work on combinatorics conundrums, and conquered most of them. Unfortunately I never calculated how the clock ticked so quickly. The light-out time passed, and I was supposed to be in my own room. I reluctantly turned off my math mode, but was caught on the way back.

Well, just another dangerous sign that I couldn't fully shake off the day's madness at the California Summer School for Math and Sciences. With a muddle of topology and combinatorics, the camp afforded me invaluable insights into the real world of math—where there was math, there was everything else. The instance I picked up my tiny, heavy companion "Notes," those Jones polynomials, Klein bottles, and trefoils began capturing the nerves in my brain. I feasted on them all.

With an insatiable curiosity, I then jumped into "Ordering the Reidemeister moves of a classical knot," a research paper written by my topology professor. After ten hours of burning the midnight oil to look up esoteric theorems and terminologies, I was very pleased that I did understand about four out of 12 pages of the paper. At the end of the camp, I peeled off a coating of math and found the number of layers inside reaching infinity.

One of the summer programs in which Ivy participated in high school was the California State Summer School for Mathematics and Sciences. Subsequently nominated by the University of California faculty based on personal achievements, project complexity, and communication style, she was invited to the coveted California Annual Nobel Laureate Dinner. There, Ivy presented a cryptography project to ten chemistry and physics Nobel laureates, and to UC board members and professors.

Ivy extended her grit to ensemble music as well. She applied herself in learning about, performing, and earning eventually a leadership role in music (percussion). She wrote a short essay about this on her college applications:

Four years ago, I only dared to tap the cymbal in a subdued whisper. A novice recruited by the conductor without faculty's consent, I faced constant disregards from the other 50 members and censures from the teachers. Lack of progress almost convinced me that the conductor's initial appreciation for my sense of rhythm was a mistake. But a virtuoso is not born overnight. Taking the train to the symphony every week—an hour-long journey—I valued every chance to eavesdrop a tip or two from others and often arrived early to practice drums by myself. Finally promoted to percussion leader in charge of the timpani by my third year, I spent more time listening to rehearsal recordings not only to acquaint myself with the melodies, but also to capture the musical spirits and subtleties. And I kept the secret that I wasn't really a musical genius.

After receiving her share of college admissions, including UC Berkeley and UCLA, and denials, Ivy chose Bowdoin College. She felt that a more intimate top-notch private liberal arts school setting and the 3,000 miles of distance from family signaled a better fit. She reflects on her Bowdoin application and admission experience:

I applied to Bowdoin because I heard that its students were among the happiest college and university students in the nation and that the food is #1. At the time I didn't give much thought to whether it would be a good fit for me, because I didn't think I could get in. With my atrocious ninth-grade record that significantly pulled down my cumulative high school GPA, I knew that for most elite private colleges and universities—where, unlike the UCs, Admissions weighs your freshman year high school record equally with the other years—my application was an easy throw-away. So when I received the letter of admission from Bowdoin, I was very surprised.

What especially surprised me was a handwritten note from Bowdoin's dean of admissions expressing appreciation for what I had gone through (as related in my personal essays), signed by his first name, Scott, below the printed lines of the letter. Later when I visited Bowdoin, I sat at the same table with Scott and a few other students at a dinner reception for admitted students. He started the conversation by asking me about my bamboo flute lessons and another student about the trip from his hometown of Albany, New York. It was the first time he met us in person, but we did not need to tell him our backgrounds and passions. It occurred to me then that every student matters at Bowdoin—starting as early as the moment we submit our application.

Gratitude and humility are also qualities in Ivy. . . .

After I transferred to Redwood Christian School and sought guidance from Mr. Ma when he was with his previous company, I was grateful that my mind-set, academic performance, skills, confidence, direction, and school and community contributions improved markedly, allowing me to become a straight-A student and emerging as a leader. After I entered Bowdoin, I wrote a letter to thank Mr. Ma for his help and guidance. Here is an excerpt of that letter:

> I want to thank you with my innermost sincerity for all that you have done in guiding my academic planning, personal development, and college applications. The scene of my first meeting you and weeping in front of you is deeply imprinted in my heart. It is by no means an exaggeration to attribute the stimulus of my turning point in life to you and your team. When I deviated from the light of learning and lost my direction with a confounded mind, it was you who motivated me to embrace my former assiduity; it was you who showed me the path to success; and it was you who encouraged me to indefatigably run toward my future. My experience with you has been a life-changing one, with or without the final results.

Today, Ivy is a college rising senior. I've asked her to reflect on the following:

To what extent did your college experience—on and off campus—meet your expectations? In what ways did your experience cause you to change your perspective on your academic career, your dreams and aspirations, and your life?

ON PROFESSORS

I first visited Bowdoin, a 1,800-student liberal arts college, during Admitted Student Weekend in April of my senior year in high school. As I was about to walk out in the company of current Bowdoin students at the end of the math class I audited, the professor stopped me to ask about my impression of the campus. How did he even know that I was a visitor? Then I realized that this place was not the big prestigious university I'd visited the week before, where I'd dozed off in a five-hundred-student lecture hall while the professor with a microphone occasionally called on "you, the blue shirt in the back," who always eagerly waved his hand to answer questions. In retrospect, I could not simply say that my college experience met my expectations—my past three years at Bowdoin went far beyond what I had been capable of expecting.

I still remember my first Linear Algebra exam. I walked into it assured that I was prepared and walked out thinking that I did well. When the professor handed me the exam back, I couldn't believe it was my name that lay next to the scarlet pen mark that read 68. The class average was a full grade higher. When I finally accepted my failure, my teary eyes noticed the neatly written line below that 68: "Ivy, come see me—Prof. Barker." In his office, Professor Barker sat down with me for an hour to go over every problem I got marked down on and helped me redefine my study strategies. With renewed confidence, I aced the subsequent exams.

At Bowdoin, building personal relationships with professors is natural. Another math professor—after finding out about my chronic neck pain—even petitioned for physical therapy funding for me from the Dean's Office. We went to many yoga classes together afterward. In addition, I decided to pursue computer science as a career only after my Introduction to CS professor saw my promise as a young woman in computer science, provided me advice and guidance, and offered me a full-time summer research opportunity my freshman summer in college.

All the professors with whom I took classes at least know me by name. I consider some of them my friends in a respectful way and sometimes get meals with them. They not only helped me shape my perspective on my academic and professional career but also helped me cope with difficulties by cultivating many of my personal qualities and skills.

ON EXPLORATION

In high school, I was set on becoming a mathematician. I thought I would take every math class offered at Bowdoin to consummate my college career. When some friends in college told me how they had explored and switched fields, I just yawned and thought: Everyone else could change his or her plans, but me? No way.

Now I'm a math and computer science double major. Although I continued pursuing math, my dreams have gone in a different direction. As I dove deeper into computer science, it struck me that I was so determined on what I wanted to be not because of how knowledgeable I was about that subject but because of how ignorant I was about the world outside of that field.

Even though most classes I have taken so far were for my majors, I'm fortunate to have a diverse group of friends majoring in different fields. Just by spending time with them, I have learned much about anthropology, gender and women's studies, classical studies, and so forth. Learning more about fields outside my comfort zone opened my mind to a much bigger world and reassured me in my pursuit of math and computer science.

Given what you know now, if you could redo high school, what would you do differently, and why?

TEN YEARS OF GAMING, TEN YEARS OF REDEFINING SUCCESS

I have been playing online games for ten years. Sometimes gaming was my way to connect with friends; other times it was my way to disconnect from reality. During my freshman year of high school, I spent hours and hours leveling up my RPG (role-playing game) character. The more I thought about my family, the more depressed I became and the more I glued myself to my computer. That year I wished I *were* my RPG character.

This summer, I spent about forty hours a week at MakeGamesWithUs, a computer science education company, developing a game of my own to publish on the App Store. Besides having had tons of fun designing, coding, and play testing, I gained more insight into the gaming industry. I now appreciate gaming in a way that I wouldn't have been able to if I were to mindlessly play one game after another. Rather than shielding me from the real world, gaming now provides me with a surge of positive energy that propels me forward in my career pursuits.

After converting a negative addiction into positive motivation, I reexamined my definition of success. Now, for me being successful means using all that I have to do all that I can. American author and motivational speaker Zig Ziglar once said: "Success is the doing, not the getting; in the trying, not the triumph. Success is a personal standard, reaching for the highest that is in us, becoming all that we can be." Whenever my achievements meet some societal standard of excellence, I would ask myself, Have I become all that I can be? Yet the moment I become all that I can be is exactly the moment when I can be more. So the answer is always no—I keep going. If I had only realized back in high school that it was possible to escape from papers and problem sets but not myself and my own future, I would have pushed myself harder in every direction. I would not have been satisfied with exemplifying definitions of success that were not my own.

Now with chronic neck pain, I wish I'd carried out my exercise plans years ago. Now always preoccupied with the variegated college life, I wish I'd practiced flute longer then. Now scrambling to gain more coding experience before submitting job applications, I wish I'd spent fewer hours gaming and more hours exploring game development and computer science.

MY OPINION ON PROCRASTINATION

I'll tell you later. Just kidding.

"Procrastinate." That's the word I heard the most from my classmates and oftentimes myself in high school. As an academic mentor in college, I continue to hear this word from my first-year and even upper-class mentees as they constantly struggle to keep up with their classes.

After I entered college, it took me only two short weeks to realize that starting a paper the night before it was due was no longer feasible. Changing my habits, however, took me two hard years. I can no longer remember how many consecutive all-nighters I pulled two years ago. What I know now is that although I'm taking more challenging classes, I'm managing my time better.

What transformed me over the past few years was something of importance that I wish I knew back in high school: forming the habit of starting work early. Habits change lives. Whether we can get into our dream school depends not on what we do the week before we submit the application but on what we do every day.

What else would you like to share with or suggest to high school and college students and why?

LEARN SOMETHING OUTSIDE OF ACADEMICS AND STICK WITH IT

Cooking. Break dancing. Juggling. Anything. Under the constant pressure of schoolwork in college, you will find that joining a sports team or practicing an instrument daily may be too time consuming; but if you have already built up solid skills in high school, occasionally coming back to these talents will relieve some stress from your fast-paced college life and even increase your productivity. While practicing a certain skill for hours every week can feel exhausting, do not have regrets because high school may be the only stage in your life outside your academic or professional career when you actually have time to fully develop these interests.

GET READY TO ACCEPT THAT IN COLLEGE, GRADES AREN'T ALWAYS PROPORTIONAL TO OUR EFFORTS

In a computer science class I took sophomore year in college, the first thing our professor warned us was that effort does not equal grade. Did she mean that we should stop working too hard and admit our inability to meet her standards? Of course not. Over time I found what this meant was that it's a horrible idea to only focus on grades. Sometimes we could get an A in a class and forget all that we learned the moment we finished that class; other times we could get an unsatisfactory grade in a class but would remember and even use the material later. In high school we aim for excellent grades to get into respectable colleges; in college we aim for excellent grades to get into respectable graduate schools or get dream jobs. Yet in reality, if instead of studying the material for its own sake we only study for the grades, we will get nowhere. When will we realize that learning, instead of meeting standards, is the real measure of excellence?

REALIZE THAT OUR FAMILY ENVIRONMENT *ALONE* DOES NOT DEFINE US

Sometimes we focus too much on what we don't have and blame our surroundings for not allowing us to achieve more. Yet every difficulty we encounter is an opportunity: If we let it set us back, we will fall and tumble until we muster enough courage to get up; but if instead we trudge against the howling wind, we will find ourselves growing stronger than ever expected. Even though we cannot control the weather, we can control our direction.

When my old self was faced with challenges, I blamed everything that was not in my power to change and fancied that some magical force could suddenly pull me out of my miseries. Over time, however, I realized that frustration, anger, and despair never provided any viable solutions. Instead, focusing on the positive aspects of life often helped me look at the negatives with a more optimistic attitude—and sometimes even turn the setbacks into motivational forces. When I couldn't look at my family without crying, I called my friends and cheered; when I started to believe that I had nothing to live for, I went outside, looked upon the stars in the night sky, and laughed at how insignificant my troubles were when the world extended far, far beyond my reach.

We cannot always prevent problems from coming, but we can always use them to cultivate perseverance, patience, and understanding in us. The harsher the trial, the stronger we grow. When we deal with difficulties, what eventually matters is not how good or bad the outcome is but how the situation comes to shape us as individuals. This depends not only on the environment but also—and in a more important way—on us. The process of learning, maturing, and adapting is not a means to an end but an end in itself, because life is nothing but an attitude.

A perfectly imperfect takeaway about Ivy:

Ivy's family environment was complicated and often discouraging, but she persevered and learned to become more mature and independent. There were times when Ivy found herself in a tight place and struggled to hang on, but she was determined to turn those situations into learning opportunities and come out with a stronger mind-set and heart. Now, no matter what happens in her life, Ivy looks upon her environment with positivity and appreciation. She still talks to her dad and stepdad sometimes, and her relationship with her mom has improved much since she started college. She has realized that the steering wheel of her fate is in only her own hands and that it is vital to never stop learning, giving, exploring, and smiling. Ivy continues pursuing her passion for learning and practicing both mathematics and computer science.

7

Kimberly Han

Filmmaker Dreaming of the Oscars

BA in Cinema and Media Studies and International Studies
(double major), Class of 2015, University of Chicago

Kimberly Han is a Korean American who was born in Columbus, Ohio, and grew up in Seoul, South Korea, and Palo Alto, California. Swept up in the Silicon Valley science, technology, engineering, and math (STEM) education craze through high school, and then tempted in college by business and law school, Kimberly did not think to pursue her true passion—film—until this past year.

From acting as a lead in a play to directing one, working at production companies, developing her own start-up film distribution company, and then directing her own short films, Kimberly has upturned her life to resist surrounding pressures and to do what genuinely excites and animates her everyday life. Currently engaged in her university's two film societies, DocFilms and Fire Escape Films, Kimberly dreams of that one day when her passion will be recognized and her movies will spark and stir people from various cultures and countries across the globe.

Know the world before creating your own.

—Kimberly Han

Kimberly Han's childhood wasn't easy, as she missed her "goose father" in Korea dearly. She reflects:

I was in second grade and my brother in third. Mom was alone with two little kids and no real friends to rely on in Los Angeles. I remember the very first international call I made to my dad in Korea when Mom handed me the phone to speak with him. I had held the phone tightly to my ear, and in a matter of seconds, I was a hot mess and a broken faucet. I wanted to speak so badly to my dad, but no sound would get past my throat. I stopped blabbering unintelligible sounds and handed the phone back to my mom, who was also in tears.

It is not a rare phenomenon for Korean immigrant families to come to America without the father. Many strongly believe that education and general life standards are better in the States, and thus work hard to settle there. However, fathers often already hold stable, promising careers in Korea that are too much at risk if they move. There is a widely used phrase in Korea—"goose father," which is meant to describe the dad who is left behind in Korea to work and send money to the family abroad. He is called a "goose" because he has to migrate long distances to see his family. My dad was a goose father; my mom was the sole family head, and I was a lucky first-generation American.

If only I knew how everything my parents did was for my brother and me only, I would have hugged them so tightly every chance I got. It's a pity that most of us don't recognize the precious people who support us until we grow older, but I am happy to finally acknowledge the beautiful people in my life to whom I'll spend my lifetime giving back.

Thinking of my parents daily, I have a confession to make: Sometimes in my spare time, I watch YouTube videos of Oscar acceptance speeches, and sob along with the winners. I dream of the day that I will get up there, take the little gold man in my shaking hands, and thank, thank, thank my parents. I am eternally sorry and grateful to Umma and Appa (Mom and Dad, respectively, in spoken Korean), who gave everything for my brother and me. For them, I am ready to fight and succeed as a filmmaker. I am ready for anything to make them proud.

But in high school, becoming a filmmaker was not yet within Kimberly's aspirations. Back then, the Silicon Valley tech vibe resonated with her. As a freshman at the highly competitive Gunn High, situated near Stanford University, she started the Girls Tech Club to help expand young women's roles in technology, and led the club through high school. Kimberly discussed this experience and why it was important on a subsequent college application personal essay. The corresponding Common Application essay prompt and her response are as follows:

Please write an essay on a topic of your choice. This personal essay helps us become acquainted with you as a person and student, apart from courses, grades, test scores, and other objective data. It will also demonstrate your ability to organize your thoughts and express yourself.

I stood cringing behind the sign, "Girls Tech Club: First meeting tomorrow at room L-14B." Before Club Day, I was a timidly excited freshman who believed that her creation was to receive great, wide acclamation from her fellow schoolmates. This day, however, the bypassing students sneered and jeered at my naïve soul. As I self-consciously slouched lower and lower to hide myself, two girls came over to my booth, conversing.

"Aren't you really tech-savvy? Maybe you should join!"

"Oh, I don't know. I guess I am but . . . Well, I don't know."

The latter girl sensed curious, mocking eyes upon her, and as if she would fall into the hands of Satan if she signed my new member sheet, she grabbed her friend's arm and walked away. I was more concerned than offended though. It was fine that the girl did not want to join the club, but I knew the reason *why* she did not want to join, and that thought weighed on me for the rest of the day.

I was greatly surprised that even in such an accepting school as Gunn High, girls interested in technology were so discouraged to pursue their interest. Moreover, I soon realized that the lack of women in technology applied not only to Gunn, but also mirrored the phenomenon around the world. I found my jumbled feelings and thoughts crystallized into the very question that I strive to solve today: Why are so few women involved in technology, and what can I do to change this?

In our society, the "norm" requires women to conform to certain career ideals that are sharp, stylish, and elegant. At the same time, many believe technological jobs to be otherwise—geeky, hands-on, and manly. Since childhood, girls watch their fathers easily manipulating computers or men teaching math and engineering. In contrast, they see the paucity of women in science. Thus, girls fear pursuing their passion for technology and standing out in a community of scientific men. The natural tendency to conform isolates women not only from men, but also from other women who believe they are unfit for technology. However, if more individual women become leaders and set examples in the fields of technology, girls will see that they can belong wherever they want to belong.

Everyone has a different personality and not everyone needs to be excited about technology. It is a pity, however, that many girls do not recognize their interest in it because they do not have the occasion to explore and encounter it. That is why I created Girls Tech Club: to give opportunities to every girl and spur any underlying passion in her. I wanted to give not only the technical skills, but also a sense of community and a forum for women to freely talk about technology.

Had I not received the many opportunities provided by my family and community, I might not have even recognized my own passion. I was fortunate enough to have a father who works at Yahoo Inc., a mother and brother who are math geniuses, and a home at Silicon Valley. My mother was especially inspiring, as she did not pressure me to choose the traditionally Korean female careers and rather encouraged me to choose my own. Women in Korea are virtually non-existent in technology, unlike in America where women are at least beginning to take influential positions in technology and even politics, such as Meg Whitman and Carly Fiorina. Therefore, I want to actualize my goal to provide opportunities for women in America and also get back to the Korean community, placing equal power in women's hands.

Ever since last year, I had felt guilty about that Club Day. Fortunately, I was given a second chance. As I was at my usual post on Club Day, I recognized the girl, Sara, who, in embarrassment, had not previously signed up for our club. She indifferently passed by our table, but this time, I called to her. I talked to her as encouragingly as I could and was finally able to convince her that any reservations should not get in the way of pursuing one's passion. She currently comes to our weekly meetings and has even brought several friends with her.

Girls Tech Club's success continued even after Sara's joining. As I set up a PowerPoint presentation for the first meeting of my senior year, more and more girls walked into the room. By the time I turned off the lights for a presentation, twenty sets of eyes looked expectantly at me. So, several years after the great crisis, I still stand behind the same booth, but with a smile, a straight back and a lifted head.

For human beings both young and middle-aged, certain little moments can yield the power to influence or redirect our interests. A moment in middle school turned out to be an omen that pivoted Kimberly's desire toward blending technology with art. She wrote about this on her college applications:

Evil assassins are pursuing Dash, the young superhero, through a forest of palm trees. As Dash zooms through the tropical forest, the foliage quivers violently in his wake . . . This vivid scene in *The Incredibles* is perhaps the foundation of my passion. I had seen animated films before, but this particular motion picture left me utterly speechless. The animators had brought Dash to life and touched me with their impossibly realistic artistry.

I went home that day believing that I would easily remake the intense action scenes in *The Incredibles*. Little did I realize how much collaboration, expertise, technology, and editing were needed to create just a few minutes of this masterpiece. A few weeks later, I watched "The Making of *The Incredibles*" feature on the DVD, which showed that talented artists had drawn 2-dimensional mockups for every scene in the movie. Learning what went into the film filled me with awe and admiration for the animators and also sparked my passion for technology and art.

Before enrolling in high school, Kimberly immersed herself in the Awesome Math summer camp at University of Texas–Dallas. A strong believer in STEM education and active engagement and learning, Kimberly loved hands-on projects in high school. She founded Girls Tech Club as a freshman and served as president for three and a half years. She served as the graphics editor and web/tech editor for *The Oracle*, Gunn High's robust newspaper. She also engaged in the award-winning Space Cookies Robotics team, an all-girls robotics team sponsored by NASA and Girl Scouts, and participated in the competitive COSMOS Biotechnology Summer Program at UC Davis.

Kimberly applied to and was admitted to a range of top-tier private and public universities. This included University of Chicago, to which she applied Early Action. (Kimberly prefers privacy regarding the details of her college admissions results.)

Truth be told, I had no idea what I wanted to do by the time that I was going to college. I was confused and clueless, like many other students of that age. I chose the University of Chicago because I was naturally drawn to its quirky and rigorous reputation. Coming out of an already academically rigorous environment in Silicon Valley, I knew that I would not be satisfied with a school that did not push me to work harder at all times.

UChicago also offered me the chance to really explore my passion by providing a core curriculum, where the students are required to take a wide range of interdisciplinary courses. Further, I had known that I wanted to attend a medium-sized or smaller private institution because I would have more freedom to get to know and work closely with professors. UChicago's liberal arts options and general quirk-accepting atmosphere drew me in to four unfettered years of soul-searching and chasing dreams.

UChicago is well known—or infamous, depending on an individual's perspective—for having quirky, if not outright difficult, application supplement essay prompts. Kimberly responded to the following prompt with an entertaining essay, which reflected her own lovably eccentric personality:

If there are two kinds of people in the world, what are they?

Have you ever had a friend who drools over the couture gowns in Vogue magazine, takes two hours to get ready for a hangout, and buys only organic, free-trade produce at Whole Foods? Have you had another friend who wears t-shirts and crocs every day, takes a maximum of five minutes to get ready for a date, and whose idea of gourmet cuisine is UFO bowl ramen? The former is a vampire and the latter is a werewolf.

Vampires have elegant and sophisticated tastes. Often found in big cities, vampires stalk about in designer clothing, high heels, and trendy hairstyles while carrying crocodile briefcases and Piaget watches. They frequent cultural events such as ballet, opera, and classical music concerts and enjoy dining in French restaurants. Vampires are brand connoisseurs; those who can afford it purchase the brand-name goods, while those who cannot covet them.

Werewolves, on the other hand, are unpretentious and down-to-earth. They go to the AMC movie theater and In-N-Out burgers, enjoy pop music, and rarely sacrifice comfort for appearance. Werewolf girls wear tennis shoes and flats, while boys wear t-shirts and denim. Larry Page and Sergey Brin, for instance, are werewolves because they are regularly spotted dining at hole-in-the-wall restaurants while wearing t-shirts and crocs. Steve Jobs also prowls University Avenue in a casual black turtleneck and jeans. For fun, werewolves enjoy hiking, cycling, camping, and other outdoor activities. They could care less about brand names, and most probably wouldn't even recognize many of them.

So are people 100% vampire or 100% werewolf? Some are. My older brother Taylor does not seem to possess a single drop of vampire blood. He wears anything that is clean, eats anything in sight, and does anything as long as it is legal. Sometimes he goes to school with lopsided hair from sleeping in an odd position, but he does not care. Unlike Taylor, most people have elements of each while still remaining majority vampire or werewolf. Since I am much more complex than Taylor, I am a mix of both qualities.

I am a vampire about fashion, food, hygiene, and lodging, so I identify as a vampire overall. Though I cannot easily afford all the trappings of a lavish life, I carefully save up my cents for years to buy that one prom dress from Neiman Marcus. Nevertheless, I am a werewolf in entertainment that I love watching comedy or action movies with my friends and family. I cannot help but fall asleep while viewing vampiric plays or concerts.

Many may believe that vampires and werewolves are archrivals, so may be shocked by my dwelling in the same house with Taylor for so long. But are the two species destined to clash in epic feuds, as in Underworld and Twilight? No, they not only can peacefully coexist, but also can complement one another. Taylor and I are two types of people who work together as a team to supplement each other's weaknesses. I introduce my brother to new cultural experiences and also improve his wardrobe, while he keeps me grounded and relaxed. We do quarrel sometimes, but we resolve the fight within the next day because we are people of different strengths and styles who learn to enrich one another's life.

Though I must say, we vampires are superior to werewolves. Or maybe I'm just biased.

Today, Kimberly is a senior at UChicago. I've asked her to reflect on the following question:

To what extent did your college experience meet your expectations? In what ways did your experience cause you to change your perspective on your academic career, your dreams and aspirations, and your life?

FROM TECH GEEK TO MOVIE GEEK

Moving forward from my tech prime in high school, I threw myself into many different fields, such as education, policy, law, finance, journalism, and so on. I did many things out of desperation to find out what my passion was. I thought that being in college would magically arrange my future, and didn't know that the search for passion would be a never-ending, excruciating process of elimination. I had to try and try again until I finally narrowed my interests down to a few.

My temptation toward filmmaking had begun early from my family's love for movies, and grew from my best friend in high school who drove us to a movie theater every Saturday, and grew even more from Sofia Coppola and Woody Allen, who caught my heart with their films. When I took an introductory film course out of curiosity at University of Chicago, I had reached the tipping point: I knew that I would not leave college without learning more about film.

Still, it's funny how long it took to finally convince myself that a career in film is possible. I loved movies. I knew specific opening dates, watched every trailer, read movie news every morning, and kept a secret blog where I'd jot down all the thoughts on the movies I watched. But I had never considered a career in the film industry because movies were just too much fun.

I had doubts about wanting to become a filmmaker. I would disappoint my parents to whom I had said I wanted to become a lawyer, and I would be unable to buy them a nice home for about twenty or so years until I get a big hit, if ever. It's not that my parents had intentionally pressured me to pursue traditionally stable and respectable careers (although they did always hope, like any parent would), it was rather that I was scared to risk everything that they had sacrificed for my education. Why did I go to the expensive and rigorous University of Chicago if I was going to be a director? Why did I study so hard, and not just go to film school? What would happen if I chose to pursue directing, and I starved for the rest of my life?

Not to mislead anyone, I am still frightened that I will fail and starve. Knowing how much I want to become a leading director meant that I would be so happy pursuing this path, but I would be terribly frightened if I failed. I realized, however, that when my parents tried so hard to educate and feed me, they did so to ultimately make me happy and not to simply mold me into an unhappy person who hates her stable but frustrating job. I couldn't imagine my life not making films, and I knew that nothing could make me as happy as being able to pursue my dream no matter what. And I believed that my parents would be happy if I am.

Furthermore, I don't at all regret going to a prestigious academics-driven university. I am tremendously thankful and feel lucky that I am able to study and learn about things that I would have never have been exposed to if not for this school. Also, movies are all about visualizing and communicating what we know about the world, so the more knowledge I have, the more material I have to make into my movies.

It eventually took me an enormous amount of courage to convince myself that I could, and would, make movies. No one in my family is involved in entertainment, however, and I hardly knew the industry. So, I put myself out there and flew to Los Angeles without having a single internship offer in hand. Starting with zero connections in the industry, I faced a foreign terrain that absolutely frightened me. But I kept thinking about the path because it excited me, too. I ended up acquiring three part-time internships and seventy business cards during the summer.

In the end, when you love something, you know from deep down that you really do love it, and you have to take the risk to admit it. I learned in college that nothing ever works out by itself. I will always be in charge of my own decisions, and I will always be the one to make the final choice. I've convinced myself to do what I love, and I am proud of this one push that will let me enjoy my every step toward becoming a leading director-producer.

It wasn't a single experience during college that changed my direction from tech geek to movie geek. My transformation was an accumulation of everything that had helped me form who I am now. The love of cinema was always in me, and I just needed the courage to find it and live life doing what I love.

Given what you know now, if you could redo high school, what would you do differently, and why?

COLLEGE ADMISSIONS ANXIETY: THE #$#%^@ AND "THANK GOD!" MOMENTS

A sum of youthful voices formed a beautiful, harmonious song in the back of my head. I could hear the distinctly loud voice of the friend directly behind me, and the slightly more timid ones of those on my left and right. But I couldn't hear my own voice. I wasn't singing.

Our conductor swung his arms to grab our attention and to indicate his further direction. I quickly stole a look at the clock above his head and then back at his face. As he threw his hands up and made tight fists for closure, I was sure I heard in silence the beating of my own heart.

The choir students began chatting as they sat back down in their assigned seats. Only I was so desperate to take a look at my smartphone, which at the time held the piece of information that could have changed my life forever. I waited impatiently after touching the Refresh icon and counted the beats of my music with the shaking of my right leg. No update. *Dammit.*

The melodious bell interrupted the music, and I bolted out of the classroom. My friends created a ridiculous chase across the school as they followed after me. They were half-nervous and half-excited to see whether this friend of theirs would end up surrounded in congratulatory remarks or . . . in shame.

I remember mistyping exactly three times trying to enter the password for MIT's application decision portal. My hands had been trembling uncontrollably. When I had finally entered it correctly and the page had loaded, it was the damnedest moment in my life. I experienced simultaneous rage and relief.

With thoughts of "#$#%^@, darn you!" and "THANK GOD," I ended the day comically bipolar. I had been heavily involved in technology in high school, and this was a game-changing moment in which I finally realized that I had never loved or even been good at math or science.

At the same time, it was impossible to neglect the fact that I had been rejected. Of course, MIT is a top-notch, world-renowned university (in fact, my own brother is an alumnus). It's just that my inner voice asked, "Who are *you* to reject me? *Me?* Who do you think you are?"

Yes, I was angry and dejected. All of the things that I'd done and learned in high school seemed to have been refuted. My efforts had failed. But somehow it was also then that I recognized that it's not that I wasn't good enough for the school, but rather that I had simply been looking down the wrong path. I had been stubborn, chasing after something I neither liked nor was necessarily good at, and I had willingly cast myself in a certain mold to get accepted into a college for its reputation.

All in all, I have no regrets and am grateful for all of the things that made me who I am now. I am happy that I became agile in illustrating computer graphics, that I got to participate in the national robotics competition, and that I fought for the place of women in technology. Lucky enough, I ended up at the University of Chicago, and I now know that I will someday become one of the world's greatest filmmakers. I have learned that even a disappointment can turn out to be the best thing to happen in life, and I am thrilled about the path that I now follow. Though it took some time into college to finally discover my true passion, now I have the rest of my life to enjoy and pursue my dream.

What else would you like to share with or suggest to high school students and college students, and why?

REFLECTIONS IN PARIS

I tasted a sweet mélange of cigarette smoke and browning crepes from tented street stands. The intricate black and gold flowers of apartment balconies reflected the weak winter sun. The mysterious mornings on rainy days moistened my face with mist. (The Eiffel Tower was also magnificent, but need I mention it? Everyone already knows that.)

I sometimes reminisce about the little things that I adored in Paris. I love traveling, exploring, and learning about the world, and I tend to remember a city by the minor details that make the city its own. Everyone knows about the Eiffel Tower and loves it, but many people dream and romanticize about this one landmark that they don't notice all the other delightful ingredients that make up the city.

"Yes, I've been to the Eiffel Tower!" I declare. "But so what," says a Parisian. "Is that it?"

The same thing often happens with our aspirations to succeed. We sweat, bleed, and cry, and try so hard to accomplish this one thing until we finally do, and we think—Now what? Likewise, dreams may often remain formidable and far from reach no matter what we do. It may actually be impossible to reach one's goal. So, we sit in our little dark corners and cry some more.

Having a dream is fantastic, as it gives us the ambition and passion to go out and do things. It gives our life purpose and gratification, but it's important to realize that there is much more to life than just success, too. Especially in a world now brimming with competition, it is easy to get hung up on a goal and beat ourselves up for not achieving it. We need to always keep in mind that it's OK to not always meet our goals. We have to realize that every moment of our lives is life worth living, and that there is so much to the world than brooding over failures. After all, the most fun comes from the process of chasing after a dream.

There will always be little things and moments around us that we can take the time to appreciate and remember. Just like how it is not only the Eiffel Tower that defines Paris, we can't let success alone define us, and we can choose to let into our lives our family, friends, favorite foods, the scent of a city, light rain, sunshine, colors, and music on the streets. . . . We can all open our eyes just a little bit more, and the everyday things in our everyday life will make us feel fulfilled and alive. We will be content to live a dream that *can* be, but never *has* to be, achieved.

A perfectly imperfect takeaway about Kimberly:

Change after change, transforming until she found her passion, Kimberly now hustles to chase after her dream. Fascinated by movies like *Beasts of the Southern Wild* and *Lost in Translation*, Kimberly believes in capturing and highlighting the beautiful moments amidst an unwieldy life. Passionate, ambitious, and full of positive energy, Kimberly wants to promote positive thinking with her movies. Although Kimberly wants to explore different stories and genres with her directing, she will ultimately make films that inspire her audiences to recognize and appreciate the beauty of life.

7: KIMBERLY HAN

8

Youyang Gu

Wall Street Hacker

BS in Electrical Engineering and Computer Science, and
Mathematics (double major), Class of 2015, Massachusetts
Institute of Technology

Having grown up in Illinois, Youyang Gu was thrust into a more
competitive environment when he moved to the Bay Area for his
sophomore year of high school. Luckily, he adjusted well enough to make
it to MIT. In his freshman year, Youyang decided to forgo the traditional
software route of computer science grads and aim for something that
has long captivated him: Wall Street. He was president of Traders@MIT,
an organization that runs the largest US collegiate trading competition
and teaches a for-credit class on finance and trading. He has interned
at Credit Suisse and J.P. Morgan, and most recently at Google. In addition, he leads the MIT THINK Scholars Program, a student-run STEM
competition that awards research grants to aspiring high school scientists and engineers. In his spare time, Youyang enjoys poker, basketball,
and sports analytics. He plans to pursue a master's degree and travel the
world after graduation.

It wasn't necessary to be the best; I just had to be among the best.
—Youyang Gu

Youyang Gu moved from his birthplace of Shanghai, China, to Urbana, Illinois, at age seven. He didn't have a clue about college admissions until he relocated to the Bay Area after ninth grade, where the competitive culture of Silicon Valley motivated his efforts to succeed academically. Today, Youyang is a senior at MIT. His reflections and advice follow.

To what extent did your college experience—on and off campus—meet your expectations? In what ways did your experience cause you to change your perspective on your academic career, your dreams and aspirations, and your life?

Walking on the crunchy ice-covered ground that used to be fresh snow, I took a look at the people around me. I knew they were extraordinary people. Valedictorians. Perfect SATs. Science-fair winners. Math Olympians. I was visiting MIT in February of my senior year. Here I am, just a semi-successful overachieving high school senior who was doing just well enough in school to be grudgingly accepted into the "smart" social group. I didn't belong here—I wasn't good enough.

It had been less than two months since I clicked on the series of "Submit Application" black holes that would determine my future life and career. I was pretty indifferent about MIT because I had mentally blocked the thought of me actually being able to attend a school like MIT. After all, I wasn't in the top of anything at my high school. Maybe top ten in Madden NFL, but who cares about that? If I set low expectations, I reasoned, then I wouldn't be as disappointed when I received that thin, crisp envelope in March.

Fast-forward six months. It is August of 2011. I set foot at MIT for the first time since February, this time as a college freshman. What used to be a frozen landscape has become a lush college campus. As I made my way to the front of MIT's Great Dome for a photo, I thought to myself, I can't believe I made it.

I was one of those kids who transferred in the middle of high school, immediately before sophomore year, to be exact. I came from a small college town in the Midwest, a place where neighborhoods were suffocated by cornfields and half the population disappeared in the summer. I happened

102

to have moved to one of the most competitive areas in the nation: Silicon Valley. There I saw students who had been preparing for college since grade school. They seemed more accomplished than me in every way: grades, test scores, extracurriculars, and so on. In contrast, I was a naïve sophomore who had not yet taken the SAT or any AP classes. I needed to catch up.

There were times during my sophomore year when I thought I couldn't do it because I was simply too lazy. I had become really good at Madden that year, and playing video games was certainly more enjoyable than studying. Fortunately, I managed to pull myself together and worked myself into the math fast lane. The following summer, I placed out of Pre-Calculus, allowing me to take AP Calculus as a junior. Knowing that I was able to more or less compete head-to-head with the best students at my high school gave me confidence to push forward.

There were still areas where I was not able to fully catch up—I didn't have time to do sports or take honors humanities courses. But the competitive environment of my high school meant that it wasn't necessary to *be* the best; I just had to be *among* the best. That is exactly what I did, and it was enough to get me into my dream school. My class saw thirteen students get into MIT, an unprecedented number for a public school. The other twelve students were among the same students whom I aspired to be like more than two years earlier.

MIT proved to offer no shortage of high-achieving people. Many of my classmates went through the same experience I had three years earlier: the sudden realization that everyone is smarter and more accomplished than you. Instead of backing away from the challenge, I look for the best students and try to model myself after them while infusing my own personal characteristics. There is something to learn from everybody. I was surprised that all the experiences that were instilled in me from high school applied the same way in college. Only this time, I had the advantage of having gone through it before.

Even today, I can safely say that I will never be able to be on the same level as some of my friends and classmates whom I look up to. And I am OK with that. Because these are the same people who helped me get to where I am today and the same people who set a bar for me to reach for. The higher the bar, the harder I will work to try to get there. My pursuit for knowledge and perfection is never-ending, because the bar is constantly rising. I might have to work harder and put in more time than others to reach the same point, but it will pay off. As long as I do not relinquish my competitive mind-set, I will be satisfied with where I am and where I am going.

Being in a competitive environment is a double-edged sword—while the environment pushes you to reach higher and work harder, the thought that you will never be good enough can be demoralizing. But I was lucky enough to find that this environment was exactly what I needed to thrive. I now realize that a large chunk of my personality and character originated not from college, but from high school. I am fairly satisfied with how everything has worked out so far. Today, I have gained valuable experiences interning for multiple companies. I am also honored to have run two great organizations, contributing my own thoughts and ideas during my tenure. Looking back, I was glad I was thrust into an environment that revealed to me all the things that I *didn't* know. Even though it took me a year or two into my college career to realize my ability to thrive in a competitive setting, I am glad MIT saw it in me years earlier.

Why computer science? And why MIT?

I didn't always like computer science. In fact, I didn't take my first CS course until my senior year of high school. For a long time, I was undecided between business and chemical engineering. But it slowly became apparent that in almost every profession, there are countless applications for computer science, and the revolution is merely starting. The more I learned about CS, the more I enjoyed it. I decided that I wanted to study computer science during my senior year of high school, and MIT seemed like an obvious choice.

I had the chance to experience MIT for myself during my visit during preview weekend for admitted students (called CPW). It is by far the best preview weekend I had attended—the campus was lively and saturated with incredible events. I was awestruck to learn that the hundreds of events had all been planned by students. Our preview weekend continues to impress me to this day, and I make sure to contribute to it. The fact that MIT is one of only five US schools that are need-blind to international applicants only made my decision easier.

In addition, MIT is extremely technical and meritocratic, and I have come to appreciate such a culture. It's not about how much money your dad has donated, or how well you can row crew. On campus, everyone is on an even playing field. Lastly, being at MIT reinforces my belief in the importance of surrounding yourself with brilliant people. The people here are extremely diligent and aspiring, and being in this environment is often humbling, but also rewarding.

In high school, Youyang participated in COSMOS at UC Davis, a competitive STEM summer program, and did research at Texas Tech University as a Clark Scholar in an intensive seven-week summer research program. He was honored as an Intel Science Talent Search Semifinalist for his research. In addition, he took math classes at Stanford, won the Toshiba ExploraVision Regionals Award, and earned a score of 5 on ten AP exams, all while maintaining a 4.0 GPA. Youyang also served as president of his high school chapter of Future Business Leaders of America (FBLA) and as vice president of Environmental Club.

While Youyang and his family were on a multiyear wait to obtain permanent residency in the United States, he applied to college as an international student, an especially competitive landscape. He was admitted to fifteen schools, including MIT, Columbia, Cornell, Duke, Johns Hopkins, UC Berkeley, and UPenn. He was waitlisted at Princeton, Stanford, and UChicago, and denied by Caltech, Harvard, and Yale.

To enlighten readers, two of the essays that Youyang wrote for his MIT application—one on how his world shaped his dreams and aspirations and the other on how he managed a most significant challenge—are included as an appendix toward the end of this chapter. I asked Youyang to reflect on this question:

Given what you know now, if you could redo high school, what would you do differently, and why?

I want to preface this section by saying that there is nothing that I wholeheartedly regret from my high school days. Learning from mistakes is merely a part of growing up. With that said, below are three things that I would have done differently.

NO RÉSUMÉ PADDING

I would have done fewer things to "pad" my college résumé. Looking back at my college application, I realized how disorganized and unsystematic all of my activities were. My mind-set at that time was: the more activities I had on my application, the better. Of course, it wasn't until much later that I recognized the importance of quality over quantity. I was appalled when I found out that college résumés were only allowed one page—my high school "résumé" was already three times that long. Since I viewed high school as a time to explore various interests, I don't regret participating in so many activities. However, I would have spent more time framing my application to reflect a more goal-oriented, decisive individual rather than a résumé-padding individual who participates in a cluster of superficial activities.

WRITE ABOUT WHAT MATTERS TO YOU

When writing my college application essays, I would have focused more on talking about what mattered to me, rather than what I thought mattered to the admissions officers. For my personal statement on the Common App, I ended up writing about an event that I thought was unique: meeting and interviewing a person who had overcome an immense physical challenge. Upon reading it years later, I realized that the essay revealed a lot about the individual, but very little about me. Instead, what had influenced me the most was my move from the Midwest to California. But I chose not to write about it in the Common App because I thought it was too cliché. If I could do everything over again, I would not hesitate to write about that experience. To sum up, write about something that actually had a profound influence on you, not about something that you think admissions officers would like to see.

SELF-REFLECT

I was so engulfed with the stress of applying to colleges that I rarely took the time to reflect on myself. What does that mean? Self-reflection involves the process of evaluating your strengths and weaknesses, and setting personal goals to work on. Question yourself. How do I want to treat my friends? My classmates? How do I want to be treated? What do I want to accomplish in life? Of course, I might have not been mature enough to achieve any sort of profound self-reflection. But I am sure it would have helped me focus more on the bigger picture. Instead of doing things for the sake of putting it on your college application, do things for your own personal benefit. In other words, don't let your life be engulfed by your college application. Now that I am in college, I still try to put time aside to reflect on my experiences and my future.

What else would you like to share with or suggest to high school and college students and why?

KNOWLEDGE AS "COMPOUND INTEREST"

I read a blog post last summer that compared knowledge to compound interest. The premise is simple: the more you learn early on, the more you will be able to learn later. In other words, knowledge is cumulative. Students who emphasize learning new material early on will get increasingly more benefit over their peers who start later, because they are able to learn more using what they have accumulated. And in the same way positive efforts are magnified, negative effects will also accrue exponentially. This is why it is essential to kill bad habits early.

Now, I am not advising that students should start learning stochastic calculus in middle school. Having a life/work balance is also incredibly important. There is no one I know who can study nonstop. The key is to not waste time. Spending time with friends and family is not a waste of time. But looking at online memes because you don't want to start on your homework is. When you're at a restaurant with friends, don't think about the problem set that's due next week. Conversely, don't think about that party on Friday when you are studying for your midterm. The most successful people I know work hard and play hard—they spend very little time in "idle mode."

Being studious is only one part of the equation. You must also actively seek out and pursue new opportunities; rarely do they just come to you without trying. I can think of numerous instances where I put my full effort into an application knowing that the chances of me being accepted is close to none (MIT comes to mind). But that's the type of mentality you must have in order to succeed. A lot of times, my willingness to pursue opportunities is directly correlated with my self-confidence. Self-confidence starts with knowledge, and builds with each fruitful opportunity. These opportunities lead to more skills learned and increased self-confidence. This is the "compound interest" positive feedback loop that I mentioned earlier.

HARD SKILLS VS. SOFT SKILLS

MIT trains some of the best engineers in the world. I have little doubts about that. From day one, we are immersed in a challenging environment and are taught to tackle tough problems with our fellow students. When students graduate, they feel ready to apply all the technical knowledge they have learned and take on the most immense of engineering challenges. But the real world is very different.

First of all, not everyone is an engineer in the real world. At MIT, it's easy to get comfortable talking about technical problems because almost everyone around you is an engineer or scientist. But these conversational skills do not translate once you leave MIT. In the real world, you can no longer start a conversation with someone from a non-technical background by complaining about the many nuances of dynamically typed programming languages or why Go is the best programming language for concurrency. Collaborating with nontechnical people becomes unfamiliar territory in the minds of MIT graduates, and that is severely delimiting in a world run by predominantly nontechnical people.

We dream of an ideal world where hard skills trump all and meritocracy dominates. All in all, this is true at MIT. Unfortunately, students get complacent and naïvely believe that the real world works this way as well. It doesn't. We disregard the need to develop soft skills such as public speaking, team cooperation, and task management. The time necessary to practice on improving on those abilities are dismissed in favor of "more important" tasks like working on a perfecting a technical solution to a problem. When it comes to obtaining influence and power in today's society, soft skills preclude hard skills for one simple reason: people are social by nature.

In much the same way knowledge can be learned, so can the ability to influence people. I believe that everyone should consistently try to find opportunities to practice and improve on his or her soft skills, regardless of what his or her specialty is. It can be as simple as introducing yourself to a classmate or as difficult as leading a student organization. The only way to improve is to step out of our comfort zones. While it is often difficult for engineers like me to spend time on something we are weak at, learning to be a better communicator is absolutely essential in today's globally connected society. In the real world, hard skills aren't everything. And they rightfully shouldn't be.

SO WHAT'S THE STORY BEHIND MY CHAPTER SLOGAN, "WALL STREET HACKER"?

I have been interested in finance since high school. Coming into MIT, I wasn't sure how that interest would fit in with my plans to study computer science. For a brief while, I put it on the back burner. But that was short-lived.

I discovered a group called Traders@MIT, a finance and trading club, during my first month at MIT (trading is a subset of finance that involves buying and selling financial instruments). I applied and became the only new board member they accepted that year. Since then, I have been very involved in Traders, culminating in my presidency my junior year. Our twelve-member executive board holds the country's largest collegiate trading competition. We also teach a for-credit, student-led course at MIT called Intro to Trading, where I was the lead instructor last year. Thanks in part to my participation in Traders, I participated in three internships for Wall Street firms, where I wrote code that used large historical data sets to create predictive statistical models.

I enjoy the trading industry because it is extremely fast-paced and result-oriented. High risk, high reward, as they say. If you do not adapt fast enough, you will lose your edge to the hundreds of anonymous predators impatiently waiting to engulf your spot. The turnaround time is also unprecedented. Instead of waiting weeks or even months to see whether or not the new version had an improvement, you can see it instantly in the form of your profit and loss ("P&L"), which designates how much money you made or lost. There is very little fluff or office politics in this business. At the end of the day, your P&L is the only thing that determines how much you get paid. This meritocratic environment is a fitting place for an individual like me.

The term "hacking" has been deeply engrained at MIT to refer to the creative process of building something, especially something that previously never existed. And being a part of a revolution to build intelligent machines to run the world's markets certainly fits the culture of "hacking". The markets are becoming increasingly automated, and the technical challenges that arise from that phenomenon are also becoming increasingly sophisticated. I openly welcome these intellectual stimulations. I find the applications of computer science in this field just as interesting, if not more so, than those in the traditional tech industry. I want to use coding *for* my job, but I don't want coding to *be* my job.

109

In a nutshell, I enjoy the unique combination of finance, mathematics, and computer science that only trading can provide. I believe that this combination is the key to driving the next generation of global financial markets. Some of the most brilliant people I know are in the trading industry, and I hope to join them in becoming the next wave of people who are challenging the old Wall Street stereotypes.

A perfectly imperfect takeaway about Youyang:

As one of the most thorough, intellectually interesting, and articulate young men who I've known, Youyang suggests, "Surround yourself with people better than you, and learn from their best qualities. Don't be afraid to reach high and fail, because one day you will reach high and make it. Be relentless in your pursuit of knowledge and your pursuit for the truth. Don't be afraid to have to put in more effort and more time than others to get to the same point. Set a high bar for yourself, and use it as a springboard to leave your own legacy. Find a path you like and leave a trail for the next generation to follow."

APPENDIX:

Below are two of the essays that Youyang Gu wrote for his MIT application.

MIT Prompt: Describe the world you come from; for example, your family, clubs, school, community, city, or town. How has that world shaped your dreams and aspirations?

"Time can't go backwards," Nobel Laureate Anthony J. Leggett said, "because it moves along in only one direction: towards decreasing entropy." Every Saturday morning, I took the #8 bus to the University of Illinois campus to attend the Saturday Honors Program, where a professor gives a lecture in the field of science. As the only junior high student willing to give up a weekend morning, I took furious notes on anything I did not understand and researched the topics at home.

Later that year, I attended the University of Illinois–sponsored high school that was located between the university's Computer Science and Electrical Engineering departments. Passing through the engineering campus on my daily commute to and from school, I was inspired to join the scientific revolution. My involvement in ExploraVision led me to work with Dr. John Rogers, a professor of mechanical engineering, who assisted me in detailing a plan for the use of stretchable silicon in nanotechnology applications. In the process, I interviewed four other professors, spent countless afternoons reading articles at the campus' many libraries, and traveled 200 miles to the Bernard Becker Medical Library at WashU to obtain a physical copy of "Ions in the Brain." I loved taking full advantage of university resources and socializing with STEM professors, which has inspired me to fervently pursue a career in science and engineering. As I look back at the questions I wrote four years ago regarding Dr. Leggett's lecture, I cannot help smiling. One day, I will find the answers.

MIT Prompt: Tell us about the most significant challenge you've faced or something important that didn't go according to plan. How did you manage the situation?

The first day at a new school is always daunting, even as a high school student. The fact that it is my sophomore year does not help ease my anxiety. As I walk into my first class, a multitude of thoughts run through my head: "Why is everyone so smart? Will I be able to keep up? What if no one likes me?"

At my old high school, I had always excelled. My self-esteem was immediately imperiled when I learned that I was moving to Silicon Valley—a region prominent for its academic rigor. As a kid who came from the vast prairies and open cornfields of Illinois, I had considerable doubts about living up to academic expectations of a notably higher standard.

I soon realized that my new school presented novel opportunities that my old school did not offer. Even though I had one less year to adjust, I vowed to try my fullest to make the best of every experience. Hence, I challenged myself to excel in the toughest classes, skipping two math lanes in the process. Since my new high school is eight times larger than my old school, I learned to take larger and more demanding leadership roles in my community.

Looking back, I have discovered that the most significant challenge I have faced is not leaving Illinois, but adjusting to my new life in California. In the end, I am proud to say that my resiliency and determination have paid off. Moving to college next year? No problem.

Act III
Seniors Stepping into the World

9

Jeremy Fiance

Relentlessly Resourceful Master of None

BA in Interdisciplinary Field Studies: Business, Engineering, and Design, Class of 2014, UC Berkeley

Jeremy Fiance is an investor and entrepreneur born and raised in Southern California. Since attending UC Berkeley (Cal), Jeremy has been fueled by the start-up world and determined to drive forward the next wave of innovation. His achievements include becoming the youngest-ever associate at Keiretsu Forum, the world's largest angel investment group, co-founding the Northern California region of the Kairos Society, a global community of top student entrepreneurs and change makers, and co-founding Dropsense, a start-up developing a low-blood-sugar alert system for diabetics.

Jeremy continues his work to drive Cal's innovation culture in collaboration with student groups and university initiatives. Most recently, he developed a curriculum for the newly founded Jacobs Institute for Design Innovation and co-founded Free Ventures, Cal's first student-run start-up incubator. Today, Jeremy is finishing his degree while investing in the best and brightest entrepreneurs as managing partner for the Dorm Room

Fund, a student-led investment fund, and an analyst at CrunchFund, a leading Silicon Valley seed-stage investment fund.

If the tools were there I found them, and if they weren't, I created them.
—Jeremy Fiance

Jeremy Fiance's strong family support system shaped him early on. . . .

MY FAMILY'S INFLUENCE ON ME

I have a lot to thank my parents for. The environment they created, as well as their dedication to my growth and well-being, enabled me to flourish. I came to understand that my father Robert's inspiration stemmed from his own unstable and unconventional childhood. His parents divorced and remarried, he had eight siblings, and he spent his life bouncing between homes in different states. He nonetheless managed to overcome this tumultuous childhood with much success. He received college scholarships for both lacrosse and football and ran several successful companies in education technology.

My mother, Beth, has thrived as a creative. She previously ran production for prime-time television shows, worked with nonprofits, and crafted some of the most memorable family holiday cards to ever hit a mailbox. Her California upbringing was more stable than my father's but almost as busy, as she grew up with two siblings and three cousins who lived ten minutes away. Our six families get together for each holiday, which helped enforce my values early on.

My brother, Alex, has always been a natural at everything he did and has seemed to shine effortlessly in academics, athletics, and social life. He has paved the way for me in many regards and puts positive pressure on me to unlock my maximum potential.

I also have a younger sister, Talia, who has an extraordinary way of connecting to others. Peers and friends consistently come to her for advice. I have enjoyed helping my sister pave her own path and she enjoys keeping me in check, unafraid to speak her mind. I see an exciting future for her as a creator and connector.

All in all, my family has taught me some important tricks about living a meaningful life.

While in high school, Jeremy learned a lot about himself and people by being a role model for numerous younger cousins and other children. He discussed this on a UC application personal essay during the college app season in his senior year. The essay prompt and a condensed version of his response are as follows:

UC personal statement prompt #1: Describe the world you come from—for example, your family, community or school—and tell us how your world has shaped your dreams and aspirations.

It was a virtual stampede; one by one, they came running down the hall. The shouting and hollering was easily audible next door; I had to do something. Crouched in an amusing, monster-like stance, I stopped them in their tracks with an audible "halt." Was this holiday different than any other? No, it was not. My mom's side, alone, includes fifteen younger cousins; the total among both sides approaches fifty, all for which, as an elder among the group, I had been named the responsible, presiding party. I have grown to enjoy my role in my very large family. It has given me the opportunity to get to know and love them all, and develop my skills as a leader, role model, and peacemaker among the children of our large clan.

Fortunately, these skills became easily adaptable in my later academic and extracurricular activities. As an example, given my desire to better the lives of children, I chose to volunteer to coach both boys basketball and girls soccer. Sports are a very important part of my life and, having had coaches far more concerned with winning than creating a positive environment had taught me a valuable lesson.

I applied my own team developing ideas and leadership abilities to assisting with the growth and athletic maturation of these impressionable young groups. Some stories stand out more than others; I'll never forget the look on a young player's face when he, as a diabetic previously unable to engage in athletics, scored his very first basket. It is truly astounding how a little extra effort can make all the difference in boosting the confidence of a child.

Jeremy reflected further on the meaning of his experiences in coaching children:

Coaching youth sports taught me the importance of patience, under-standing, and personalized approaches in teaching, leading, and collab-orating. This ethic was carried further through my work with kids at a low-income housing development and serving as a summer camp coun-selor. Throwing myself into these varying social roles has proven important to developing a sense of who I did and didn't want to be.

On another account, Jeremy never thought that a fun-loving backyard barbeque game could become a cutthroat sport of physical intensity and mental trials. He was trying out for the Jewish Olympics table tennis team. He recalls, "You really have to see it live to believe it! I needed to step up my game, so I trained for months with a fifty-year-old former Russian cham-pion named Bella who absolutely kicked my butt." Ultimately, Jeremy earned the last ticket to the games in Detroit.

He wrote about his follow-on experience via another UC application personal essay. The essay prompt and a condensed version of his response are as follows:

UC prompt #2: Tell us about a personal quality, talent, accomplishment, contribution or experience that is important to you. What about this quality or accomplishment makes you proud and how does it relate to the person you are?

When it was time for matches, my anxiety escalated. I was uncertain of what to expect; after all, I had only trained for a relatively short time compared to some . . . and how good would my new opponents be? I lost my first seeding match, but, for the next fifteen straight matches, I was unstoppable and . . . undefeated! My lack of fear of losing was my greatest competitive asset; I was different in that I was at the games for the experience, the culture, and the stories.

But, now, I actually had a chance. I kept my focus and played all the way to the Gold Medal match where I found myself facing my teammate, Josh, a player I had yet to beat in practice. We both knew he was better, but again, I wanted it more; minutes later, standing on the podium with the gold medal glistening around my neck, I truly knew that obstacles were only as large as one envisions them to be.

Amidst forging international relationships, representing my faith and my country, and achieving a feat even I had thought impossible at times, I realized that fear was the ultimate impediment toward progress; this knowledge will forever change my perspective toward challenges.

Jeremy reflects on this challenging but confidence-adding experience:

Though I had lacked skill and experience, I worked hard to bring out the best in myself with the tools I had, working to my strengths and bringing an unconventional style to the game that would give me a leg up. Given the pursuit of table tennis was unfamiliar and challenging in a completely new way, it was an early confidence builder in making me believe I could tackle whatever I was up against.

Jeremy has always been a man of various interests, including early explorations in athletics, film production, finance, and technology. In high school, he was recognized as US lacrosse All-American, black belt in Tang Soo Do karate, and gold medalist for table tennis in the Jewish Olympics. Jeremy also started both investing in stocks and producing short films, including the school's television show. He honed his leadership skills as captain of the lacrosse team, officer in the Film Club and Jewish Club, and a youth sports coach.

Just before high school graduation, I was hospitalized and suffered amnesia after an aggressive opponent's titanium-laden cross-check blow to my head, which amounted to four hundred pounds of force. Despite this setback that ended my lacrosse career and created cognitive challenges, I kept moving forward.

After learning about the college admissions results during his high school senior year, Jeremy chose to attend UC Berkeley in hopes of facing a new intellectual challenge, escaping the security of the SoCal suburbs, and exploring a campus of unknowns and endless opportunities.

Today, Jeremy is about to graduate from UC Berkeley. I've asked him to reflect on the following.

To what extent did your college experience—on and off campus—meet your expectations? In what ways did your experience cause you to change your perspective on your academic career, your dreams and aspirations, and your life?

When I was entering UC Berkeley, I had trouble remembering things, lost my focus, and found myself in one of the most academically rigorous institutions in the world amid a sea of 25,000 Einsteins who had done everything I had and more to get here. The tools I had weren't enough, and I was seeking inspiration.

I joined a social fraternity, planned to enter the prestigious Haas School of Business, had a finance internship, and kept in touch with my high school sweetheart. That all might seem great, but I felt stupid academically, lost socially, unexcited about the future, and wanted to leave Cal.

I had two choices: I could sit back and go through the motions or accept a new reality and take it by the horns. Fortunately, I did the latter. I learned over the last four years that a common trait among successful people I've met is taking control of their destiny and never quitting. A few important decisions in my college career taught me valuable lessons that have shaped who I am today:

SPARK YOUR FIRE

When I got to college, I was astounded to realize that I was on a campus and in a part of the world that touched the daily lives of the rest of the planet by way of technology. I met a few students who were already creating breakthroughs—and they were my age! At the time, I was completely intimidated, thinking I was certainly no brilliant inventor, genius scientist, or entrepreneur. To my surprise, these students were lone rangers with nowhere to go or uncertain direction. This was my way in to start engaging with these individuals.

I imagined a place like the coffeehouses during the Enlightenment, where unfiltered discussions of intellectual topics and crazy dreams and ideas could collide. When I found out about the vision of the Kairos Society, a community of young founders sparked by the question "What if today's world leaders were friends twenty years ago working to solve the world's problems?" I knew it was the perfect platform for me to get this vision off the ground.

With thousands of undergrads and limited experience as a new sophomore, I had no idea where to find these outliers and no relevant network to fall back on. I threw myself into every start-up event, joined clubs focused on technical topics I knew nothing about, and talked to people at coffee shops and bus stops. Starting Kairos on campus wasn't easy, as I challenged Cal's cultural norms of risk aversion, bridged some of the stand-alone organizations and pitched students, some of whom included good friends who just didn't understand why I was spending so much time on a student group.

Those who saw the vision are now part of a community consisting of the most ambitious entrepreneurs, creators, and leaders on campus. These folks have unlocked technical innovations, launched creative products, raised millions of dollars, and inspired countless peers to think differently and create.

For me, starting Kairos Society Northern California was a spark that spread into a fire of opportunities and unleashed my entrepreneurial potential. As a community, Kairos has broken down barriers for amazing individuals to pursue their passions through mentorship, resources, and a strong support system.

Ultimately, I just found a way to create something many wished had existed, and by surrounding myself with these inspiring people and ideas, a new world unveiled itself. Today, my brother Alex runs the Kairos Society globally, and it's been an adventure working together to take the magic at Berkeley and create similar communities around the world.

BE HUMAN

Despite the great global exposure I had with Kairos, I was still lacking a deep understanding of both others and myself—especially since I had grown up in somewhat of a suburban bubble. Last year, I took a course called Facing You, Facing Me at Berkeley where Professor Dave Stark brings together sixteen student leaders from different races, religions, nationalities, genders, and sexual orientations to challenge one another and societal norms head-on—we were thrown together like the motley *Breakfast Club* cast and ultimately unified in a similar way.

I prayed, sang, and confessed at an all-black Christian church—I'm Jewish. I walked through the most crowded quad on campus holding hands with another man—I'm straight and had friends awkwardly texting me about it asking if I had a boyfriend. I had to live off $5 for a whole weekend: Try it. I failed. I heard stories of hate, love, abuse, life, death, racism, sexism, wealth, poverty, and beyond. We all shared deeply personal stories and beliefs, some of which we'd kept from our closest family and friends. These were individuals who were all on a seemingly happy, successful track, yet we were all so far from perfect.

After taking this class, I now force myself to rethink first impressions, challenge assumptions, reevaluate my own beliefs, and do things that I was previously afraid of. College is a unique place to gain exposure to people of many types in somewhat of a controlled environment, and it marks the start of a lifelong journey of accepting my own imperfections and those of others, and exploring what it means to be human.

CAST A WIDE NET

One of the best decisions I've made in college was declaring an interdisciplinary field studies major my sophomore year, working with a professor to create my own major comprising three fields of study.

I realized that I wanted to expose myself to as much as possible both in and out of the classroom. From biology and sociology to consumer behavior and web development, I found that there was no better time and way to learn so many subjects just for the sake of learning. To many, my new major sounded scattered. I became quite literally a master of no subject, but I had and still have true confidence in this unique path I have chosen for myself.

With this academic journey, I challenge myself in a new way every day: I have done everything from building a smart toaster to developing an economic model. My diploma won't tell you exactly what it is that's in my tool kit, but what I can say is I've learned how to solve problems and execute plans. Though not everyone has the luxury of developing their own major, there are creative ways to run educational experiments, both in and out of the classroom, to find their true calling. Though I'll be focusing my efforts on investing in and working with early-stage start-ups coming out of college, I plan to keep casting the net wide as a lifelong learner.

TAKE A LEAP

The college ecosystem is a sandbox for creation, and those who take initiative thrive. I was fortunate to learn this my first semester at Cal by getting up before a class of 150 students and pitching—with hands shaking, voice cracking, and sweat dripping down my freshman face—an idea in the start-up competition.

I was a finalist in that competition and over the next few years worked on several start-up ideas that taught me everything not to do and helped prepare me to start Dropsense, an idea my friend Steve, who is a type-I diabetic and brilliant engineer, had. Together, along with a third founder, Vikram, we developed a non-invasive low-blood-sugar alert system using wearable biosensors, mobile technology, and machine learning to detect hypoglycemia, a major fear and health risk for diabetics. These guys were easily the smartest I'd met at Cal; they constantly inspired me—and I believed I could bring out the best in them.

At the start, I had little to no experience in healthcare or hardware. Without fear, I did everything and anything to learn and push the idea forward—cold calling countless regulatory consultants, interviewing endocrinologists, and reviewing research studies. We would spend late nights in the hackerspace (a campus workspace where tech enthusiasts build, learn, and collaborate) working on hardware, software, and product design. Eventually, the world would take notice as we pitched at leading health-tech conferences, were covered by the press, got into the campus accelerator, partnered with major medical companies, and had funds committed for what seemed to potentially be a billion-dollar business—if the stars aligned.

The story sounded great, but it recently came to a screeching halt. My co-founders pressed for a pause to pursue research and graduate school, and it didn't make sense for me to continue without them, given each team member's vital role in our efforts. Thus, Dropsense is on the shelf for now. I look back and laugh, realizing how deep I got into various new areas I knew nothing about. In every project I join, I have become incredibly resourceful in overcoming challenges and relentless in equipping myself for every battle, armed with preparation and knowledge.

I've yet to create something that reaches my aspiration to touch millions of lives, but I'm certain each leap has compounded on the one before to prepare me for the next.

COLLEGE CONCLUSION

Though I didn't realize it when coming into Cal, I needed a catalyst to point me in the direction of a space wide enough for broad exploration, but focused enough to get my hands dirty. I found this with entrepreneurship. Founders fearlessly face the unknown and must adapt and reinvent themselves and their pursuits to forge new paths. I wasn't certain where I was headed, but I launched with the entrepreneur as a model and started constructing a better-equipped me than ever before.

Given what you know now, if you could redo high school, what would you do differently, and why?

If I were to find myself in high school again, I'd still follow a similar journey, but I'd place more focus on the elements that positively shaped me and be less afraid of taking a few detours along the way. It turns out many of the same lessons I uncovered in college had precursors in my youth. My four principles—(1) spark your fire, (2) be human, (3) cast a wide net, and (4) take a leap—would have applied to high school as well.

SPARK YOUR FIRE

Growing up I was obsessed with card collections and their worth. My brother and I would save up our allowance every week and beg a parent to take us to SportsCard Outlet. Alex and I would track card values in *Beckett* magazine, seeing them go up and down depending on player performance and market speculation. The collection buzz would get out of hand, as we inadvertently began diversifying our assets investing in Beanie Babies, WWE action figures, and most notably, Pokémon cards.

When I convinced Alex to collect with me, he assured himself and me that it was for the money. The craze took off and a few times Alex mentioned we were going to sell. I refused. Eventually the Pokémarket would crash. So would the Beanie Babies bonanza. Our hundreds invested were worthless and my mom was left with boxes of paper and stuffed animals. We always said they'd come back, like my uncles who'd invested in Microsoft, but we all were kidding ourselves.

Despite my loathing for the stock talk that sometimes took over family events, my grandfather gave me a copy of Benjamin Graham's *Intelligent Investor* when I was in high school and started a program for my siblings and me called the Good Savers Club. At the end of each year, he'd match our savings. Let's just say that I put the club out of business because I saved so much. My siblings won't forgive me for it to this day. Soon after, I entered the stock market.

My brother and I always found creative ways to make money. My favorite example was our family business as the top guinea-pig breeder in the area. Since my parents wouldn't let us get a dog, we settled for little "piggies" named Smarty and Furrball. Smarty was not so smart, got knocked up before we bought her, had a baby male, and the rest is history. We probably sold over sixty pigs to the pet shop.

All in all, I just followed what got me excited, and I encourage high school students to do the same. The more time I put in, the more I learned, which opened up new ideas. Today, I continue to follow my interests and to apply my acuity for finding value in places others miss in the start-up and investment worlds.

BE HUMAN

I've always prided myself on being good with people, but the truth is, when I hit puberty and had pimples and when other boys started becoming men in sports, the world was becoming uncertain and awkward. In middle school, I was incredibly self-conscious, best indicated by my full head of bleached-blond hair and baggy pants sagging to my ankles. I asked one of the cutest girls to the first middle school dance and got blatantly turned down. The climax of embarrassment came when I ran for school president and tried to do a rap. I started a clap and a few mean dudes purposely messed it up by yelling obscenities. These and other early failures helped me learn to bounce back stronger.

High school proved to be a better transition, as I found myself jumping across many activities and social groups including athletes, academics, and creatives. Though high schoolers sometimes fit the stereotypical cliques, I pushed the boundaries to be part of several communities, and my closest friends were able to do the same. This is something I believe has benefited me throughout college, as my connections have expanded beyond my imagination.

CAST A NET

Exploring creative outlets beyond school has always been essential for me to acquire new skills and knowledge. Growing up, I'd rush to complete my homework so I could get back to some project. My mom spread her artistic joy at home with a table full of markers, paper, glue, clay, and the works for crafting. I would become well known in high school for my distinct doodling, placing characters conveniently on my homework, notes, and the yearbooks of all that I signed.

In a more formal fashion, I developed an interest in creating short films during high school, running the TV station with my friend Garrett, and taking an animation class. This project-based, learning-by-doing enabled me to pick up skills in technical editing, design, production, writing, and storytelling that would prove useful well into the future. I was at my best in high school when I wasn't afraid to draw outside the lines.

TAKE A LEAP

I have always been up for a game with anyone on the street, field, or court—quite often creating new games from my imagination—and maintaining a distinct fearlessness. The earliest example I can remember was setting up mattresses and pillows, pretending I was a pro wrestler, and doing flying elbow drops off the top bunk onto stuffed animals. As I aged, I still maintained this energy but harnessed it for games, practices, and moments that could use that extra emphasis.

One of my favorite examples of fearlessness was during a varsity lacrosse playoff game my freshman year. I got in with a tie score and a few minutes left. I knew my chance was coming. I'd practiced martial arts most of my life, which taught me to intensely focus on the moment and notice things that others would miss. With three seconds left I'd break free, catch, shoot, and score to win the game, a moment that would set the stage the for rest of my lacrosse career.

HIGH SCHOOL CONCLUSION

On the academic front, my high school years became defined by a track where I was in class to learn, acquire the grades, and then get into college. To get there, I realized it was more a matter of putting in the time and getting A's, rather than testing true mastery of a subject. I did what it took to succeed, so I could get to the activities I noted. The reality is that I wouldn't be at UC Berkeley if I hadn't worked hard, and my life would be very different if I hadn't found myself there.

That being said, today's educational journey leads most students like me to fall into the trap of learning to get grades. I recommend trying to truly learn for the sake of learning and doing it both in and out of the classroom. Curiosity is an all-powerful king that continues to present new questions to conquer. Answering one question only leads to another. Don't be afraid of the unknown.

What else would you like to share with or suggest to high school students and college students, and why?

STEP OUTSIDE YOUR COMFORT ZONE

I've needed to enter seemingly scary and uncharted territories. In reflecting, it was from these scenarios and decisions, when I put myself off the track, that I truly grew the most, had experiences I'll never forget, and became prepared for the next chapter. When I stepped outside my comfort zone, the experience generally took form as a new kind of education that I helped create. At the time, what I really did was just follow my new interests. What I realize now is I had put myself in the scenarios where magic could happen and I could help produce it.

SURROUND YOURSELF WITH A STRONG COMMUNITY

Many of the experiences described were told starting with "I" but they were defined by "we." My greatest triumphs wouldn't have been possible without the support of friends, family, and others who have helped me or took me under their wing. I have tried to surround myself with amazing people, recognized the opportunities to rise to the occasion, and put in the necessary work to succeed with the power of *we* behind me. I've done my best to stay away from those who bring me down and surround myself with individuals who help raise my ceiling of possibilities.

ON SUCCESS: BE RELENTLESS AND RESOURCEFUL

I have absolutely overdone it in college. I have pushed myself to the limit, and I don't regret it for a second. I'm one of those who believe that you can do it all. We're young. We have energy. There are so many opportunities in the world ahead. The destination may seem unclear right now, but it will appear with time and focus. Exhaust your tank to achieve your goals, but don't forget to refuel.

In many of my pursuits, I started with little background in the challenge or activity before me, but I was able to define what I hoped to accomplish, figure out how to do it, and would stop at nothing until I gave it my all. If the tools were there, I found them, and if they weren't, I created them.

I've failed more times than I can count. My greatest triumphs couldn't have happened unless I fell flat on my face a few times. I can say with certainty that I'm no table-tennis master nor health-care practitioner, and neither will I be the next Spielberg, but in anything I have committed to, I take it upon myself to be relentlessly resourceful and go for it. Success is going to sleep knowing you did your best and waking up happy, healthy, excited to be alive, and ready to win the day.

A perfectly imperfect takeaway about Jeremy:

Jeremy is obsessed with the art of the start-up as a vehicle for pushing the world forward. This led him to start multiple companies, build communities to support young entrepreneurs, and invest in game-changing businesses. He loves meeting people and is fueled by new ideas. Today, as a young venture capitalist, he continues trying to break down barriers for the next generation of entrepreneurs just crazy enough to believe they can change the way we live.

9: JEREMY FIANCE

10

Max Song

Gritty Data Scientist

BS in Applied Mathematics-Biology, Class of 2014 (on leave
after the end of junior year), Brown University

Max Song is a biologically minded mathematician fascinated by emergent systems. He grew up in Chicago, Beijing, and Shanghai before attending Brown. Freshman summer, he worked at NASA Ames to create a proof-of-concept of biocementation with Martian soil simulant. The project won Best New Application at the World Championships of the International Genetically Engineered Machine (iGEM) Competition. Sophomore year, he co-started and ran Venture Labs, Brown University's first (and student-run) venture accelerator, and worked as a Teaching Fellow at Singularity University.

Max has organized workshops for the Kairos Society and the Thiel Foundation Summit and has delivered presentations at the iGEM Opening Ceremony and the White House Education Datapalooza. Recently, after a life-changing taxi ride in Moscow as part of 100 Young Innovators, he decided to take some time away from college.

He currently works full-time as a data scientist at DARPA-funded topological machine-learning company Ayasdi, and is co-author of *The*

Data Science Handbook, a compilation of 25 interviews with some of Silicon Valley's best and brightest data scientists. In his free time, Max loves to build communities; he led student coordination for Brown's Year of China and co-organizes a weekly intellectual gathering in Palo Alto called the Salon.

> *Figure out what you want to do, then do it until it works.*
> —Max Song

Adversity has a way of making people stronger. Max reflects on his childhood and a high school experience in which being "the dumbest person in the room" forced him to accelerate his learning and stretch his tolerance.

PART 1: GENESIS

My childhood was marked by frequent travel—I spent half my life in Chicago, and another half in Beijing and Shanghai. The experience of constant relocation left me with a strong sense of self-reliance and an appreciation for the common threads of humanity that span cultural and geographic divides.

During seventh grade, my father lost his job at the University of Chicago, and from then on our idyllic middle-class life was never the same again. For two long, agonizing years, my father was unemployed, and the experience left a deep psychological impression on me. From a family that had been able to vacation in Europe, we started shopping at low-cost grocery stores.

Much of my drive and ambition came from that difficult period and the subsequent relocation back to Beijing, where my father had found a teaching position at a Chinese university. The experience shattered my naïve sense of security in the world. I learned that the world does not take care of you—that you have to fight for what you want. In an empty parking lot in front of our house, filled only with tears, I promised myself that I would learn whatever it took to prevent this from happening again. The tenacity of my family during this difficult time was a constant source of inspiration. Even as our financial resources dwindled, the care that my parents devoted to the education of my sister and me only grew, and for their sacrifice I am forever grateful.

You can say that through those uncomfortable years, I lit the fire of my ambition. For those of you reading who have tasted hardship and discomfort early in your own life, I celebrate with you. It is not a misfortune but a blessing in disguise. Take it and use it to make yourself stronger. Have something to prove to the world and work harder than everyone else.

PART 2: WHAT IS TO GIVE LIGHT MUST ENDURE THE BURNING

Transitioning back to high school in Beijing was jarring. After nearly a decade in Chicago, the names of rappers were more familiar to me than Chinese characters. Both the language and the culture felt foreign. Yet my instruction—first a brief stint in a bilingual school and then at RenDaFu-Zhong (RDFZ), one of the premier pressure-cooker high schools in China—demanded a native level of proficiency to even begin to be comprehensible.

For the first time in my schooling, I failed the tests I took in school. Not one, not a few, but every single one of them. Unknowingly, over the last nine years of schooling, I had built part of my sense of self on my academic achievement, and now as that edifice began to crumble, so did my self-confidence. The public ranking system RDFZ employed amplified the frustration and embarrassment I felt. Every week a bulletin of school academic standing displayed the ranking of each student in that grade, spanning from 1 to 564, and I was the reluctant resident of box #547. The steely resolve I committed myself to in Chicago was put through a furnace of failure and alienation, as over the course of many sleepless midnights, I slowly seared Chinese characters into my brain.

From these experiences, I developed an appreciation for "crash-course learning" that informed many of my choices later in life. In three months, motivated by my parents' encouragement and with the gracious help of my classmates, I learned more Chinese than in three years' worth of language school. I came to understand and master my surroundings, and rose from that bottom box. Crash-course learning has many benefits: the pace is accelerated and the sense of urgency acts as a constant motivator, but you must be willing to pay its costs. It requires that you become intimately familiar with the taste of failure and the "nothing to lose" mentality.

When I was a straight-A student in Chicago, I hesitated to take risks for fear of losing my reputation or academic standing. But when I was failing every single test at RDFZ, I discovered a joyful obliviousness to my apprehension for asking stupid questions or displaying my ignorance. Since then, I've tried to always place myself in situations where I have no business being, where I am the dumbest person in the room, and where I have no reputation to protect. It is never an easy experience, but I know that it is a surefire way to accelerate my learning.

Through the four years of high school, Max transferred through four different schools in Chicago, Beijing, and Shanghai. He did not have the chance to be consistently involved in activities at each school. Instead, he focused on getting up to speed academically in each new academic setting. Because his father found a better job in Shanghai, Max's family moved again. During the last two years of high school, he earned a 4.0 at Shanghai American School, and graduated valedictorian of the class. He achieved a 2370 on the SAT, received 5s on nine APs, a 7 on International Baccalaureate High Level (IB HL) Math, and 800s on the SAT Subject Tests (SAT IIs) for Math, Biology, and Chemistry.

Max reminisces on his college choice:

During my senior year of high school, I developed a love for literature. I read in the *New York Times* a review of a book called *The Brothers Karamazov*, which the reviewer endorsed as teaching him "everything [he] knew about life." Intrigued, I bought a copy and lost myself in an intoxicating story, exploring interwoven themes of love, reason, and faith.

As Tom Stoppard wrote, "I don't think writers are sacred, but words are. They deserve respect. If you get the right ones in the right order, you might nudge the world a little." *The Brothers Karamazov* nudged me to develop a deep appreciation of the power of writing in communicating ideas and remains to this day one of my favorite books, especially its story-within-a-story called the "Grand Inquisitor."

When the time came to choose a college, my choices were between the University of Chicago and Brown University. Having grown up by the doorstep of UChicago, I wanted to go somewhere new, to reinvent myself. Brown, with its renowned Open Curriculum, felt like a place that could give me freedom to enrich both the scientific and literary sides of my brain. It also offered a first-year seminar on *The Brothers Karamazov*. I was sold.

Today, Max would be a senior at Brown University had he not taken a leave after his junior year. I've asked him to reflect:

To what extent did your college experience meet your expectations? In what ways did your experience cause you to change your perspective on your academic career, your dreams and aspirations, and your life?

THE SINGULARITY UNIVERSITY EXPERIENCE

Looking back, each remarkable period of my life came from a combination of luck, hustle, and building on top of past experiences. I'd like to share the story of how I worked at Singularity University my sophomore summer as a taste of this dynamic.

The closest thing to describing Singularity University (SU) is perhaps Professor Xavier's School for Gifted Youngsters in *X-Men*, except instead of mutant superpowers, attendees were gifted with a fluency in technology and an entrepreneurial drive. Another way to describe it would be a six-week nonstop TED conference followed by a four-week start-up accelerator. Founded by space entrepreneur Peter Diamandis and futurist Ray Kurzweil, SU was one of the densest concentrations of smart people and big-picture thinking I have encountered in my life. To get into their annual summer Graduate Studies Program required an extensive application period, competing in a countrywide Global Impact competition, and all of that without even mentioning tuition.

A session at SU not only exposed you directly to the movers and shakers of Silicon Valley but also asked you to come up with your own ideas about how to apply exponential technologies on major world problems. Every summer class was eighty students large, usually representing thirty or more countries, with an average age in the late twenties or early thirties. Many of the attendees had previous experience in entrepreneurship, or were pursuing advanced science and engineering degrees.

Like the start of many incredible experiences, the first time that I visited SU was almost by accident. I was in NASA's Ames Research Center in Mountain View, conducting bioengineering research for the International Genetically Engineered Machine Competition (iGEM). One night after work, I was curious to investigate what went on in the building next to our housing and just walked through the doors. In the middle of a tight-knit group of pod chairs, a distinguished Indian American man sat on a stage, sharing philosophical insights about entrepreneurship.

As this gent talked more, I learned that he was legendary venture capitalist Vinod Khosla, co-founder of Sun Microsystems, from which we have the Java programming language. I took a seat next to a bearded gentleman and was surprised to find him later swarmed with people carrying MacBooks. He was none other than Steve Wozniak, co-founder of Apple Computers. Sitting amidst a handful of people personally responsible for the technological underpinnings of our world, I thought to myself, I'm going to find a way to come back here.

Flash-forward to the end of that summer. I wrapped up our iGEM research at Ames and prepared to go back to Brown, but I also visited SU a few more times to get to know the people involved. One person, with whom I hit it off with immediately, was Raymond McCauley, head of the Biotechnology Track.

For our community outreach project for iGEM that year, I had the idea to interview various people in the space and bioengineering community to ask their thoughts on opportunities and challenges of using synthetic biology for space exploration. That included a chance to talk to Pete Warden, the center director for NASA (who as legend goes, would occasionally dress up for formal meetings in a full Viking outfit, complete with helmet and battle-axe. One can imagine that budget conversations always began a little nervously). Of course, we also asked for the opportunity to interview Raymond McCauley as well, and when he said yes, I was ecstatic.

I remember the important moment at Specialty's Café, where we went for lunch after the interview. I told him: "I'm happy to do whatever it takes to come back to SU next summer. If it means volunteering to do physical labor, I'll do it to be able to sit and watch the sessions." He looked at me thoughtfully and said: "Perhaps there is something else that I can use your skills on."

I went back to Brown. Later that year, I heard from Raymond McCauley about the role of a Teaching Fellow. Most Fellows were PhDs or MDs in the track they represented, but Raymond said he saw potential in me and wanted to take a chance. Even as I was still finishing my finals at Brown at the end of sophomore year, I started preparing for the Biotechnology Track.

As a Teaching Fellow, I was responsible for bringing the track chair's vision for the summer program into reality. For those in computer science, I like to joke that my job was to solve "NP-hard scheduling problems"—from coordinating group visits to biotech companies like Genentech and Amyris to inviting and organizing visits from cutting-edge researchers. At one point, we were making calls to the Israeli embassy, to expedite the passport process of a DNA-programming researcher so he could fly in on time. In my free time, I had a chance to learn and expand my knowledge from the other tracks—Robotics, Energy, Design, and Medicine. At the end of the summer, the Biotechnology Track was a great success. We brought in top-notch researchers and entrepreneurs in the biotechnology space, organized workshops and site visits, and opened up an appreciation of biology within the students' minds.

The summer was not without its challenges, though. In addition to the time pressure of coordinating a densely packed program, I also wrestled with a strong case of imposter syndrome: at twenty, I was legally not old enough to drink, and yet here I was, "teaching" and sharing knowledge with doctoral students and entrepreneurs. Fortunately, from my previous lab work, I did have something to contribute. Synthetic biology (and the process of rationally engineering biological organisms) was a hot topic in our discussions about the future, and my summers of wet-lab benchwork allowed me to lead workshops on pipetting and DNA transformation. We took petri dishes of *E. coli* and transformed them to glow fluorescent. It was a simple procedure, but one that opened the eyes of the students with more powerful possibilities. To mutate a line from Arthur C. Clarke, screenplay co-writer for the movie *2001: A Space Odyssey:* "Sufficient enough knowledge transforms magic into technology."

Given what you know now, if you could redo high school, what would you do differently, and why?

MY LESSONS LEARNED AND TIPS ON COLLEGE PLANNING AND ADMISSIONS

As a rule of thumb—you are the average of the five people you spend the most time with. When choosing schools, one metric is to see whether or not the environment will automatically surround you with smart, motivated classmates and with teachers who care about the craft of teaching. If the environment does not amply provide you with such a context, think about what you can do to create your own microcosm of curiosity and motivation. Even if it is hard, you will have learned a valuable skill that will stay with you for the rest of your life. Learning how to build a community for yourself in any context is a much more valuable experience then being handed on a silver platter.

This advice is particularly poignant for you readers who grew up wearing the mantle of success, who have gotten good grades your entire life, who go to a reputable high school, excel in your class, and lead your clubs. I was very much like you, until my experiences in China forced me to reconsider what you lose when you play the prestige game. What they don't tell you in school is that your true potential is only revealed when you walk off the beaten path and try to pave your own. Otherwise, you might end up chasing other people's definition of success your entire life.

Today, having accumulated more life experiences, I would tell the bright-eyed version of my high school self the following:

1. Good grades are the table stakes. They get you in the door of consideration, but they by no means compel a decision. When Shanghai American School organized an alumni panel at which current high school students could ask questions of their older brethren, I was shocked to hear how many bright, intelligent young people asked about how minuscule differences in SAT or AP scores factored into college admission decisions. I only had three words to give them: "Do Epic Shit."

2. To rise above the ocean of perfect test scores, you have to do something real and meaningful. This is challenging because even with the Internet at your fingertips, it's hard to know what to search for. I know that I didn't have good role models for what I should (or even *could*) be doing. Here's what I'd do now: go on the Internet and look up the Thiel Foundation to find the stories of kids punching above their age range. Their stories will give you a better sense of what is possible. Once you overcome your initial sense of shock and awe, ask yourself: "What is it about these kids? Are they born with superpowers? Or have they just been spending their time doing interesting things instead of playing video games?"

3. Really get to know and demonstrate interest in your college choices. Visit the school you are applying to. Take the official campus tour, but sneak away in the middle to create your own unofficial tour. Talk to as many students and professors as you can. Tell them about yourself. Tell them about your hopes and dreams and what you like about the school. For those who can't travel to visit the school, go hunt down people who have gone there. Read about the school online. Send e-mails to alumni who took the classes you want to take. Be relentless in your research, and show that you really understand what the school is about (and I mean more than you can find on their Wikipedia page).

P.S. It turns out that these tips are also exactly the same for getting the job you want. A quote by Neil Kendall captures this sentiment perfectly: "Some people follow their dreams, others hunt them down, and beat them mercilessly into submission." Dream schools, dream jobs, and dream lifestyles all operate with the same rules.

What else would you like to share with or suggest to high school students and college students, and why?

From my blurb, you can tell that I had a busy time in college. In fact, it was perhaps the first time that I really got a sense of what one could do with time and experience. I have three simple lessons to share:

WATCH OUT FOR YOUR HEALTH (YOU CAN BURN THE CANDLE AT BOTH ENDS ONLY FOR SO LONG)!

I had a pretty fiery sophomore year. Between working as student coordinator for Year of China (a year's worth of campus-wide events that brought Chinese culture to Brown's campus), running Brown Venture Labs, and taking hard engineering classes, I found going to bed at two or three a.m. a daily occurrence. During one intense week, the last few days before our presentation for iGEM was due, I stayed awake for three days straight—going to classes during the day and working through the night on the website and our research summary. I felt like Superman, able to do everything at the same time and still hold it all together.

The boundaries of my mortality came calling soon after. I developed a really bad case of repetitive strain injury (RSI) in my hands and had a difficult time typing or even just using the keyboard. To write my final essay for a class, I had to resort to two pencils, taped to each hand, with which to stab at the keyboard. I was also taking computer science classes that semester, and needless to say, it was not a fun experience.

The lesson here is to take good care of yourself. Don't overdo it. Exercise regularly, and remember that skills and abilities take time to mature. (And yoga, it turns out, really does change your life.)

LEAD SOMETHING THAT YOU ARE PROUD OF. WORK WITH CLASSMATES THAT YOU ADMIRE. PROJECTS ARE THE BEST WAY TO REALLY GET TO KNOW SOMEONE.

It's good to participate in the organizations of others, but you really learn about the trials and tribulations of leadership when you are the one making the decisions. The stakes in college are terribly low. There is no cost to trying to start your own interest group or even business venture. Sophomore year, I co-founded Brown Venture Labs, an incubator for student ventures, with my good friend Adrienne Tran. She had worked at a Silicon Valley start-up the previous year, and I had met and talked with many entrepreneurs during my own visit. We wanted to create a program to encourage and expose our peers at Brown to entrepreneurship.

We saw Brown Venture Labs as our own venture, and the participating students like our customers. We learned how to network, how to organize and host events, how to enlist advisors and mentors who believed in our cause, and how to gather legal and financial resources for our members. And that was the first semester. Over the course of my tenure, we graduated twelve student teams: a few went on to raise money, one became an Echoing Green fellow (one of the most acclaimed awards in social entrepreneurship), and others are still actively working on their ventures today.

GET SOME WORK EXPERIENCE BEFORE YOU "USE UP" TOO MUCH SCHOOL

My first real job came after taking a leave of absence from Brown. It is actually the one that I'm still at right now—data science at Ayasdi. I had been in research labs most of my life, and ironically, it is really only when you leave school that you come to appreciate how interesting and useful school is.

Here's why school is a rare and valuable place. These words will be interesting, but not "true" for you until you disembark from the pre-planned voyage of school and test the waters yourself:

1. Rarely elsewhere in the world is your only responsibility to purely just "learn" and pursue what interests you.

2. Rarely elsewhere in the world do you have people whose jobs mostly consist of answering your curious inquiries and teaching you things you want to know.

3. Rarely elsewhere in the world are you constantly surrounded by young, motivated, and enthusiastic peers, who believe in the future as much as you do, and who challenge you intellectually. Peers with whom the only competition is grades: not money, job security, or a livelihood.

Only by removing yourself from college do you really take control of your education. One way is to intern during the summer and come back energized and motivated to learn new things. Another way is to take a leave of absence as I did—which is totally underrated as a tool in one's educational tool belt. I love my current job. I work with some of the smartest people in Silicon Valley, but I also get to see the shortcomings in my knowledge. If I decide to return to school (I have not made a decision at this point), I intend to fill in some of these knowledge gaps.

Real learning happens when you marry experience to theory. An effective way to approach one's education, in my mind, is to oscillate between work and school, experience and theory. If you have a chance, find a program at your college/university that allows you the structure to do this. If it does not exist, create your own. Enjoy the self-confidence and financial security that working in the real world provides, and then go back to school to do a deeper dive on things that piqued your interest. If you rinse and repeat, you will never have a dull moment in life.

A perfectly imperfect takeaway on Max:

Starting from his experience at the RDFZ high school in Beijing, Max developed a taste for challenges that push him to the edge of his abilities. His near-term goal is to continue growing as a data scientist and learn more about the nuances of entrepreneurship. Max adds, "Leaving university did not signal the end of my learning; rather, I look at work as the natural continuation of my education." Max feels as though he is training for the marathon of entrepreneurship. He cautions: "There is a mad rush around entrepreneurship right now, and some people say that it is overhyped. It's overhyped if you are blindly going into it without a clear plan. Prepare yourself by finding high-quality learning opportunities. Embrace the pain that comes from growing quickly and remember: 'What is to give light must endure the burning.' "

11

Sophie Mann

Strategic Planner from NYC

BA in Economics-Mathematics, Class of 2015, Columbia University

Originally from Manhattan, Sophie Mann grew up only three blocks away from Columbia University. In high school, Sophie was passionate about debate and, as captain, led her team to win the New York City Championships. She also had a keen interest in math and thought highly of her math teacher, who is a former investment banker and who first sparked her curiosity for the finance industry. She has since been involved in a variety of organizations and projects on and off campus centered mainly on her business interests. At Columbia University she leads the largest pre-professional group on campus, the Columbia Economics Society, where she has organized events introducing freshmen and sophomores to the business world.

Since she was a college freshman, Sophie has served as an equity partner at a start-up aimed to create a marketplace for college women to buy and sell clothes. After a sophomore summer internship in the finance industry in a rotational Sales & Trading Program at an investment bank, Sophie decided to pursue an internship in consulting in her junior year and received an offer to intern at a top consulting firm. Recently, Sophie received an offer to return to the same firm as a full-time hire after graduation and has decided to accept.

Achieving a balance is the most difficult but essential skill to learn in college, and it is the one I see as being the most important to achieving long-term success.

—Sophie Mann

Born and raised in the Big Apple, Sophie Mann is grateful for her parents' encouragement and support through the years.

My parents are scientists. They both received a PhD in biology, and have instilled in me the importance of hard work and education from a young age. From middle-class upbringings, both of my parents worked very hard individually to succeed in their fields. I count myself lucky to have such terrific role models as parents—they brought me to museums, encouraged me to read books, yelled when I watched too much TV, and gave me the optimistic idea that all could be achieved if I worked hard enough. No problem was insurmountable; they have helped me with everything from applying to colleges to getting a stain out of my shirt. They also gave me their trust. I explored New York City at a young age without them.

Through this independence, I became comfortable in strange and unpredictable situations and speaking to people I didn't know—two skills I feel have helped me navigate the business world (and were especially helpful when going through the rigorous finance and consulting interview process). I navigated high school with their support but with enough distance to make my own choices and mistakes, and solve problems on my own. Though my chosen career path has brought me far away from the sciences, my parents' influence and encouragement have allowed me to succeed.

In high school, Sophie maintained a 4.0 GPA and participated in many extracurricular activities. In school, Sophie was president of the Debate Team, ran track and cross-country, and was a member of the ARISTA Honor Society, a group open to students who meet the grade and community service qualifications. Outside of school, Sophie devoted her energies to playing violin, which she had started when she was seven years old. She also explored her interests through various internships, working at the dress design division of Ralph Lauren and gaining a taste of the nonprofit world at Math for America, an organization dedicated to supporting and encouraging public school math teachers.

To which colleges/universities did Sophie apply and to which was she admitted? Why did she choose Columbia?

I was admitted to Columbia University, University of Pennsylvania, Johns Hopkins University, Emory University, Washington University in St. Louis, and the University of Chicago. After much thought, I chose Columbia University for two main reasons.

The first was that I was already somewhat interested in the finance industry and felt that Columbia would be the best place from which to pursue internships and further my career goals. I was worried that if I went to the University of Pennsylvania (where I was accepted to their Arts & Sciences College), I could be overshadowed by students at Wharton (their business school, which has an undergraduate division). Furthermore, since Columbia was in New York City, I was in close proximity to many of the banks and consulting firms to which I was applying for internships.

The second reason, which was perhaps the most important, was that Columbia made the most sense financially. Attending Columbia would cost significantly less than any other college, and I could not justify spending considerably more money on what I saw to be a comparable education.

Today, Sophie is a rising senior at Columbia. I've asked her to reflect on the following question:

To what extent did your college experience—on and off campus—meet your expectations? In what ways did your experience cause you to change your perspective on your academic career, your dreams and aspirations, and your life?

NOT EVERYTHING CAN BE PLANNED IN ADVANCE, AND SOME OF THE MOST IMPORTANT EVENTS CAN BE COMPLETELY UNEXPECTED

In high school, I was always well organized. I methodically planned out my days in my color-coded planner to schedule in everything I wanted to get done—go to class, go to track practice, finish up an assignment, and so on. Not a moment was wasted in downtime, and the only time I took a break was when I was finished with everything else I had planned. I was so prepared for college applications that I finished applying to my chosen twelve colleges by the end of August, just a couple weeks after the Common App had come out. My guidance counselors in high school would bring me into their meetings with other students so I could explain the college application process to my peers.

Once I decided to enroll at Columbia University, the planning began immediately. I decided to be an economics and philosophy major, and promptly made an Excel spreadsheet of all the classes I would be taking in the next four years. I left very little room for any electives or classes in subjects I was interested in exploring.

When I arrived at Columbia in the fall, I discovered how badly I had miscalculated my well-thought-out plans. I found that I really didn't like the introductory philosophy class I was enrolled in, and realized that unless I wanted to spend my remaining seven semesters taking philosophy classes that I couldn't stand, I would have to give up on my predisposition to plan everything for the next four years. Though this sounds trivial, it took me a while to come to terms with this and to understand that my "plans" would—and most important *should*—change multiple times throughout my years in college and more generally in life.

Furthermore, the best things that happened to me and that defined the past three years at Columbia were the ones I didn't plan and that appeared at times when I least expected them. I was encouraged to join the Columbia Economics Society by my wonderful freshman-year resident advisor. As context, the Economics Society is the largest pre-professional group at Columbia, with over a thousand members, and I had been too intimidated as a freshman to even apply. It was my RA's encouragement and help that gave me the confidence I needed to apply.

I met and became heavily involved in a start-up by sitting next to the future co-founder in my introductory economics class. The relationship began as a mini-internship where I helped research and assess market demand for the idea, and it morphed into much more when my contributions helped change the direction for the company. Opportunities come when you least expect it, and I had to learn to let go of my habit of planning everything.

NON-ACADEMIC PURSUITS ARE EQUALLY, IF NOT MORE, IMPORTANT THAN CLASSES AND GRADES

This piece of advice can be further broken down into three distinct parts: (1) making and maintaining strong friendships, (2) pursuing extracurricular activities, and (3) exploring various internships. All three are exceptionally important for maintaining a well-balanced and happy life while in college.

1. Friendships. My friends have easily been the best and most welcome distraction to my academics in both high school and college. I found that time spent with friends is infinitely more enjoyable than time spent alone. All my friends are equally busy leading their own separate lives, so it is definitely a challenge to find times that work for everyone and it is easy to neglect or underestimate the importance of staying in touch. However, this is a necessary challenge to undertake, as my friends throughout high school and college have been the ones to support me through all the unexpected difficulties that have come up over the past years. I find time to spend with my friends during meals and while studying at the library, and always make an effort to leave weekend nights free.

2. Extracurriculars. Though my extracurricular activities during the school year took away time that could have otherwise been spent studying, they were crucial to keeping a balance in my life and kept me somewhat sane during the demanding and exhausting semesters. Being a part of the Columbia Economics Society, and especially being co-president as a junior, taught me numerous lessons in being a leader. Several disasters were narrowly avoided (or not) due to small mistakes in technology or room scheduling—I learned to keep calm during mini crises and that the ability to move on from mistakes was significantly more important than the actual mistake. Our weekly Monday meetings were easily what I looked forward to most at the beginning of another taxing week.

I also prioritized exercise, participating in sorority events, and spending time alone reading for pleasure or just relaxing. I would not trade these thousands of hours that could have been spent studying for anything; they are the hours that defined my college career and made me a happier person.

3. Internships. Especially during the summer, they are important not only to gain work experience to put on a résumé and talk about during interviews, but also to provide a relatively risk-free way to experiment with your likes and dislikes in a job. I believe the latter is the most important. For example, working with a start-up has been one of the most challenging and rewarding parts of my college career. I have been involved with the company since the first couple months of its conception, and helped transform the original idea through several iterations. I have had a variety of responsibilities throughout my three years. Among many highlights would be working on the strategy and business plan of the company, formulating and implementing the Campus Ambassador Program at select colleges, and analyzing important metrics tracking our progress and the effectiveness of our various expansion strategies.

Though I thoroughly enjoyed all experiences working with the company, the uncertainty and stress of being part of a start-up taught me that I was not ready to work in such an unstable environment at this early stage of my career. However, it could be a step I may be interested in taking later in life.

My internship during the summer of 2012 (after my freshman year) was at a small, federally funded consulting firm that provided free business advice for aspiring entrepreneurs and current business owners. I had landed this internship through a recommendation from a fellow Economics Society member. It was a relatively relaxed internship where I spent my time organizing their filing system and building up my bosses' trust enough to listen in and eventually participate in their various client meetings. I was able to help our clients write business plans and seek funding for their ideas via loans and grants.

It was both a rewarding and frustrating summer. I felt excited when my clients would receive loans they had applied for with my help, but frustrated as both of my bosses were leaving the firm at the end of the summer and were thus relatively unmotivated and uninspiring to work for. The internship taught me that I was interested in consulting as an idea, but I wanted a larger work environment with higher-profile clients.

Internships as pre-professional consultants at large firms are practically nonexistent for college freshmen and sophomores. So for my sophomore summer, I applied to banks in their Sales & Trading divisions. I was interested in exploring something new—after all, how could I be sure consulting was right for me if I never tried anything different? I was intrigued by the mystique of the trading floor and wanted to learn more. My internship in Sales & Trading during the following summer was at a bulge-bracket bank (that is, a multinational investment bank). I had applied to this internship (and various others) online and completed several rounds of interviews before receiving an offer to work there for the summer. It was a ten-week internship with three rotations through different desks for three weeks each. I rotated through a sales, trading, and structuring desk—a great experience because I got a brief taste of all three facets of the Sales & Trading division of a bank. I loved working in a high-energy corporate environment with intelligent coworkers but found that I enjoyed working on longer-term projects.

When it came time to look for junior-year internships for the summer of 2014, I was able to narrow my search to places I knew I would enjoy working because of both of my previous summer experiences—and was ecstatic to accept an offer to intern at a top consulting firm.

In sum, I believe that students who focus only on achieving straight A's in college at the expense of having little to no extracurricular and internship experiences ultimately achieve less (be it in outside-the-classroom educational experiences or top jobs upon graduating) than students who balance grades and extracurricular activities but give up on the idea of a perfect 4.0.

This is crucial to understand, especially when starting college. In high school, I found it relatively easy to achieve both extracurricular and academic success without sacrificing too much. In college, this won't be the case: academics are significantly more difficult and the other students are equally as high-caliber as you. In this sea of intellects, what helps keep my sanity are my non-academic activities and my friends.

I have also learned that extracurriculars and internships can give students the grounding and support necessary to be successful and, more important, to maintain a happy college experience. My advice would be this: realizing sooner rather than later that in college you cannot have perfect grades, outstanding extracurricular activities, a social life, and get enough sleep—and that this is OK—will allow for a more fulfilling and well-rounded college experience.

Achieving a balance is the most difficult but essential skill to learn in college, and it is the one I see as being the most important to achieving long-term success.

Given what you know now, if you could redo high school, what would you do differently, and why?

TAKE EVERY CLASS SERIOUSLY, EVEN DURING SENIOR YEAR

By taking classes seriously, I am mostly referring to the importance of actually absorbing and understanding the material presented, and less so the actual grades. For college admissions purposes, grades matter significantly less in the second semester of your senior year of high school. Seniors should take advantage of this term as an opportunity to relax before college begins. That being said, however, one of my biggest regrets in high school was not taking my second-semester senior-year classes seriously enough and consequently having gaps in some basic knowledge when entering college.

For example, during my senior year I took AP Calculus AB. Because I loved my teacher, I continued to pay attention in class throughout senior year, and studied hard for the AP exam. The result, besides achieving good grades and an AP score that exempted me from Calculus I in college, was that I understood the fundamentals of calculus. I was able to use this strong foundation when taking other math classes in college, allowing me to understand and enjoy most of my college math classes and it ultimately led me to declare an economics-mathematics major.

As an opposing example: I also found out what happens when you do not pay attention to a class in high school. I took three years of Spanish in high school, and unfortunately found that I achieved decent grades by memorizing choice words and tenses without actually practicing the language. Once arriving in college, I could not place out of my language requirement (as I had also opted out of taking the AP Spanish exam), and it was mandatory to take two Spanish classes to fulfill this requirement in college. These classes were exceptionally difficult for me because I generally lacked some Spanish basics, and I truly regretted not putting more time and energy into learning the fundamentals while in high school.

Furthermore, I regret not being conversationally fluent in a language besides English in general. Apart from how much the fundamentals would have helped me in my college Spanish classes, I wish I knew another language because it is a great skill to have (in this case especially given the constantly growing Latin American market).

The bottom line is that high school classes provide important fundamentals needed for college classes, and so every effort should be made to actually absorb this information, otherwise you will be at a disadvantage in the future.

What else would you like to share with or suggest to high school students and college students, and why?

"NETWORKING" IS EXTREMELY IMPORTANT

This piece of advice is geared more specifically toward those who are interested in finance or consulting, because those are the two fields that I have become most familiar with during my time in college. When I started college, I knew I was interested in finance. However, since both my parents are scientists they knew next to nothing about the industry. Though I could have accepted this lack of information and contacts as a huge disadvantage, I instead turned it into one of my greatest strengths.

Because I knew little about the finance industry, I was eager to learn anything and everything I could from anyone who was willing to answer my endless questions. Those willing to help first were older students who had been through and understood the finance or consulting interview/internship process. I also reached out to many people already working in finance or consulting after meeting them at various firm events; I made an effort to attend as many of these events as possible, even as a freshman and sophomore.

The word "networking" is in quotes above because it is one that I generally dislike. To me (and to many other students) it connotes a calculated relationship that is initiated just to get ahead. This is not what I think networking should be about. Instead it should be used as a way to gather information and advice from people whose careers you genuinely respect, admire, and are interested in, and not as a way to get your résumé to the top of the interview pile. So my "networking" advice is this: find a few people whom you sincerely admire and keep in contact with them—not because you think it will help you get an internship but because you really want to get advice from someone who has succeeded in a way you want to. Though you may ultimately have fewer contacts than the students who speed-date to increase their network, your relationships will be more fruitful and more rewarding.

As an example: my aforementioned high school math teacher who first sparked my interest in the finance industry is someone with whom I make an effort to keep in contact because I respect his opinions and greatly value his advice, not because I think he can get me an internship. He has since retired from teaching high school and moved out to California, but I have stayed in contact via e-mail and was even able to grab a quick lunch with him during a recent trip to California.

I would also advise you not to treat "networking" contacts as people who are only useful to you to get an internship or job, and then discard them when you decide that the firm is not right for you or when you get rejected by the firm. Understand that even if those people cannot help you with your immediate goal of finding an internship or job, they are still very successful and intelligent people who have tons of great advice. These people—who took time to give me invaluable advice and without whose help I would not be where I am today—are people I genuinely admire and ones with whom I truly intend and hope to stay in contact far beyond college.

A perfectly imperfect takeaway about Sophie:

Sophie no longer has a five- or ten-year plan for the future. She wishes to explore options as they present themselves. What she does know and value are the friends she made in both high school and college. She realizes that no matter what is next to come, she will stay in touch with them all and their support will be vital as she continues her career and life. The experiences Sophie has gained in college—both academic and extracurricular—have been instrumental in shaping her interests and future career. She is excited to enter senior year with a full-time job she loves already lined up and to spend her final year enjoying all that Columbia and New York City have to offer.

Act IV
Graduated and Making Their Way

12

Angela Wang

Long Mohawk

BA in Sociology, Class of 2014, UCLA

From becoming Associated Student Body (ASB) vice president to being an Advancement Via Individual Determination (AVID) tutor, Angela Wang actively contributed to various facets of her school and community. She was active in Interact Club, Varsity Badminton, school dance, and service clubs she initiated. Weekdays, she took piano and Kung Fu lessons and participated in local competitions. Weekends, Angela volunteered at the River of Life Church, Second Harvest Food Bank, and other non-profits. These experiences occurred over a period in which she gave herself a defiant Mohawk haircut and opened her eyes to a world that constantly lacked love. This realization fueled her passion for helping others, creating smiles, and delivering happiness.

At UCLA, Angela served as executive director of Student Group Outreach under the Undergraduate Students Association Council (USAC) Internal Vice President's Office. She also interned at two award-winning, event-planning firms. To give back to the community, Angela has decided to pursue something dear to her heart—educational counseling at a high school, a college, or an educational academy.

Taste freely, breathe deeply, love fiercely, embrace openly, and rejoice in every moment of every day, because it is all so worth it.
—Angela Wang

Born and raised in a suburb south of the San Francisco Bay Area, Angela Wang grew up suffering abuse and trauma through middle and high school. She reflected on these intense experiences via the following UC application personal essay submitted as a high school senior (slightly edited by Angela).

UC personal statement prompt #1: Describe the world you come from—for example, your family, community or school—and tell us how your world has shaped your dreams and aspirations.

Harder. Better. Faster. Stronger. To some, these words merely fill the chorus of Kanye West's new rap. At my school, they are the catch phrases that echo throughout our rallies. In my world, however, these four words instantiate my unbridled passion for change and love.

My life has been a veritable war. Even before I had stepped onto the battlefield, I was immediately shoved onto the ground. Stop! I shouted. Stop. But my mother offered no sympathy. [Readers: I've deleted a sentence here—too personal.] She vitiated my will to live. To her, I was nothing, but I knew I wasn't. Harder. I just could not live this way. I stared into my enemy's blood-shot eyes and screamed "Enough." For the first time in my life, I had defied; she was stunned. From that day forth, I learned the meaning of Harder. To survive this war, I had to stand up, stand tall, and stand firm.

Harder did I learn, but harder did I fall.

My abused spirit fell into a deep coma of depression. I mindlessly passed through my middle school years in a blur of suicidal thoughts. With cuts slashed unto my arm and rope marks burned into my neck, I surrendered my lifeless spirit to the doctor's notepad. However, through my beloved expressions of dance, sports, music, and lithium, I was able to hear the soft symphony of "Better" reverberating in my ears. This melody sounded so sweet, but I was too far away to taste it.

Up ahead, a familiar face runs towards me and I am joyous at his presence. I think he could help me but I am wrong. [Readers: I've deleted two sentences here—too personal.] At school, rumors are morbidly twisted.

Slut! They called me. Whore! My parents neglect me, and my friends leave. I was unfairly wronged. I was alone in my world—a pariah with no purpose and no vitality.

Better. Harder. During a California School Counselors conference I discover the concept of leadership and my perspective on the world radically shifts. Through its power, I begin to learn the root strength of my being and begin to forgive the world. Faster. Through clubs, I hold the tools to serve the environment that had once abused and ridiculed me. Faster. Through my position as class secretary, I desperately strive to transform my school and my community—the very places that once shamed me.

Harder, Better, Faster, Stronger—the actions in my life instantiate these ideals. Every time I start a committee, initiate a club, sign a petition, or organize a proposal, I express my insatiable hunger for positive change in my world. From my past sufferings, I have learned the gift of empathy and forgiveness. Because of my once hopeless world, I am now more sensitive to the pain and suffering that pervades my city.

My dream is to open a community shelter aimed at helping the poor, the homeless, and the rejected. I want to show them a hope that leadership has once shown me—a hope that life is worth living. Through this shelter I want to provide people relief from their own bloody battles. Together, we can bandage our wounds and together we will be Stronger.

In high school, Angela daringly shaved her head bald and when her hair grew a little, gave herself a Mohawk. She wrote about what these defiant yet symbolic acts meant and how they related to her character, on her other UC app personal essay:

UC prompt #2: Tell us about a personal quality, talent, accomplishment, contribution or experience that is important to you. What about this quality or accomplishment makes you proud and how does it relate to the person you are?

ZZMM. With each broken strand of hair, I lose the core fibers that have once built me up.

There is a moment in everyone's life when she realizes that she needs to change herself, and my day came when I took my mother's razors and shaved my head. I can still remember the black hair as it gently kissed the ground. To the world, my hair gave me the appearance of a cute, geisha doll. But to me, my hair made me look weak. Because of this childish hair, nobody took my leadership ambitions seriously, nobody noticed the strong passion in my eyes, and nobody listened to my suggestions. Almost everyone pushed me down.

After my hair grew 3 inches longer, I chose to give myself a Mohawk because it was more than a hairstyle. It symbolized my resilience and the true nature of my life. Never again did I want to be "flattened" and pushed down again; I wanted to "stand up" with strength and power. Every strand of my hair was gelled high into the air, broadcasting its splendor. At first, passersby stared; boys mocked; teachers kept their distance; and my parents hung their heads in shame. As a student, dancer, daughter, and Christian, I was everything they despised. People who saw me instantly stereotyped me as a punk rocker, a band druggie with no potential or promise. The insults initially hurt me . . . THIS was not the person I was trying to be. However, I gradually embraced my hair's eccentricity and soon transfused this uniqueness and power into my bloodstream.

The new hairstyle sculpted my face into a sharp and mysterious shape, and I was inclined to dress in an edgier style. However, this hair had not only changed my physical appearance but also my inner core. My perspective on leadership, schoolwork, and extracurricular activities evolved. I initiated locker petitions, the 180 Committee (a school based community club), the Make-A-Wish Club (a school beatification club), and joined leadership conventions. My goal was to change the school, and nothing was going to stand in my way. When my petitions and school-based clubs failed, I started more. When the office rejected my school improvement ideas, I initiated student committees. My ambitions to change the school manifested themselves as my hair gave me the self-confidence and personality to act upon my desires.

Through my actions, other students conjured up the confidence to start their own petitions and clubs—some even began to Mohawk their hair. No longer was I considered a sweet girl. I was the rebellious and ambitious girl who would try everything to reach her goal. Though my hair has now grown out, I know that the fire of change within me has never died. In fact, it has grown stronger. This ongoing power manifests itself in my current role as ASB Vice President: I have focused on improving school recycling and teacher unity. My hair gave me the initial confidence, but it did not give me the potential. I had it within me the entire time. As I continue through life, my fire will not die. But if I need some inspiration along the way, well, my hair can always spare a few inches.

In high school, Angela contributed heavily to student government, including starting various initiatives to better the school (for example, recycling, fund-raisers, and petitions for lockers). She was also active in dance teams, school sports, and other club organizations, in many of which she held officer positions. During weekends, she volunteered to hand out food to the underprivileged while taking piano, dance, and Kung Fu classes. Despite dozens of hours of extracurricular activities per week, she maintained a 4.0 GPA.

Angela applied to University of California (UC) campuses, Wellesley, and Brown. She was accepted into all the UCs, including Berkeley and UCLA, waitlisted for Wellesley, and denied by Brown.

The reason I chose to go to LA over Berkeley was that I wanted a fresh start. I felt like UCLA had the environment, people, education, and resources that I needed to get that fresh start.

Angela recently graduated from UCLA. I've asked her to reflect on the following:

To what extent did your college experience meet your expectations? In what ways did your experience cause you to change your perspective on your academic career, your dreams and aspirations, and your life?

My high school years were a blur, a battlefield, and a distant memory I can only hope to forget and leave completely behind me. But, at times when I'm alone, I still reflect on what I have been through to get to where I am today, and needless to say, I am beyond grateful for the vigor and life that college has given me.

Unlike my application essays, this short story is my story of hope, reform, and change.

I came to UCLA as a scared and nervous freshman, desperate to meet friends, to live independently, and most important, to start my life over, to rebuild myself, and to discover my purpose. What drives me? Why am I here? After joining an Asian sorority, I found a group of girls who would go to hell and back to see me grow. They sat patiently and listened to my darkest insecurities, gave me advice, protected me, and talked to me whenever my past would manifest its ugly face again. These girls gave me the bonds that I so desperately lacked from high school, and from that I was able to build my confidence, my ability to trust and love again, and my desire to let go of the past so that I can finally move forward.

During my second year in college, however, I learned the value of family after a devastating event ripped through my family. My mother was diagnosed with bipolar disorder after a depressive state nearly cost her her life. She was in the mental hospital for weeks—and I had no idea. Where was I when my mother needed me? I was too busy wallowing in my pity, crying about the scars that my mother had inflicted on me, whining about my past; all the while, my mother had been suffering a mental illness that had gone completely undetected because of my neglect. Who, then, was the real monster?

To say that I was angry with myself that year would be a complete and disgusting understatement. However, the following year was the year that my mother and I reconciled and put aside all ill feelings we had toward each other. For the first time, in so many years, we were finally able to hug and say "I love you" to each other. Come vacation time, I was *excited* to go home. Most important, I was able to realize just how immense and unconditional familial love was. It would be my base, my motivation, my strength, and my optimism for the coming years.

After my mother started taking medication, drastic changes began to take place at home. No more would it be dreary and dark, but it would be filled with laughter, serenity, and "blue"—in reference to the blue curtains at our new house that would shade and cast a delightful peace throughout. Conversations would consist of funny gossip and future plans of taking vacations. My mother, especially, would talk of how proud she was of my brother and me and how she is so blessed to be living her incredibly lucky life. One time in particular, I remember sitting in the backyard with my brother and mother while we looked through our old baby pictures, laughing at how silly we all looked. My father, cleaning the swimming pool beside us, would occasionally chuckle to himself. It was a lazy summer Sunday, and the warm breeze was gently blowing on all of our faces.

The storm that had ripped through our family had finally died down. The dust had settled. The sun was coming up, and it was time to rebuild, this time with a newfound vigor and perspective on life, love, and peace. I involved myself with Teach for China as a UCLA ambassador, and with USAC (the UCLA student government). I met amazing people, experienced amazing things, and saw my work directly affect the student body. I had supportive friends and a supportive family and was so unbelievably happy. Every day I woke up with a purpose and a drive. I prayed this feeling would never go away, and it never has. And with good reason.

During a phone conversation with my mom, she said: "Daughter, do you know what your Chinese name means?" My name was 王悦洋 (Wang

Yue Yang), and I had never given it a second thought. "No, what does it mean?" I replied.

She continued: "Daughter, let me give you four explanations of why I gave you that name. The last two characters 悦洋 (Yue Yang) quite literally means 'Happiness' and 'Ocean.' I had such a horrible childhood, and I just wanted my children to be happier than me. I wanted you to have happiness as wide as the ocean. Another way you can see those last two characters is 'happiness found on the other side of the ocean.' I left China in pursuit of happiness in America. And I have found it with you and your brother, my most beautiful blessings. My third explanation is biblical: the words Peace and Happiness comes up in the Bible many times. I have named you Happiness and your brother Peace so that you two can always remember to live a God-like life of peace and happiness. The fourth translation relates to the Chinese belief that it is good luck to have a son in every generation with the character 洋 (Yang) in his name. But because you were born a girl, we have the word 悦 (Yue) in the front, which also means to pass over. So if there were any bad luck, having that character in your name means it would pass over you and you would continue to bring luck to our family."

It was at that moment that everything made sense, all at once. And all I had to do was understand my own name. My name literally embodied all the irony, expectations, and struggles that had been my life till now. Before her diagnosis, my mother perhaps never thought she would ever find happiness, and wanting her children to have what she never could, she gave me that Chinese name so that she could give me every chance in discovering my own journey toward happiness.

So what does it mean to be happy? To me, it is to forgive and to love selflessly. Cliché, right? But how many of you can really attest to how easy that is? Forgive, and let go of all ill feelings that can narrow your mind. Let your heart, soul, and mind finally *breathe*. Love selflessly, so that you can go beyond yourself and see the bigger picture, the greater pain, and fix it! Nourish your heart, soul, and mind.

I sure am not an amazing entrepreneur who can start her own business, who is cunning enough to earn millions. It would be quite a breakthrough if I could even survive one college math course. But if there is one shred of wisdom that I can offer to the new generation of students entering college, it is this: Live a happy life. Yes, use your college years to build your résumé, get good grades, build your future. But when you ever have some time to yourself, just think about your purpose in being on this Earth. What makes *your* life poetic? What excites you? What drives you? Once you figure that out, ask what you can do to improve your life so that you can live happier.

You only have one life; don't live for anyone else but yourself. Taste freely, breathe deeply, love fiercely, embrace openly, and rejoice in every moment of every day, because it is all so worth it.

Having graduated from UCLA, I am pursuing a career in educational counseling to help children and teenagers reach their goals by tapping into their potential as students and as members of society so no dream of theirs will be out of reach. This is my plan, and I can think of nothing else that would make me happier.

My name is Angela Wang, and I am a graduate from UCLA. I had a Mohawk back in high school. Now my hair goes down to my hips. It flows in the wind when I want to feel free. And it can be tied up in a bun when need be. This was my story of how I found my happiness. Now go and find yours.

Given what you know now, if you could redo high school, what would you do differently, and why?

Looking back, I wish I had lived, laughed, and forgiven more freely. To generalize it even more, I wish that instead of focusing on the little things (that at the time seemed really big), I could have just taken a step back and really reevaluated what would be worth focusing on in the grander scheme of things.

In high school I was focused too much on the short term. I was determined to get into a good college, and I needed to do everything I could to impress these strangers who would be in charge of my acceptance. I thought I *was* planning ahead because I was thinking about my future in education and how that would lead to a better job and a brighter future.

But in the midst of this, I skipped out on hanging out with friends, bonding with family, and going to social events. I thought that by making these sacrifices, I would be more respected, not just by my family, but also by my peers, who would witness my successes and essentially be proud of my accomplishments. But in hindsight, I feel as if these little decisions in my high school career really stunted my ability to form long-lasting relationships, to understand the importance of family, and to understand what it means to care, love, and cherish everyday moments.

If I could go back, I *would* study less so I could go eat yogurt with some friends. I *would* stay a little longer in badminton practice to joke and fool around with my teammates. I *would* take some study breaks to just talk with my parents and brother. I would do all these things and more if I could make up for those times I had neglected my family and friends and hurt them in doing so.

I'm definitely not saying that you should neglect your studies completely, but it will serve you in the long run to find that fine balance. Even in college, I wish I had taken more time to network and get to know people instead of studying. Yeah, grades look good, and they *can* put you ahead of the competition, but finding a good job and maintaining a good career also has a lot to do with *who you know*, your social skills, and your charisma in leadership.

Just remember that when you are on your deathbed, you are not going to want to hold your trophy, your certificate, and your money in your last seconds on Earth. You are going to want to hold onto your family, your friends, and the people in your life who made it worth living. So don't ever take them for anything less than what they mean to you!

What else would you like to share with or suggest to high school students and college students, and why?

During my high school career, I made *a lot* of mistakes. I stressed. I failed, sometimes horribly. I lost. I got rejected. At the same time, I have also succeeded, and I have been incredibly happy with these successes. But what I've learned is how little of an influence succeeding can have on your future, and how much more *failing* can have.

By failing, and getting knocked down to the ground, I was able to truly take a good look at myself and find ways to improve myself. This reflection gave me character, and it gave me the strength to overcome whatever other stresses life would throw at me. This pressure that I give to myself then pushes me to strive for perfection. In the times when I succeed, I tend to overlook my flaws and just be content with the person I am, but this complacency leads only to stagnation.

So don't ever be afraid of failure. In fact, you *need* to fail to improve yourself. Just remember to *always* get back up after you fall. Realize your mistakes. And don't make them again.

Another lesson I have learned the hard way is to just accept the circumstances that you are given and optimize your abilities to the best of their potential. When I was a child and a teenager, I would constantly compare myself to those who were smarter, prettier, or more talented than I was. And I would beat myself up over why I couldn't be like that. But the more I lived my life, the more I realized that everyone is blessed with different abilities and different talents. I may not be the smartest (far from it), but I know that I tried and did my best. I put my best foot forward, and wherever it lands shall be a destiny that I *earned* for myself.

Your successes are particular to *your* life and your destiny *only*. Comparing them to others will only hinder your growth. No one has ever walked in your shoes. They have not seen, felt, or endured anything you had to go through. So, the standard you set for yourself should come only from you and apply to you, and no one else!

A perfectly imperfect takeaway about Angela:

As a young girl, Angela was too damaged to see her own worth (and gave herself a Mohawk to symbolize her rebellion). In college, however, she forged her own path and earned the respect and admiration of others. Now Angela walks with inalienable confidence—her head held high and her heels clicking and clacking on stone floors. Her crooked smile still offers a peek into her broken past and her tremendous efforts in mending the cracks. Having overcome the crippling grip of her past, Angela walks only forward now toward the bright future, her hair undulating in the wind with every step she takes: *click, clack, click, clack.*

13

Enrico Bonatti

Citizen of the World

BS in Applied Economics and Management, and International
Agriculture and Rural Development (double major), with
minors in International Relations and Entomology, Class of
2014, Cornell University

Prior to studying at Cornell University in the United States, Enrico
Bonatti lived in six other countries, spanning the globe from Switzerland to Venezuela to the UK. A third-culture kid (TCK) who grew up in
multiple countries outside his parents' culture, he attended schools with
very different educational systems and learned six languages. Enrico's
double major and minors reflect his broad interests and passions.

In college, aside from his academic pursuits, Enrico was deeply involved
with AIESEC, the global youth network changing the world through
leadership development experiences across 124 countries and territories.
At Cornell, he served as president of the International Students Board, an
umbrella organization that monitors and distributes funding for all graduate and undergraduate international students organizations throughout
the university. Additionally, he was twice elected as the international
liaison in Cornell's undergraduate student government.

Enrico completed summer internships across the globe—business development in Jakarta, overseas business in Seoul, and investment banking in New York City. Most interested in international relations and finance, he has begun his career in finance in New York City.

Travel far and wide. Don't be prejudiced about places you visit or people you meet—if something seems weird to you, there's a chance you might be the strange one.

—Enrico Bonatti

Enrico Bonatti grew up in an unusual kaleidoscope of international cultures and environments.

Growing up wasn't easy, but I wouldn't trade those years for anything in the world. As a child I lived mostly across Europe and South America, continually moving from country to country and following my parents, who often relocated for international work. As a result, I lived most, if not all, of my life as an expatriate and third-culture kid (TCK). To me, a TCK is an individual who moves between cultures before he/she has had the opportunity to fully develop his/her personal and cultural identity—thus creating a new kind of transnational culture.

This continual moving meant switching not only among different school systems but also among diverse languages, such as French, Italian, and English. At times it was a real struggle, as subjects like math were hard enough already, let alone having to learn and relearn all the terminology in three or four different languages! The hardest part was having to say good-bye to the friends I had made just two years earlier while getting ready to leave for a new country—and start the whole process all over again—six times. I remember the day when I saw my primary school friends in Venezuela for the last time. After years growing up together, I still haven't seen any of them in person since (at least we have the internet though!).

This experience nevertheless taught me, more than any school or teacher ever could, the power of firsthand learning. I learned and studied more than six languages. I adapted. Having traveled to approximately forty different countries around the world, I came to better understand and appreciate very different cultures and develop my own perspective on the world. Life is always about trade-offs, but despite my moments of difficulty, those were the times that really defined who I am today. And I must thank my parents for this gift: they were strict when it came to academics, pushing me to do better, and at the same time they were encouraging when it came to letting me try new activities and giving me, from an early age, the responsibility and freedom to travel and learn new perspectives early on.

Enrico spent his high school years in three different countries, from Italy to Scotland. He graduated from the United World College of the Atlantic (UWC), a unique boarding school with a mission to "make education a force to unite people, nations, and cultures for peace and a sustainable future," along with students from more than ninety different countries. During high school, Enrico received the Duke of Edinburgh Award and was a qualified NaRs Pool and Beach Lifeguard, all while studying for the International Baccalaureate (IB).

Throughout high school, Enrico completed more than five hundred hours of community action and service ranging from lifeguarding at a public beach in Wales to working with the Scottish Coastguard. Additionally, he co-founded his high school's current-events debate club, became a first-aid instructor, looked after the school's honeybee colonies, and volunteered at a local hospice.

During the college application season, Enrico applied to both UK and US universities. The underlying theme of the personal essay on his US college applications was about the ways in which his experiences as a TCK affected his view of the world and allowed him to grow.

He reflects on his college applications, his admissions experience, and his reasons for choosing Cornell:

As I initially thought about staying in Europe so I could be closer to home, I applied to universities in the UK, including University College London and Imperial College London, both of which subsequently gave me conditional offers (meaning that entry to that university is guaranteed depending on achievement of certain final exam grades). Learning about the liberal arts environments of US schools and wanting to keep my options open, I decided to apply to US universities as well. I submitted applications to just a few universities in the United States. When Cornell admitted me, I decided to enroll there right away.

What attracted me to Cornell were the liberal arts education and the amazing opportunities, both academic and extracurricular. I chose Cornell also because of its dynamic student life and a more tight-knit campus environment made possible in a college town away from big cities. Finally, I enrolled there mainly because Cornell did not restrict my broad interests to one single major. I wanted a more flexible curriculum and Cornell, with its seven different colleges, offers this flexibility. I don't think I could have made a better choice, as I graduated with a double major and two minors in quite distinct fields—which I chose mostly based on interest.

Shortly after college graduation, Enrico began a career in finance in New York City. I've asked him to reflect on the following:

To what extent did your college experience—on and off campus—meet your expectations? In what ways did your experience cause you to change your perspective on your academic career, your dreams and aspirations, and your life?

To be perfectly honest, I didn't have any clear expectations of what was waiting for me in college, aside from my eagerness to learn new things and meet new people; most of what I knew about the college experience in the US came from books or movies (clearly not the best way, but it made it all the more exciting). I vividly remember how lost I was arriving on campus for the first time as a freshman, having never visited the campus before and not knowing anyone there. But, like many times before, I assumed, the formula was repeating itself: new country, new school—nothing new in that. However, having always been in small schools with just a couple hundred students each, going into a college environment where I was surrounded by thousands of very motivated students was not only different but also extremely stimulating.

Now, having finished college and having started a career in finance, I find myself in a similar situation again. Until a couple years ago I would have never imagined, for instance, that I would end up working in finance. But I realized that, aside from its being a very interesting industry, it is one that allows me to improve on many personal aspects, such as work ethic and analytical skills, and it allows me to keep my options open for the future—all while being surrounded by exceedingly smart and motivated individuals.

Below are some of the biggest lessons I learned in college;

BE PURPOSEFULLY ACTIVE OUTSIDE OF CLASSES

While schooling and living across Europe and Latin America, I always thought of university as an exclusively academic experience, one that would allow me to learn about specific subjects in great depth. Nevertheless, having just completed my four years of college, I realize just how far this was from the truth. College is so much more than just taking classes. While I had amazing professors and learned more than I would have ever imagined, most of the life and people skills that I possess today come from my non-academic experiences while in college.

These non-academic experiences can be irrelevant to acquiring a degree (and the corresponding knowledge) *per se*, but are critical for one's personal development. By heading the main organization for international students on campus, for example, I had to set the future path of the organization, learn how to manage people, and deal with difficult situations, such as resolving conflicts or having to dismiss someone from the organization—pragmatic lessons that I would never have learned in a typical class. This is the reason that, while I support innovative educational tools, I remain somewhat skeptical about the Massive Open Online Courses (MOOCs) now being offered at more and more top universities. MOOCs lack some of the most important factors of the college experience, mainly learning to work with and around other people directly.

In college, I was privileged to serve in several "public" roles and university-wide leadership positions, to which I was elected and that required significant accountability and transparency. I would rank these as some of my most highly formative experiences. I decided to partake in these activities in order to bring meaningful change to the university community, and was able, for example, to persuade the university administration to open up a large university-wide program to international students, who had previously been excluded because of funding restrictions. This example shows just how much one can do in college, other than studying for exams, of course!

TRAVEL FAR AND OFTEN

Non-academic experiences also include summer internships and travel, and I will never regret having taken full advantage of school breaks to travel and try new activities. Traveling, by myself or with friends, to places far away from home, has been one of my most transformative experiences. Having traveled to developing nations, particularly in the global south, I realized not only how fortunate I was, but also how little I knew about the world. These humbling experiences pushed me to learn more and made me want to make a positive difference in the world.

During the summer after my freshman year, for instance, I traveled throughout Southeast Asia, thanks to an internship opportunity at a small social enterprise in Indonesia. As an intern there, I helped rural communities escape loan sharks and grow rice in more sustainable ways, as well as finding a market for it, on top of learning about new societies, cultures, and lands previously little known to me. Alas, as a student, traveling can often be difficult because of financial constraints; however, college is arguably the best and easiest time to do so. This is both true financially and time-wise because of the availability of study-abroad opportunities, grants, and international internships that cover the cost of travel. So, it really pays to start thinking about how to spend your summers early and make the most of it!

DO SOMETHING YOU ACTUALLY LIKE

It is critical for you to remember that you should engage in something based on your curiosity and natural interests, not based on peer pressure or what might look good on your résumé. If you do anything with the latter mind-set, it will be hard to be truly passionate or to give your hundred percent. Instead, join organizations you are truly interested in, or explore widely until you find something you truly like—no matter what it is. That is the only way to enjoy yourself while becoming the very best at something.

Going from Europe to college abroad and studying at an Ivy League university like Cornell changed my life. I traveled far out of my comfort zone, I learned new things, and I joined groups I was previously unfamiliar with. I can't emphasize enough the importance of always making the most of every opportunity and giving it your best shot. College can be either a decent four-year academic experience or a once-in-a-lifetime opportunity to learn, lead, and serve all at once—all the while being surrounded by great people in an environment that won't condemn you if you fail.

The experiences I had with my activities in college taught me more than I had ever expected. They shaped my interests, my aspirations, and my perspective on life. In fact, I had no idea of the sheer scope of organizations that were even available prior to my arrival there. Anything I have ever achieved has mostly, if not all, been the fruit of venturing out of my comfort zone, of working hard, and of trying new things until I found what was perfect for me.

Given what you know now, if you could redo high school, what would you do differently, and why?

If I were to step into a time machine and return to my fourteen- or fifteen-year-old self, I would certainly change a few personal and educational decisions. But overall, my trajectory would remain the same—with plenty of instances of falling down and getting back up. That is what life is about: trying, making mistakes sometimes, learning from them, succeeding, and continually striving to do better.

MAKING MISTAKES IS A GREAT WAY TO LEARN

Many of the mistakes I made in my high school and college years have been instrumental in shaping me into the person I am today, so make mistakes and learn! They can be anything, big or small, but making mistakes, even though it's sometimes painful, is one of the best ways to learn something well. While it sounds clichéd, you would be surprised at how many people get stuck in a vicious cycle of ever-repeating errors—always hoping that "this time" things will work out and be, somehow, magically different. One mistake that is easy to make is to remain static and wait for "good things" to occur. But, if you really want something, you need to step up and actively make it happen.

I definitely wish I had procrastinated less, focused more on the task at hand, and thus been able to have more fun later. This is a very easy mistake to make. For example, if you go to the library to study, make sure you use that time to actually study and not watch videos on YouTube (or procrastinate in a similar way); that way, you will be done sooner and will get to actually go out and properly enjoy yourself. High school and college are the last years of your life when you can truly devote yourself to almost anything you want, so treasure your time and have fun!

FOCUS ON WHAT REALLY MATTERS

All in all, I would also focus more on what really matters. Sometimes it is hard to identify what those things are, but stepping back and looking at the big picture helps. In fact, we are often distracted and get caught up in the small things, losing sight of that larger scheme. This happens often in college, where one can easily get overwhelmed between classes and extracurricular activities and end up underachieving in both. I wish I had worked harder for certain things and achieved better results. On the other hand, I wish I had known when enough studying was enough and enjoyed life a little more. Being a bit of a perfectionist, I can remember countless sleepless nights finishing assignments in the library. While most of those all-nighters were for legitimate reasons, many were definitely unnecessary (although seeing the sunrise might have made it worth it), and I wish I had dedicated a little more time to family, friends, and personal interests instead.

What else would you like to share with or suggest to high school students and college students, and why?

LIFE IS ABOUT BALANCE

Study hard, or you will regret not learning or performing well academically. Have fun, or you will regret not enjoying yourself. Remember: you can go to college when you are eighty, but you can't get your youth back. That being said, a healthy life is about balance, but few people, including me, remember to follow this advice. If you study too much and don't allow yourself some downtime, you will burn out and your work/study sessions will be less productive. Spend too much time having fun, and you will likely fail academically. Sleep can often be left out of the equation, but remember that if you are unproductive and stay up late, or pull too many all-nighters, you *will* crash. It goes without saying that social and sporting activities are also essential, so do both—make friends and stay fit. As the Romans said, *Mens sana in corpore sano*: In order to have a healthy mind, you need a healthy body (and vice versa).

SPEND SOME TIME (QUIETLY) BY YOURSELF

In college, setting aside enough time for yourself can be challenging. I, however, find spending time by myself extremely helpful—away from phones and other electronics, I use this downtime (at least fifteen to thirty minutes a day) to help me prioritize and reflect. I like to write down what matters to me, be it getting good grades or having a fun weekend, and to go for a short walk to clear my head. This can also help you strategize. When things get tough, and I was stressed because of an exam for example, instead of sitting there and thinking how I wished I had studied more beforehand, I found it very useful to stop for a few minutes, take a walk outside, and create a plan to tackle the issue as efficiently as possible.

READ AND BE PRODUCTIVE

Always take advantage of any free time to do something useful. Have a thirty-minute break between classes? Don't just watch the clock hands turn. Do something productive. I don't necessarily mean that you have to get started on that dreaded problem set (although you might as well), but do something that will add to you as a person, such as practicing the guitar or reading a newspaper (with regard to current events, I personally recommend the BBC online or *The Economist* if you are interested in economics and international issues). This is especially important in college, where one is often enclosed in a "bubble" where it is easy to lose touch of what is happening around the world. Being up to date with current events is essential, given such an interconnected world where something that's happening in another country likely affects yours, too.

VOLUNTEER TO HELP OTHERS

Broad academic and leadership experiences in college have taught me a great deal, not just about myself but also about the world, in particular about many of the world's problems that need fixing. Plenty of things in the world need improvement, and I feel it is not just one's duty but should also be one's desire to help, be it by volunteering at a local soup kitchen over the weekends or by making it one's life's calling. No matter what job I did, I found few activities more rewarding than helping other people without getting anything in exchange; seeing a smile of gratitude on a person's face can make hours of work feel like seconds.

SURROUND YOURSELF WITH DOERS

I can't stress this enough. I always had rather varied groups of friends, some of whom were more relaxed about schoolwork or life goals than others. While both types had significant, positive influences in my life, without the drive and competition that I saw in the more "focused" ones, I wouldn't have worked as hard or been as inspired to accomplish what I have, such as getting involved in student government or starting an organization at the university. Friends influence one's habits, so make sure they are the right ones.

This doesn't mean that you should select your friends artificially according to how successful they are, but that you should make an effort to go out of your way to meet different kinds of motivated people. A good and easy way to do this is by joining new organizations and clubs in your school, as well as by simply being welcoming and open to people—allowing them to find you, too.

Is there anything else you would like to share?

STRETCH YOUR BOUNDARIES AND BE PERSISTENT

Traveling so much has taught me the importance of seizing every opportunity because often you will not be given a second chance. This is true in many societies around the world. In addition, with improvements in education and a growing global population, if you are not fast enough and qualified enough, the chances are greater that you could easily be replaced. While this might sound scary, it is also beneficial, as it means the world is becoming more meritocratic and mobile.

Despite all of these concerns, don't think that if you fail once, you are doomed. Very few people succeed at their first try at something. Life is a process of purposeful actions and trial and error, and the ones who make it are the ones who are flexible and who don't give up! I definitely learned this in so many ways, from academics to personal experiences. For instance, if you run for a position and are not selected at first, don't be discouraged;

instead, you should be all the more motivated to improve and to get what you want on the second try!

BE CURIOUS AND ADAPTABLE

Various experiences have taught me not only to adjust quickly to new surroundings and environments, but also to learn how to interact and respond to various stimuli in different organizations and cultures. Every time I travel to a new place, I try to learn as much as possible about it beforehand. I always try to take up the local customs and learn as much as possible by speaking to local people, such as shop owners or taxi drivers. Not only will they really appreciate that you took the time to learn about their language and culture, but you would be surprised how much you can learn or what you might experience along the way. I have met scores of amazing people this way and was able to have more authentic experiences in the places I traveled to.

A perfectly imperfect takeaway about Enrico:

Growing up as a third-culture kid (TCK) and having traveled the world in search of his authentic self, Enrico suggests: "Take chances. If in doubt, just do it. You have more to gain than to lose. Keep track of what is going on in the world and read the news every day. Travel far and wide. Don't be prejudiced about places you visit or people you meet—if something seems weird to you, there's a chance you might be the strange one. If you fail once, try again, and again. Life can be unfair, but if you persevere, the chances are that you will eventually make it—so don't give up."

14

Leila Pirbay

Anthropologist from Madagascar

BA in Social Anthropology, and minor in Economics, Class of
2014, Harvard University

As a sophomore at the American School of Antananarivo, Madagascar, Leila Pirbay founded an NGO, Keelonga, to improve the public educational system in rural areas. At Harvard, she co-founded the Francophone Society to enhance and deepen the common linguistic, cultural, and political interests of French-speaking students. She received the Harvard Foundation's Insignia Award for her "Unique Contribution to Intercultural and Race Relations" as a result of her leadership within the organization. She worked for one of Infosys's NGOs in India after her freshman year and consulted at A.T. Kearney in Turkey and Italy the following summers. While preparing to publish her thesis on women in business, she attended the Summer Institute for General Management at the Stanford Graduate School of Business.

Leila is currently working to extend the reach of Edukasyon, a Philippines-based social enterprise to Madagascar, aiming to improve access to higher education. She is also interning at Experience Morocco, a travel venture based in Casablanca, Morocco, and is participating in a collaborative inquiry art project entitled "here, without –" that seeks to examine the relationship between outsiders and the Israel-Palestine conflict. Her aspiration is to return eventually to Africa, improve the region's economic stance, and help reduce the digital divide by providing inexpensive but excellent Internet and television services to the unconnected.

Civic avoidance prevents meaningful interaction, and it is only by engaging actively with genuine interest and empathy that we can truly learn to appreciate and leverage diversity to find creative solutions to our problems.

—Leila Pirbay

Leila's maternal Italian roots, juxtaposed with her paternal Indo-Malagasy background, created a truly eclectic cultural, linguistic, and religious environment in the family. She grew up celebrating both Christmas and Eid-al-Fitr (an important Muslim holiday, celebrating the end of Ramadan) wearing both dresses and saris, listening to both the violin and the valiha (Malagasy tube zither), and involving cousins from both sides during festivities.

As a child, this meant receiving twice as many gifts! This plurality of cultures made me value—and seek—diversity. Both sides of my family now have a heightened appreciation of cultures, religions, and languages that are not their own, and advocate cross-cultural understanding and a reduction of miscomprehensions, which are still far too common.

Leila was fascinated by the history and cultures of her home country, Madagascar, an island nation situated East of Africa and known for its unique biodiversity and for the animated film named after the country. She reflected on this via a personal essay when applying to US colleges as a high school senior:

Growing up in Madagascar, I was told countless tales about the mysterious Vazimba people. It is said that these dwarves live in the Tsingy—unique limestone "forests" that emerged from the erosion of ancient geological formations covering the western part of the island. It is also said that those who do not find their way out of the limestone labyrinth are not lost but captured by the Vazimba.

I became enthralled by these mysterious creatures and wanted to know more. However, my high school's curriculum did not cover the early history of Madagascar, and even less so that of the Vazimba, which were dismissed as mere folkloric constructs. But for me, the Vazimba were becoming a riveting topic, one that could delineate the roots of my country. In an attempt to learn more, I visited all of the museums in Antananarivo and spent days discussing the Vazimba with curators and university history professors who talked about them as real, and not mystical, people. I was thrilled to find people who helped me consider these remote ancestors in a historical perspective, and was even lucky enough to visit the Tsingy during a school field trip, which made me appreciate the birth of the legends concerning these strange yet beautiful geological formations.

The more I learned about the Vazimba, the clearer it became that I would not fully understand their history if I did not first take into consideration their origins. What was initially a curiosity about the tales of my childhood suddenly became the subject of rigorous academic research. With the help of a history professor from the University of Antananarivo, I began to research in tenth grade how migrants settled in Madagascar and started forming their own unique culture. I learned of the most improbable encounter between the Bantu people of Africa and navigators from Southeast Asia. I discovered how they met and mixed in what was a new and foreign land for both of them. I was fascinated by how they were able to converge toward a symbiosis that led to the formation of a new language composed of Bantu and Indonesian vocabulary and syntax. The origins of numerous indigenous traditions, such as the cult of ancestors and the history of our music, were suddenly brought to light. Most interesting to me was the history of a particular local zither called the *valiha*, an instrument I happened to play.

I began to chronicle the populating of Madagascar and the history of the Vazimba and submitted my research paper to *The Concord Review*, which published the paper in December 2009. Though I started this research hoping to uncover the origins of the Malagasy people, I learned much more. Studying the migrations of travelers from different continents to Madagascar helped me connect my isolated island to a global history of endless migrations. Thanks to my journey, I now have a sense of humankind beyond local differences and a growing appreciation of our common and interconnected history.

The Vazimba are no longer mysterious, magic dwarves living in the dark Tsingy forests, but they are no less fascinating. Over time, they became even more appealing to me as they taught me that an exceptional society can be born from the improbable fusion of different cultures.

Leila was also passionate about righting the wrong of many public schools being glaringly underprivileged in Madagascar. She elaborated on the Harvard application supplement how she purposefully and resourcefully took actions to improve the situation:

When I told him my plan, the mayor of Anosiala leaned back in his chair and sneered. Although he gave me his accord, he did not believe in me.

After seeing what remained of a school that had been hit by a cyclone, I decided to do something about it. All I could do then was collect chalks, pencils, and other supplies for the students of what remained of the school, but how could that be enough? I then serendipitously met a former staff member of the Minister of Education, Mrs. Esther, who shared my desire to help establishments in similar situations. She took me under her wing, and together we visited a few rural schools in the village of Anosiala, located two hours away from the capital.

There I saw the most urgent problems: a severe lack of teachers and shaky infrastructures. A few days later, I met an old family friend who had previously been a contractor. Following our conversation, Mr. Gilbert offered to help repair the schools if I financed the materials and the workers. The cost to thoroughly rehabilitate five schools was less than $8,000, a sum I was determined to gather to revamp the schools.

I took care of the fundraising by going to the offices of a number of corporations and knocking on the doors of friends and acquaintances to tell them about the schools. Regularly showing my progress with pictures and facts nurtured trust and encouraged donations. I then began to define an action plan based on my budget and the work that was most urgent. I bargained for the construction materials, hired Mr. Gilbert's team, and initiated the restructuring of the schools.

Mrs. Esther found competent teachers and I hired the best eight. The latter were supervised by Mrs. Esther and met with me every other week in order to keep them motivated. With the equivalent of $14,000, I was able to completely renovate five schools, hire eight teachers for two years, and provide thirteen other schools with basic supplies such as desks and textbooks.

After successfully completing these first projects, I researched the proper type of juridical body for my initiative in various government offices. What had started as a few boxes of chalk turned into page rolls, spreadsheets, and a website. The concept of a "not for profit" organization is not clear in Madagascar, but I managed to get all the authorizations and register my project as a NGO called Keelonga ("children" in Malagasy).

My goal by 2010 is to improve the kids' hygiene by providing water wells to these schools as most of them lack running water. I have enlisted the help of the Rotary Club, the United Nations Children's Fund (UNICEF) and the UN Water, Sanitation and Hygiene Initiative to help me in my endeavors. The mayor of Anosiala no longer doubts my drive to improve schools nor the viability of the project, and in fact does what he can to help.

In addition, a sociopolitical experience really shook up Leila after she took the SAT during a period of political unrest in Madagascar:

King Julien from the movie *Madagascar* must have inspired our young president, Andry Rajoelina, to take over a real country. This recent coup not only transformed the political and economic situation of Madagascar but also changed my perspective on my own life and future.

I took the SAT Reasoning Test on a Saturday in January in Antananarivo. That day, I was thinking about nothing else but getting a good score on the test, but three days later, I found myself hiding with my family behind bamboo trees in the back of my house, in fear for our lives. All around us were thousands of people shouting, looting, burning, and destroying everything in their path. I was terrified. The very idea of attending college someday had become a nonissue; all I wanted was to be safe.

Two days after I took the SAT, it was like the entire country caught on fire: there were riots and lootings in all the major cities for days. People started pillaging stores, burning cars, breaking into houses, and kidnapping individuals for ransom. From the first day of the unrest, we started to go to bed dressed in day clothes, with a small bag containing a few clothes, documents, and food ready by the bed so we could make a quick escape. How ironic that the normally peaceful country of Madagascar, known as a tropical paradise where friendly zebras, hippos, giraffes, and lions from New York City's Central Park Zoo frolic, now looked more like *The Happening*—even the lemurs were getting restless.

One night my father woke me up as people approached our house. I quickly got up and followed him with the rest of my family outside the back door. We rushed behind the bamboo trees in my backyard in an attempt

183

to protect ourselves. After a few hours that seemed infinite, the tumult ended. Thankfully, the looters had left without breaking into our house.

I had forgotten about the SAT. In those days, I discovered another value of life that was more important than the pleasure of learning: dignity. Having your life threatened by machete-wielding bands of looters is the kind of experience that can only teach you that the safety and integrity of your loved ones is far more important than anything else.

I now know that attending the college of my dreams cannot be an objective per se as it once was for me, but a step toward building a safe and dignified life. I want to learn even more, not only for the sake of learning but to contribute to a better life for the people in my country so that we do not have to live through this kind of political unrest anymore.

I've chuckled at Leila's college application process. These days, high-achieving high schoolers normally apply to eight to twelve colleges. But Leila applied to more than twenty, a formidable number for most mortal souls. In her case, her energetic efforts paid off.

She was admitted to Harvard, Yale, Stanford, Brown, Dartmouth, University of Pennsylvania (Wharton), Columbia, Cornell, Duke (Angier B. Duke Scholar finalist), Johns Hopkins (Hodson Trust Scholar), Amherst, Williams, Middlebury, Pomona, UC Berkeley, UCLA, Barnard, Wellesley, University of Chicago, and Northwestern. Only Princeton and MIT denied her.

I decided to enroll at Harvard because it offered the best African and African American Studies Program, my intended major. I'd attended a summer program at Harvard when I was in high school, and thus knew I was a good fit for both the college and Boston. I was also eager to participate in the myriad conferences and attend talks by prominent individuals at the Kennedy School and the Business School.

Today, Leila is a newly minted Harvard graduate, I've asked her to reflect:

To what extent did your college experience—on and off campus—meet your expectations? In what ways did your experience cause you to change your perspective on your academic career, your dreams and aspirations, and your life?

My high school was tiny—there were only eleven students in my graduating class. Harvard Yard holds 1,650 freshmen. Two orders of magnitudes apart—a little overwhelming!

I was awestruck by the number of classes Harvard offered—more than five thousand in the Faculty of Arts and Sciences alone. We are required to take thirty-two classes over four years, or four per semester, and I halfheartedly realized that I could take fewer than 1 percent of the classes offered. I knew that college was the time to deepen my interests and find new ones, so I enrolled in classes that sounded intriguing, and several unlocked new academic or career interests. During my freshman year alone, I satisfied my curiosity by exploring fields I had never considered before: I took a class in philosophy, visual arts, history of science, math, Hindi, writing, history, and Islam. Through these classes, I learned to discern my interests, the teaching methods I enjoyed, and the skills I had—all of which informed my subsequent choices.

A vast array of classes impressed me in both content and format: I had a virtual classroom in Understanding Islam and Contemporary Muslim Societies, studied the physical and chemical reactions that take place in the kitchen in Science of Cooking, and partook in negotiation simulations, business case studies, and coding hackathons that enriched my learning experience. Professors also made these classes unique. For example, I took an economics class with Professor Summers, who had been chief economist of the World Bank, secretary of the Treasury, president of Harvard, and director of the National Economic Council. Hearing from Professor Summers as he discussed regulations and agreements he'd helped frame and adopt was one of the most striking memories of my undergraduate experience because of the unique perspective he had and the introspection he engendered.

Although the sheer number of classes taught by world-renowned professors alongside bright peers was daunting at first, it was all made possible thanks to the surprising amount of attention and help I received from formal advisors, other students, and the faculty. Friends proofread my essays. Professors introduced me to businesspeople. Alumni helped me find internships. Tutors helped me craft résumés. The administration supported my efforts to co-found a club, and the list goes on. A lesson I learned was never to hesitate to ask for help, advice, or guidance—I needed it more than I thought.

While the help I received was abundant, I failed more than ever before. I was rejected by student organizations, firms, and graduate programs, even though I applied with the same enthusiasm as I had applied to college.

Sometimes I did not even participate in competitions, for I thought I had no chance against my peers, and several times stopped believing in myself—maybe the Admissions Office had made a mistake in accepting me? These failures, while painful, attest to how my peers propel me to keep moving forward. I am surrounded by individuals who are the best in their fields, and such talent pushes me, extends the boundaries of what I think is possible, and makes me want to try harder.

I was exposed to an astonishing caliber of people. As Cervantes wrote, "It takes all kinds to make a world"—but also to make Harvard. From the most liberal to the most conservative, from the most religious to the ardent atheist, from a variety of socio-economic backgrounds, from all corners of the world, I could hardly imagine how diverse my peers' backgrounds were. Even more impressive were their accomplishments: behind all-too-common T-shirts and sandals often hid music prodigies, scientists on the verge of finding a cure for a disease, and presidents in the making.

Needless to say, Harvard's guest speakers were also fascinating. Some individuals I was lucky enough to see and even meet were Argentinian president Cristina de Kirchner, Grameen Bank founder Muhammad Yunus, former Indian president Abdul Kalam, Palestinian Liberation Organization member Hanan Ashrawi, and European Central Bank President Mario Draghi, among others. Their speeches were inspiring, controversial, and thought-provoking, and after each speech I found myself with a renewed sense of trust in what we can accomplish.

As I attended the commencement ceremony, I grasped the richness of the history, traditions, and legacy that will never leave me. The community created in this institution is surprisingly strong, and I feel imprinted with the name Harvard to an extent that I did not anticipate. While it is an honor to wear the Harvard ring, it is also a responsibility, for I represent and am represented by this institution—and sometimes these two are at odds: as an example, I might not embrace all its investments or policies, but I am nonetheless affiliated with them.

Given what you know now, if you could redo high school, what would you do differently, and why?

If I could go back, I would be more entrepreneurial, explore more things, and encourage my peers to take on more responsibilities.

The high school I attended was too small to offer the breadth and depth of extracurricular activities that can be found in the United States. While I participated in Model United Nations (MUN) conferences, I felt unprepared, as my school did not provide appropriate training for the conference. We were barely exposed to the issues we were supposed to debate and were ill prepared to take a stance on them. If I could go back, I would establish a debate club, or a MUN conference for schools in Madagascar, which would have taught us to use better rhetoric and improve our public-speaking skills.

My friend Zach Hamed (at Harvard) nicknamed me "Dora," not only for the short haircut I had as a college freshman but also because I explored so much in the past four years. I attended conferences, talks, presentations, and tried a plethora of new activities—sailing, salsa dancing, business clubs, theatre, and many others. In high school, I was as interested in exploring these activities, but not nearly as committed to trying them. I would encourage my younger self to venture out of her comfort zone, to try new things, and seek new passions.

Another thing I would do if I could go back is to encourage my peers to take on more projects. Instead of solely encouraging donations from friends and relatives, I wish I had motivated my peers to start a social venture of their own, or expand Keelonga. While Keelonga had a positive influence—it catered to more than 2,500 students in eighteen schools and increased their success rate at the national primary school exam from 65 percent to 90 percent thanks to the teachers employed and the new infrastructure—I can only wonder what could have been possible had I encouraged my peers to do the same.

I learned about working in a team mostly by co-founding and presiding over the Francophone Society at Harvard, and I wish I had made more of an effort to collaborate for a common goal earlier. Thanks to the Francophone Society, I learned to identify and leverage my team members' unique abilities to effectively collaborate and create events that no board member could have single-handedly conceived. I discovered that empowering individuals to organize their own events fosters efficiency, enthusiasm, and mutual enrichment, and it is through collaboration that farther horizons can be reached. This realization enabled me to become a much better team member for both class projects and internships. I am still acquiring this skill, and I wish I had started to develop it in high school by working more effectively on group projects, an invaluable asset to have in both the academic and professional realms.

What else would you like to share with or suggest to high school students and college students, and why?

CONNECT

A pearl of wisdom that I grew more appreciative over the course of the last few years is: "Don't compare—connect," as Michael D. Smith, dean of the Faculty of Arts and Sciences, urged during the convocation of Harvard's Class of 2016.

Connecting and collaborating, rather than competing and comparing, enrich us beyond imagination. The wealth of the conversations I had in college—from politics to art to science; the countless debates I listened to and participated in; and the sheer number of different minds, interests, and fields of study—have enabled me to challenge my beliefs, explore new ideas, and form a better and more nuanced understanding of our world.

ENGAGE AND DISCUSS

Protests—whether in-person demonstrations in front of President Drew Faust's office or micro-scale ones on social-media platforms, happen daily with invigorating energy. They improved my understanding of how different people view and act upon certain issues, which allowed me to craft new or better-informed opinions, and to revisit and think more critically about the issues I cared about. From Occupy Harvard to a movement for divesting from fossil fuel companies to asking for greater inclusion of minorities and the LGTBQI community, students are passionate, vocal, and ready to take risks to fight for what they deem is right. Find what interests you and become actively engaged in the cause. It is extremely rewarding to inform, question others' beliefs and your own, and convince or be convinced. There is so much that you can help improve, and college provides you with the perfect opportunity to be a more informed and engaged citizen. Do not let that chance slip by!

Rather than competing against those you disagree with, or comparing yourself with those around you, I would urge you to talk and discuss with those you think you disagree with and with those you admire. With respect and a positive attitude, you can only learn from these conversations.

BE HUMBLE

Have an open mind and discuss, share, and connect with those around you, but do not forget to keep some humility. Toward the end of my senior year, I attended a barbecue in the courtyard of the Kennedy School. At some point, a professor approached the friend with whom I was talking to greet her, and we all conversed for some time. He was from Ecuador, so we discussed immigration in Ecuador before he asked about the recent elections in Madagascar. He hugged us good-bye, and when he could no longer hear us, my friend said, "You know that was the former president of Ecuador, right?" I was astonished—he had introduced himself simply as Jamil, and was so eager to talk and socialize with us. My serendipitous encounter with him reminded me that humility and kindness are the driving forces behind effectively connecting and exchanging, not only in an academic setting but in all aspects of life. They make one even more admirable.

DO NOT SPREAD YOURSELF TOO THIN

At one point in my college career, I was involved in twelve extracurricular organizations, was taking five classes instead of the regular four, had a job, refused to forgo my social life, was applying to internships, and was preparing for the GRE. I failed at many of my responsibilities because there were only twenty-four hours in a day, when I needed at least ten times as many. But I learned, albeit the hard way, that choosing one battle, focusing my efforts on it, and winning it, are far more rewarding than trying to fight ten wars and losing all but one. I would advise my younger self to explore new things, but to do so wisely and not blindly.

BE INDEPENDENT

Take into consideration all pieces of advice; but remember that the final decision is yours and yours alone. Even if you make the wrong decision, you will be the one to blame and will learn from your mistakes, rather than blaming others. You should be proud of your decision, and not act to please others or to fit somebody else's definition of success. Success is so subjective that I do not have a definition applicable to all. For me, it is when you *surprise* yourself with what you've achieved in all aspects of your life—personal, professional, and academic.

EXPRESS GRATITUDE

Finally, be grateful, and acknowledge the people who have helped you along the way—be it those who have encouraged, advised, financed, connected, or challenged you. I know I would not be where I am today without my family, friends, professors, and other individuals along the way who believed in me.

I have encountered numerous people who have inspired me because of their accomplishments, drive, or kindness, but it is not always easy to let them know the impact they have had on our lives. I would encourage you to do so because it not only strengthens your relationship and is gratifying for that person, but also makes you more aware of the qualities you would like to have and the traits you want to emulate.

Is there anything else you would like to share?

As Michael Sandel said during one of his talks a few months ago, "We need pluralistic engagement instead of civic avoidance," which has become one of my favorite sayings. I have always strived to engage in others' practices and beliefs by trying to see the world through their eyes. For instance, I was interested in learning more about India, so I joined the South Asian Association and went to Pune for an internship at Infosys after my freshman year to experience, albeit for only a summer, what being Indian meant. I have learned tremendously from trying to put myself in other people's shoes, and I would recommend you to do so, whenever possible. It is not always easy or pleasant, but it is only by doing so that we can promote understanding and foster collaboration. Civic avoidance prevents meaningful interaction, and it is only by engaging actively with genuine interest and empathy that we can truly learn to appreciate and leverage diversity to find creative solutions to our problems.

A perfectly imperfect takeaway about Leila:

Leila hopes that she can continue to connect with people who are different from her and help others to do so as well in the years to come. In order to facilitate mutual understanding and collaboration, she aspires to expand her family's telecommunication business, which seeks to distribute integrated low-cost Internet and television services. She says: "My wish is to economically improve the region by spreading the business model developed in Madagascar across East Africa, helping reduce the digital divide— the current frontier of intercultural information exchange, cooperation, and appreciation between these unconnected communities."

15

Ngan Pham

Happily Depressed Two-Time Dropout

BA in Interdisciplinary Studies: Business, Education, and
Women's Studies, Class of 2014, UC Berkeley

As a student, Ngan Pham was an award-winning leader who focused on public education, youth advocacy, and women's rights while attending UC Berkeley ("Cal"). At Cal, she co-founded ServeFund, which aimed to help students effectively fund-raise by providing microwork in return for sponsorships. Her work was featured at the Clinton Global Initiative University and Opportunity Nation Summit. Along with Opportunity Nation, a bipartisan, national campaign dedicated to expand economic mobility and close the opportunity gap in the United States, Ngan lobbied on Capitol Hill, urging legislators to fix the student debt crisis and support career technical education courses.

An advocate for mental-health education, Ngan also openly discusses her depression and solutions with her peers, having dropped out of UC Berkeley not once, but twice, to take care of her mind, body, and soul. After reenrolling at Cal, Ngan founded Cal's Aspiring Entrepreneurs, a global support network comprised of more than 650 entrepreneurial students and alumni of UC Berkeley, and is its chief community organizer. She is helping to bridge the diversity gap in technology by creating a safe and inclusive community for women and minorities.

A UC Berkeley graduate, Ngan is currently attending a six-month immersive software engineering fellowship at gSchool in San Francisco. While gaining experience in the technology industry, she aims to become a tech business leader before starting her own venture.

Where there are birds, there is hope.

—Ngan Pham

Born in Compton (a city in Los Angeles County), California, and raised in Phoenix, Arizona, Ngan Pham comes from a humble Vietnamese family.

"BOAT PEOPLE" PARENTS

My mom and dad first met during the Vietnam War, after Saigon fell to the Northern Communist regime. My dad escaped reeducation camp—essentially a prison camp where the South Vietnamese were forced to learn the "ways of the new government." He ran barefoot through a nearby forest as he heard consistent gunshots behind him. For seven days and nights, his only compass was climbing up the tallest tree and following the city lights that lay ahead in the distance. Months later, he met my mother in a fishing town, where he forged documents that officially proclaimed him as a fisherman. After creating these documents, my parents salvaged buckets of gasoline on their boat for months before fleeing Vietnam.

My father; my mother, then pregnant with my older sister; and fourteen other refugees, including three children, family members, friends, and strangers, fled Vietnam to what they always described as freedom. My parents are some of the infamous "boat people"—they floated aimlessly on the vast, deep ocean for four days and nights. They were part of the lucky 10 percent of Vietnamese refugees who remained alive after encountering Thai pirates. My parents have always had a keen fascination with birds: they have always told me, "Where there are birds, there is hope." Years later, I would discover that it was the birds they saw while on their boat that finally led them to the nearby land.

My parents' story is the foundation of who I am today. As a young teenager, my parents always told me they risked their lives for the kind of freedom the Communist regime did not provide and seized opportunities to escape poverty. In a recent visit to Vietnam, I discovered horrific accounts of murder of family and friends by the Viet Cong, the Vietnamese Communist Army. My mother's brother was stabbed to death while resting by a local shop in his village in retaliation against my grandfather, who supported the South Vietnamese and assisted the Americans. Her sister was killed during a stampede when the Viet Cong raided her village. Both of my parents had family members who were buried alive.

My parents have made it their life's mission to teach their children humility and generosity. They have always taught us to be kind and to do no harm, even to those who have wronged us. They have taught us the value of education and instilled the gift of giving into our hearts. I remember when I was ten, we took a family vacation to Vietnam, the first time my parents had been back since their escape. They always made sure my siblings and I were the ones giving the money our family donated to their former village. I remember thinking to myself, They have two hands. Why can't they give it themselves? Looking back, I laugh. I had no idea what a beautiful lesson they were teaching me.

In high school, Ngan was the Arizona state vice president for Health Occupation Students of America (HOSA). Her interest in health care was largely influenced by her parents, who'd lived in small villages in Vietnam where medicine was nonexistent and many died from preventable diseases. A huge proponent for education and career exploration, Ngan also lobbied for career and technical education courses at the State Capitol (and later on Capitol Hill as a college student). She co-organized district-wide leadership seminars to engage student leaders in advocacy and civic involvement. Ngan valued public service, dedicating her summers to volunteering with her local hospital and at Special Olympics basketball tournaments.

Ngan recounts her college decision and why she chose UC Berkeley:

I applied to in-state schools—Arizona State University (ASU), University of Arizona, and Northern Arizona University—and to other University of California campuses. I chose UC Berkeley mainly because my parents wanted me to be a doctor. The fact that UC Berkeley had an amazing molecular biology program made it the best choice. I thought that not only seizing the opportunities offered on campus would be worthwhile but also experiencing a new city would allow me to open my mind and gain new perspectives. Although I ended up not pursuing a medical career, I am happy I attended Berkeley.

Ngan recently graduated from UC Berkeley. I've asked her to reflect:

To what extent did your college experience—on and off campus—meet your expectations? In what ways did your experience cause you to change your perspective on your academic career, your dreams and aspirations, and your life?

CAUSES OF MY DEPRESSION

I'm a two-time college dropout from UC Berkeley. In the summer of 2010, five of my friends were victims in a rollover accident, including my childhood best friend. I fell into a deep state of depression and became a prisoner of my own body and mind, unable to sleep, eat, or think. There was a time when I contemplated suicide, to the point of researching different gun stores. Thankfully, I never went through with it.

Looking back, I wouldn't say I became depressed after my friends died. I have always been depressed, but the car accident was the tipping point. I am still on my journey to understand why I was depressed. It continues to be a struggle, and I do not know if I will fully understand it. It has a lot to do with my identity crisis (more on this later), cultural barriers between my parents and me that often put us into conflict, having a distanced relationship with my family, and other matters too personal to share.

When I was twelve years old, I locked my bedroom door, downed a bottle of thirty or so pills, and sprawled out on my bed slowly, awaiting my death. I cannot remember if there was a specific incident that made me do this. All I remember is that I did not want to live anymore. At that time, I was not close with my family, so I did not care to live, and I was too embarrassed to tell my friends that I tried killing myself. I never told anyone until college, when I sought professional medical help. I then told my family, and I have made amends with them since my childhood.

I choose to share this now because hearing other people's stories of mental illness has helped me realize I am not alone. It encouraged me to seek professional help. Depression was an illness I was too embarrassed to share, and that in turn made me more depressed. By sharing my story, I am coping with my demons and hope to alleviate the stigma associated with mental illness.

My depression went public my second year of college. The overwhelming stress from the academic rigor of being a pre-med molecular toxicology student, coupled with heartbreak from an incredibly unhealthy relationship and my inability to understand the sadness that shadowed me, became evident through my failing grades and excessive drinking.

After my friends' accident, the depression hit a critical threshold and unraveled at an exponential rate. It was an out-of-body experience where I went to class, but was never present. I distanced myself from the world and even lost friends I thought would be friends for life. I cried uncontrollably at random times, like when buying school supplies. For a month, the only food my body allowed me to consume was nutritional shakes. Anything else, I threw it all up.

My mind constantly raced. Thoughts like "Why am I sad?" and "I should not be sad. I'm a college student studying at a prestigious university. I have it all . . ." kept spinning around in my head. It wasn't until later I realized that I was also human. I have been conditioned to believe there was a set path to success. I call it the Henry Ford assembly line of success: graduate from high school, earn a bachelor's degree, obtain a master's degree, and finally have a PhD or MD certificate in hand. Only then would I have finally "made it." This mentality only added fuel to the fire. I constantly compared myself to others who were "on track," creating a mentally abusive and unhealthy lifestyle for myself.

TURNAROUND TOWARD HOPE AND EXPLORATION

It took me six months to finally seek the help I so desperately needed. I was feeling hopeless. Everything I once loved to do felt like a burden. It wasn't until my friend shared with me his dad's story of mental illness that I realized I was not alone. My friend insisted I go seek medical help. Four days before the first semester of my sophomore year was officially over, that same friend and my little sister walked me to the Tang Center, UC Berkeley's student health services. I went during emergency hours and sat with a psychologist for what was supposed to be a fifteen-minute assessment session but, instead, lasted for an hour and a half. I cried the entire time.

"You've been taking care of people all your life. Let me take care of you," said my psychologist. This was the turning point. This simple statement finally made me realize that I did not need to save anyone but myself.

With the support of my family and friends, I officially dropped out on medical leave during the spring of my sophomore year. During this time, I explored different career paths: researching with a toxicology lab at Cal, volunteering at both Tang Pharmacy and the Berkeley Free Clinic. I got a job tutoring student athletes with the Athletic Study Center, and I also audited classes. I returned to Berkeley that fall only to drop out for the second time on the one-year anniversary of my first withdrawal. I relapsed in my depression, only this time I was hospitalized for three days. I realized I was pursuing opportunities for all the wrong reasons. I was so enthralled in "keeping myself busy" to "remain competitive," that I never took care of the most important person: myself. The second time I withdrew, I made an honest effort to create the change I wanted to see.

My goals evolved. I dropped all activities that did not make me feel inspired. I loved teaching and mentoring, so I continued to work as a tutor. It proved to be worthwhile because I was promoted to assistant director for student-athlete development for the Cal football team. I also fell in love with the tech and start-up community because being around smart, ambitious people gave me life again. I also took the time to take care of my health. I exercised more, experimented with meditation, and started cooking healthier meals. I slowed down, and I learned how to love myself. When I re-enrolled at Berkeley, I changed my major from molecular toxicology to interdisciplinary studies focused on business, education, and women's studies. I was not yet fully certain of what future this multidisciplinary major would lead to, but it felt right and I was OK with that.

The past six years have been incredibly colored with failures and triumphs. I learned that it is OK to diverge from what I originally thought was my pathway to success. Looking back on all of these experiences, I am grateful because I discovered what makes me happy and what does not. Most important, I understand that before I can move forward with my academic career, dreams, and aspirations, I must take care of myself.

Given what you know now, if you could redo high school, what would you do differently, and why?

IF THE CLASSIC "BECOME A DOCTOR" PLAN PLEASES ONLY PARENTS AND NOT YOU, SAY "NO" EARLY

In Vietnam, doctors hold the highest honor and have opportunities that are typically unavailable for the average Vietnamese citizen. Since my parents came from a society that did not provide freedom or opportunities, they wanted their children to pursue a career that not only gained respect, security, and prestige, but one that would also make us advocate for social justice.

The advantages of having parents with high expectations is that I took my education very seriously. In high school, I was a straight-A student, a member of the National Honor Society, and held the Arizona state vice president position for HOSA.

However, the disadvantages can be immense. In hindsight, I was doing things for my parents' happiness and the number of people who praised me for being a future doctor because I "fit the part." I was scared I would be considered a failure in my parents' eyes if I did not pursue a medical profession, so I made excuses and talked myself out of exploring the creative arts, technology, and business. I put myself on track to be accepted into a prestigious university in hopes of increasing my chances to attend the best medical program ranked by *US News and World Report*.

By having this mentality, I was closed-minded to opportunities that could have potentially unveiled skills I thought I never had or to my true passions at an earlier age. As a child, I never danced, acted, or tried to learn computer programming, but I wish I had. As I matured, traveled, and experienced different environments, I often changed my mind about what I wanted to be.

LEARN AND EXPLORE RESOURCEFULLY, BUT AVOID THE TRAP OF RÉSUMÉ BUILDING

Reflecting on what I would have done differently, I wish I had lived in the present and actively explored all opportunities available to me. If I had, I would not have limited myself to preparing for a future career, especially one that I was not sure I would actually love. I later realized, during my college graduation ceremony, that my parents' happiness comes from their children's happiness and success regardless of their studies.

A great thing about life is that it is never too late. In this day and age, the advancement of modern technology has allowed people to be entrepreneurial without being an entrepreneur. Massive open online courses (MOOCs) have made it possible to learn programming online at your own pace. Social media has allowed ordinary people to build and engage an audience with shared interests. By simply watching YouTube videos, I am learning how to play the ukulele at home. The opportunities are endless, and we have the resources to explore. So, students, utilize it all and discover your abilities.

But be careful. Do not fall into the trap of résumé building. Explore avenues that excite you. The opportunity costs for saying yes to something that does not electrify you compromises time and energy for activities that could make you happy and the plethora of opportunities that may arise from them. If you don't know where or how to begin: Google. Then take initiative. Reach out to your networks and ask questions. You'd be surprised at how many people want you to succeed.

What else would you like to share with or suggest to high school students and college students, and why?

LOST IN IDENTITY

For the past twenty-three years, I've been struggling with my identity. I was born on US soil, so I am innately a citizen of this country. However, I have never felt like an "American."

Being named Thuy Ngan Vo Pham with fancy accents on the top of each vowel perpetuated my identity crisis. Every time I typed my name into a Word document and watched the red squiggly line immediately appear under it, unable to recognize my foreign name, made me feel alienated from this country I call home.

My almond-shaped eyes and long, black hair have caused many to misinterpret my ethnicity. Some think that I am a citizen of Asia or China. Yes, *Asia*—a diverse world sector of dozens of countries, in which almost all peoples have black hair. Yes, China, a large Asian country that is not Vietnam, the country from which my parents emigrated (or escaped).

For instance, when meeting new people, some insist that I must be from China, or what they like to call my "Mother Country." When I interject and say that I was actually born in Los Angeles, they persist with the gut-wrenching question that, to this day, makes me question whether ignorance is truly bliss: "No. I mean where are you *from* from?" they ask unapologetically. I never understood the emphasis on the first "from"—like it's supposed to make it sound culturally sensitive. In fact, it emanates the completely opposite emotion. My identity crises continued to develop whenever I had to answer "Vietnam" in one conversation but "Los Angeles" in another.

My parents also fit the stereotypical role of Vietnamese immigrants here in the States. They own a successful nail business called Nails "R" Us. They have a loyal clientele, some of whom have grown with my parents' shop since its inception fourteen years ago. As a young girl, I was embarrassed to divulge my parents' profession. Many kids who do not know my family always laughed at the "coincidence"—the fact that my parents fit the stereotype of Vietnamese-owned nail salons. To feel better, I always told myself, "Well, they just don't know my family's story."

As a teenager, I became restless, irritated, and angry at the snide remarks. But deep down, I was ashamed of myself for letting these ill-informed comments get the best of me and instigate my condescending behavior toward the very two individuals who have worked tirelessly to provide me with endless opportunities. Now as a twentysomething, I'm practicing my new mantra: "Confront your demons, forgive yourself, and appreciate your parents."

THE ART OF FAILING AND BEING VULNERABLE

I was traveling the world with Semester at Sea, a global study program that takes students around the world by ship. For 115 days, I voyaged with the *MV Explorer* to eighteen cities and sixteen countries along the coast of the Atlantic Ocean while also earning fifteen semester credits that went directly toward my major. I was living my own magical fairy tale while also earning credits for my real-life occupation as a student.

During our two-week-long stretch traveling from South Africa across the equator to South America, we had the honor of welcoming Les McCabe, president of the Institute for Shipboard Education. When he asked a group of students what characterizes a great leader, we offered up the most common, predictable answers: courage, a sense of humor, and the ability to engage others. But he surprised us with this: "All leaders embrace their vulnerability." By definition, to be vulnerable is to be susceptible to physical or emotional attack or harm.

Too often, I hear successful CEOs share with their audience anecdotes of the art of failing to eventually reach their successes. But how do we overcome our fear of failing so that we can embrace our vulnerability and vice versa? As I began to dissect the answers, I realized there was more to it than just failures and vulnerability.

In the spring of 2011, I had the privilege to attend the annual Clinton Global Initiative University, part of former President Clinton's promise to help young leaders bring ideas into action. My friend and I founded ServeFund, which aims to help students effectively fund-raise by providing employment opportunities in return for sponsorships and which CGIU recognized. During the closing plenary, President Clinton shared with our honored guest interviewer, Jon Stewart, along with 1,000 international students driven to create positive change, a moment he had with the late President Nelson Mandela. When asked if he had hatred toward the parties who put him in jail, Mandela had responded:

"Well, of course I did. I was full of hatred. I had not been free in so long. But I realize that if I hated them after I got in that car and got through that gate I would still be their prisoner. I wanted to be free. So I wanted to let it go. So should you. So should everyone."

It's a profound moment when a prominent individual who was jailed for twenty-seven years chooses to restore justice instead of seeking retaliation. President Mandela was able to release himself from the prison of his own body being jailed by anger and hatred through forgiveness. For me, it was accepting my depression. It took me a while, but I finally let go of the stigma of dropping out of school, because I realized my well-being deserved much more attention than what I was giving it. I actively stopped comparing myself to others I thought were doing "greater and better things."

Instead, I became proud of my colleagues *and* of myself. An essential first step I needed to take was confronting my demons and recognizing I had been mentally abusing myself. Only then could I release myself from built-up negativity and use that energy to appreciate my accomplishments. Once I did that, my self-confidence dramatically increased, which gave me the courage to put myself in vulnerable situations like sharing with you my story—a story I have been embarrassed to tell for so long. The art of failing is not just to fail, but to learn from your failures so that you become stronger, try again, and improve.

If there is one piece of advice I want to leave you with, it is this: convert the energy that has caused you harm into something positive. Do not forget any of your wrongdoings, but confront them. Then learn to forgive yourself and to forgive those who have wronged you. Embrace your successes.

Thank all the people who have supported you, but also thank the people who have doubted you. Once you can be honest with yourself, you will start to build self-confidence. This will help you understand and apply the art of failing and being vulnerable toward your success. It requires both courage and humility.

BUILD RELATIONSHIPS

Do not network, but build relationships. Before reaching out, do your research. I usually make a list of industries I want to explore. Then, I Google to learn more about those industries and read online articles, making a note of who wrote the article and what names were mentioned. I then search more about these people to learn about their background and to try to find out how they got to where they are now. Typically, I find their information through LinkedIn, personal blogs, and websites.

For students, utilize your university and college. Start researching different majors and professors on your school website. In Excel, list the professors you want to reach out to in one column and some talking points in the neighboring column. You can ask questions related to their respective industry, their research, what classes they took during college, or all of the above.

When you are finished researching, take initiative, follow through, and maintain the relationship. Typically, I cold e-mail, Facebook, or LinkedIn message with a nice introduction about myself and ask if they can take fifteen minutes for an informational interview either over the phone or for coffee, whichever is most convenient for them. For school professors, some of them may have open office hours, or you may have to schedule a personal meeting. Do not be surprised if for every ten cold e-mails you send, you only get one response. Also, do not be deterred if someone replies that they cannot meet with you. People may have very busy schedules, and you just have to carry on. With persistence, you'll find someone who has time for you.

Make sure you are on time and prepared for interviews or meetings in person, by phone, or online such as Skype, Google Talk, or FaceTime. In the unlikely event that you will be late, as a courtesy, call the person you are scheduled to meet, let him/her know you'll be late, and apologize sincerely. You don't want the person to form a bad impression of you after the fact for being late and disrespectful of his/her time.

If you've done your research, you should already have talking points. There may be times when you won't even need them because the person you're interviewing may drive the conversation. It's a case-by-case basis, but always remember to be prepared. At the end of the conversation, there's usually an "ask." I typically ask for three more contacts to further explore a specific industry. If there's an internship or job opportunity, I'll respect-fully ask if they can refer me internally. And of course, always say thank you when you end a conversation.

Maintaining the relationship means sending a follow-up "thank you" e-mail or letter. This person has graciously offered their time out of their busy schedule, and you want to make sure you are appreciative of their time. Building relationships can be intimidating, but if you do your research and are excited about your future career, it can be very fun.

Start reaching out and talking with people early on. Here is my experience and what I've learned:

1. **Explore career options.** I came into college as a molecular toxicologist because that's all I knew. My parents wanted me to be a doctor, so I wasn't familiar with any other industries outside the medical field. It wasn't until I started conversing with people from other fields that I realized my passion is in education, business, and entrepreneurship.

2. **Get mentors.** Oftentimes, I've had no idea what to do with my life. There have been times when I was completely lost about the direction in which to go for my career, and that's where a mentor could come in handy. Mentors are the people who understand what you're going through and can offer you invaluable advice. Just like an evangelist for a product or start-up, a mentor will be an evangelist for you. They will help guide you through your career and introduce you to the people you should know.

   For me, I have multiple mentors from different industries, functions, and locations. I have so many interests that each one of these people offers a unique perspective to their respective fields or functions. If you are interested in a particular field in which you don't have any connections, do not be afraid to reach out. Research the people you want to reach out to and make sure you understand why you want to reach out to them.

3. **Leverage existing relationships in a job search.** A colleague of mine who worked at a large entertainment company once told me there are three types of applicants: (1) applicants who come from partnered colleges, (2) applicants who are referred internally, and (3) applicants who apply independently online without any connections. By

the time the hiring managers get to the third type of applicants, all the positions are filled. Try to be in groups (1) and (2).

Knowing someone within a target company may dramatically increase your chances of getting an interview. I have used this technique to get the opportunities I have had while attending Berkeley and for my first job out of college. Be proactive in building relationships and leverage your relationships when opportune.

A perfectly imperfect takeaway about Ngan:

Ngan is "happily depressed." She embraces her depression rather than fighting it in order to move forward and alleviate the stigma associated with it. She says: "I have to thank my depression, and my family and friends, for forcing me to take the time to reevaluate what's important in my life. Depression has allowed me to privately address the deep-rooted issues that ate at me for years. This contemplative and active process has rejuvenated my excitement in the meaning of life. Without this meaning, I don't think I would have had the confidence to explore the tech and start-up communities, find the mentors I have today, and pursue a software engineering fellowship. There's no doubt I'm still depressed. But I'm working on things that matter to me, and for that, I'm happy."

16

Ryan Mango

Midwest Wrestler Chasing
Olympic Hopes

BA in Human Biology, Class of 2014, Stanford University

A Midwest native, Ryan Mango quickly found his niche as a wrestler. Compiling an impressive track record at Whitfield School, his high school, Ryan quickly became recognized as a top recruit by a plethora of colleges across the nation. He committed to Stanford University, where he continued his success on the mat, becoming the fifth two-time conference champion in school history and finishing his career fifth on the all-time list of wins (111). He was also the fifth two-time All-American in program history.

After graduating from Stanford in 2014, Ryan has completed the Summer Institute for General Management at the Stanford Graduate School of Business, and has given back to local wrestling communities by leading camps and clinics, and coaching the Stanford Wrestling Team. A recent move to Minneapolis has allowed Ryan to focus on training for the 2016 Olympics with the Minnesota Training Center. He hopes to follow in the footsteps of his brother, Spenser Mango, a two-time Olympian (2008,

2012) and five-time World Team Member (2009, 2010, 2011, 2013, 2014). Additionally, Ryan hopes to pursue an MBA and expand on his ability to help businesses ethically and efficiently deliver health care, education, and life-support resources to inner-city families.

Even at a young age, you can influence your community by reaching out, taking ethical risks, and being unafraid of failure. Understanding the fragility and diversity of life can help you gain an appreciation for the challenges that emerge and learning opportunities that follow.

—Ryan Mango

Soon after Ryan's birth, his father passed away. His mother's strength, resilience, and dedication to the education of her children shaped Ryan's and his older siblings' values profoundly early on.

MY DAD

It was a brisk autumn morning, September 15, 1992, and the Mango family was already up, buzzing with morning activities in the hardscrabble 3900 block of Natural Bridge Avenue. As my father, Thomas Lee Mango, left the house to head to work at Union Electric Co., my mother finished getting my older brother of five years, Spenser, and my older sister of six years, Natasha, prepared for school, all while balancing thirteen-month-old me on her hip. Needless to say, my parents had their hands full taking care of three children in a neighborhood that was often turbulent, all while my father worked as a blue-collar pipe fitter and my mother was finishing up nursing school.

Just after six that morning, the doorbell rang. When my mother answered the door, she was met by two police officers. "I heard the gunshots," she said. "But we lived in a neighborhood where gunfire was nothing out of the ordinary."

One police officer asked my mom if she knew Thomas Mango. He added: "Mr. Mango wasn't robbed or anything. They left his wallet, his watch, his ring, everything. They didn't take anything." The officer sighed and continued: "Except his life."

My father, Thomas, had just been ambushed and shot four times as he was getting into his vehicle in front of our home, tragically setting the sun on his short thirty-seven-year life. Much grief and mourning followed my family, and we three kids were relying on the strength of family, friends, and mostly my mother at this point.

Growing up without a father since I was a baby, my imaginations of what my dad was like have stemmed entirely from the memories of his kind heart and genuine personality expressed by my family. I developed many questions surrounding the incident itself. How had my mom coped with this situation? How did she become so strong? What was I missing out on? How could I help my mother? How could I help others who were facing the same challenges as me? As I grew older, these questions set the larger stage for my success. My genuine pursuit of answers, centered on our family values, guided me through the many challenges of growing up in a single-parent, blue-collar, Midwest family.

MY MOM

Growing up in the Midwest, I will never forget the influence my mother had on me as a young, malleable soul. I often describe my mother as a "Woman on Fire," as she was instrumental in bringing our family together, never forgetting the plans she and my father, the late Thomas Lee Mango, had for raising their children. They recognized the need for schooling and pledged to send us to private schools, where college attendance rates were much higher. Deborah Mango was resilient in her pursuit of our education, but this wasn't without motivation, as its foundation was the death of my father. My mother worked hard to achieve this goal, moving us, early in my life, into a new home and new school outside of the rough city center.

My mother worked the night shift as a registered nurse (RN). She would then return from home from working all night, fix breakfast, take us to school, run errands and fix dinner, pick us up from school, take us all to sporting practices, pick us up, have dinner, then go back to work. As I got better at wrestling, she would get dressed for work before getting me from school, drive me an hour and twenty minutes to the best club and partners, and sleep in the car in order to drive me home afterward and head straight to a grueling shift of work. This is one small example of the many ways my mother provided for our entire family, which collectively taught us to come together as a team and support one another in moving forward by embodying the values of hard work, teamwork, sacrifice, and humility.

I honestly to this day do not know when she found time to sleep, and I am extremely aware and appreciative of her sacrifices. There's no doubt I am a better young man today because of the values my mom instilled in our family.

LIFE IS DIVERSE AND OFTEN FRAGILE

Experiencing the many struggles my family endured, lost, and conquered, I gained an advanced understanding for the fragility and diversity of life. When I was young, we often visited our scattered family members in the St. Louis area. My mother, influenced largely by my grandmother, did what she could with her nonexistent free time to keep our family together and connected. Most of our relatives, some of whom had chosen troubled paths in life, still lived in the city center of St. Louis, unable to escape its detrimental clutches.

The issues to which I was exposed were cumulative, mainly caused by a lack of education, health care, and general support systems. The experiences in my immediate family had paralleled these larger issues. I lost my father as a result of the crime that festered. Many of my relatives were struggling, being exposed to the influences of inner-city life. My own sister had also strayed from our family for a stint in her life, during the time I was in high school, moving from place to place, neglecting school, and making poor life choices.

Although I was young and my mother had paved a more established foundation for me, these early life events had a large influence on the rest of my life, athletically and academically. My understanding of the fragility and diversity of life grew into an appreciation for the challenges that emerged and learning opportunities that resulted.

In high school, Ryan compiled an impressive wrestling résumé, including winning three Missouri Class 1 State Championships, going an undefeated 95–0 during his junior and senior years, and leading his high school team to consecutive Missouri Class 1 Team Titles in 2008 and 2009. He also compiled five Cadet and Junior Freestyle and Greco National Titles. In 2009, the Missouri Officials Association recognized Ryan as the Missouri Wrestler of the Year. Additionally, he was able to travel to Beijing, China, twice during high school, the first trip as part of a Junior Olympic Team. The second trip was particularly special to Ryan, as both he and his mother together were able to support his older brother, Spenser, in the 2008 Olympic Games.

Ryan earned his place as a heavily recruited star athlete. He reflects on this, including the reason for choosing Stanford:

In my high school senior year, I became a top recruit in the nation and was grateful that a plethora of universities showered me with attention. I received hundreds of letters and many calls, but eventually used just three of my five official visits—touring Stanford University, the University of Michigan, and the University of Indiana. Initially, I struggled in deciding whether or not to attend a school with NCAA wrestling (for example, Stanford), as I could forgo this option and attend Northern Michigan University (NMU), where my brother went and trained Greco-Roman full-time. At NMU, he benefited from being able to accept prize money and sponsors, travel the world, and focus on making international gains in wrestling early on rather than transitioning to professional wrestling after collegiate wrestling, as would be the case at Stanford.

In the end I applied to Stanford and NMU. After being admitted, I humbly committed to Stanford because of its strong combination of athletics and academics and its location in the heart of innovation in Silicon Valley. But one thing made Stanford stand out from the rest of the colleges with which I had briefly been acquainted: it was the only school on this list where I truly felt like I was part of a family, which was vital to my success given my delicate past.

Growing up, Ryan lacked a father. He recognized this intrinsic human need and challenge as an opportunity to pursue father figures in other ways.

FAMILY AND FRIENDS

Early on my father figures came mostly in the form of family and friends. I always had a special relationship with my brother, who is five years my senior, and he looked out for me as we spent a lot of time together. He has been instrumental in my growth and is an individual whom I have revered.

Outside of my brother's support, I also built a relationship with Orvelle Hughes, who was a close friend of my mother's and acted as a father figure for me as well as a beacon of emotional support since the time of my father's passing. To this day, my mom, siblings, and I consider Orvelle dearly as part of our family.

TEACHERS OR COACHES AS MENTORS

When I arrived at Whitfield, I was largely unfamiliar with the open, innovative culture of the school. I developed a strong bond over the years especially with Buddy Smith, the assistant wrestling coach at the school. Buddy was a familiar face during a time of transition for me, as well as a pillar of support for which I am grateful. The moral is, set aside time to get to know people, as this is a worthwhile investment. He was a mentor and teacher who acted as a father figure for me during high school.

The wrestling program at Whitfield was also ideal for me, not because it was wildly successful but because I had the opportunity to contribute significantly to building the program. I embraced the challenge to integrate my passions and see my effect on the community as well as the community's effect on me. I wanted to become not just another name on the wall, but a part of something to be remembered. I was the face of Whitfield Wrestling, leading our team on the mats and in the Whitfield community by embodying and sharing the values passed on by my mother. We grew our wrestling team, not placing in the state my freshman year but eventually winning Missouri State Titles during my junior and senior years. We also built a wrestling community that is deeply integrated and active within the school to this day, consistently performing well during the season, sending student athletes to college, and growing an unpopular, ancient sport in an innovative, contemporary school and changing the sport's reputation.

Today, Ryan is a Stanford Class of 2014 graduate. I've asked him to reflect:

To what extent did your college experience—on and off campus—meet your expectations? In what ways did your experience cause you to change your perspective on your academic career, your dreams and aspirations, and your life?

EMERGING "FATHER FIGURES"

In leaving the modest Midwestern culture of St. Louis and embarking on a new journey to Stanford University, I assumed I had to work hard and try to keep my head down in order to accomplish my wrestling and academic goals concurrently. As my undergraduate career matured, I realized that many of my past "father figures" would be my lifelong mentors and friends, while new figures also emerged. Collectively, they continually set me up for success, affecting my life in a positive way.

STANFORD UNIVERSITY: CO-PURSUIT OF ACADEMICS AND ATHLETICS

Early in my undergraduate career, it was clear that my goals were to reach the pinnacle of wrestling by winning an NCAA National Championship and becoming an Olympic Champion. This resonated with the coaching staff, as they wanted to reach the pinnacle of coaching by winning an NCAA National Team Title. The themes of goal setting and striving for greatness radiated on the Farm (the nickname for the Stanford campus), among all associated individuals.

This set Stanford's athletic department apart from all others. After all, Stanford sent more athletes to the Beijing Olympics than any other college in the United States, and it would have tied Japan for eleventh place in the medal count if it were its own country. Every individual not only shared these aspirations but also understood what it took to get there. This common understanding created synergy between individuals across the entire community, and the positive aura made it easy to develop relationships, as the entire system worked together to support one another—just like a family. Personally, I found this to be a breath of fresh air, as I knew I was not alone in this challenge. My personal values and aspirations and the entire athletic department's culture clearly overlapped, but more interestingly these values were also consistent across the academic environment.

With that said, I had my share of character-enhancing struggles. During the ten-week winter quarter of my sophomore year, I was in the heart of what the coaches and I hoped would be a breakout season. Unfortunately, I tore my lateral collateral ligament (LCL), damaging my knee structure, while I was studying hard for the academically challenging "human biology core" and spending a lot of time serving my fraternity, Omega. So, I was slammed with the "big three"—academics, athletics, and social life.

With the big three pulling what was left of my mind and body in separate directions, I had no other choice than to force myself to be more efficient and resourceful by actively reaching out to others for support and by applying lessons about friendship and perseverance learned from my fraternity. After physical therapy, my knee was still injured going into the NCAA tournament. Determined, I managed to power through the tournament on a torn LCL, reaching All-American status for the first time in my career. I also finished the pledge process and joined my fraternity shortly after the tournament, ending one of the toughest but most fulfilling quarters in my undergraduate career.

At Stanford, each individual had his or her own goals, driven independently. Stanford is synchronized in that every individual, despite having different goals, is humbly pursuing excellence to some degree. In this way the culture and community at Stanford made it possible for me, a Midwestern wrestler with a broken past, to pursue my academic and athletic goals while being socially engaged. This speaks to the importance of the cultural fit of the college and the individuals that comprise it across all departments.

This type of experience provides every student athlete the opportunity to build relationships in non-athletic settings, resulting in the pursuit of relationships and passions outside of athletics.

USA WRESTLING: TRAVEL

I believe that pursuing opportunities to travel is one of the best means of gaining understanding and perspectives on one's own life as well as others' by stepping outside of one's comfort zone. Fortunately, thanks to wrestling, I have visited numerous US cities and traveled abroad periodically over the last ten years of my life. Recently, I traveled to Tehran, the capital of the geopolitically unstable Iran, to represent the United States in the World Cup. Through the city, we saw scattered remnants of propaganda and the crumbled US embassy building lying untouched. One section of the embassy's demolished brick wall displayed a painting of the Statute of Liberty as a skeleton, holding a gun in place of the torch.

This imagery quickly triggered concern within our group, who represented the United States for Iran's most popular sport. Luckily, the people of Tehran quickly and definitively doused these concerns through their incredible hospitality and genuine pursuit of friendship. The first day of competition, we arrived at the wrestling arena where the competition was held only to be met with a spectacle. As we approached the venue, displaying the US flag on the front of our bus, fans began to crowd around, first on small motorcycles alongside the bus, then on foot. As we got close, the bus came to a complete halt, as it was surrounded not by angry antagonists but by overjoyed bystanders. This became a daily routine as security carved out a small tunnel through the enormous crowd, through which we would run into the venue. Once inside the venue this camaraderie would continue as we had a chance to interact with the fans, signing autographs and competing with their support.

Yes, the Iranian wrestling fans were supporting us, the US team. In these moments, along with countless others from the trip, the true essence of the Iranian culture emerged. Despite the many economic and political battles that Iran endured in the past and present, in particular with our country, I gained valuable life experiences and built genuine relationships with locals on this trip. In particular, I learned that it is valuable for Americans to experience other cultures firsthand, squash false assumptions, and let on-the-ground experiences refine beliefs.

My international trips:
- Beijing, China (2007, 2008 Olympics)
- Prague, Czech Republic (2010)
- Moscow, Russia (2010 World Championships)
- London, England (2012 Olympics)
- Frankfurt, Germany (2013)
- Budapest, Hungary (2013 World Championships)
- Tehran, Iran (2014 World Cup)

OMEGA PSI PHI FRATERNITY, INC.: THE FRATERNITY DEBATE

During sophomore year, I pledged in and earned membership to Omega Psi Phi Fraternity Incorporated, alongside four men with whom I shared an experience and journey that had a cumulative effect on my life. Even before the successful resurrection of the Alpha Mu "Morning Thunder" Chapter of Omega Psi Phi at Stanford University in 2011, after four years of on-campus absence, we had all been touched by the far-reaching hand of Omega.

For me, Buddy Smith, the assistant wrestling coach at my high school, personal friend, mentor, and member of Omega Psi Phi, grew my interest in the fraternity through truly living his creed centered on the fraternity's four Cardinal Principles: Manhood, Scholarship, Perseverance, and Uplift. Seeing the value the fraternity provided Buddy, specifically the avenues through which community service and involvement were integrated with the fraternity's principles and high aspirations, captivated my interest and resulted in my pursuit of Omega.

Arriving as a freshman on campus, I saw no Omega men. Seeking out like-minded individuals at Stanford as well as at San Jose State, Berkeley, and other surrounding colleges, other students interested in joining the fraternity and I eventually met with representatives from local graduate chapters as well as older members of the Alpha Mu chapter still living in the area. Our process of seeking representatives took about one year. After resurrecting the Alpha Mu chapter of Omega at Stanford, we hung no signs on campus promoting its rush events and held no ice-cream socials. Omega wasn't hoping to passively lure in college students by being appealing but rather was striving to create a genuine pursuit of the fraternity. In this way we were all devoted and invested in our relationships with one another and with Omega.

Omega will always be a part of my life and a means for me to make a difference in the community acting as a bridge builder, as well as in the lives of other young men whose values align with those of Omega. It also serves as means for me to stay connected to the black community in a positive way. My journey with Tyler Alston, Terrence Stephens, Jamal-Rashad Patterson, and Khalil Wilkes into Omega, as well as countless national interactions with members of Omega and other Black Greek Letter Organizations (BGLOs), represent relationships that are invaluable.

My experience with fraternities has not been plagued by common perceptions centered on social stereotypes, but has added deep meaning to my life. I chose to continue participating in the life-enriching fraternity activities against the Stanford Wrestling Team Rules, which saw fraternities as a distraction and explicitly discouraged wrestlers from joining them. My coaches knew that I was passionate about wrestling and valued friendship as being essential to the soul, and I was confident that they trusted my judgment. I eventually unveiled my secret life of pledging when I arrived at the bus with a bald head as we were off to the NCAA tournament my sophomore year. My coaches were surprised, but most important, supportive.

DON'T BE AFRAID OF CHANGE, EVEN LATE IN THE PROCESS

Entering my fourth year as a human biology major, my studies concentrated mainly on human performance, which was something I was interested in but not fully passionate about. My passions centered heavily on the early life experiences I'd had with my family and friends in St. Louis, and to this point I wasn't satisfied in my ability to give back to individuals by knowing the difference between the respiratory quotient and respiratory exchange ratio or calculating rotational forces on baseball pitchers. I was, however, sure of the many possible applications of medical ethics, particularly in a world where digital systems are becoming increasingly integrated into health care, especially with respect to delivery.

Heading into my final two quarters at Stanford, I decided to adjust my concentration to include medical ethics. The Human Biology Department was consistent with Stanford's overall culture, being flexible in their willingness to work with me on adjusting my concentration, ensuring both the department's requirements as well as my own aspirations were met. Through the diverse challenges I had already faced in my life, I felt prepared for a late change in major and knew I had built a support system of father figures who were there if I needed them. I had also taken advantage of a learning opportunity that I likely would have overlooked in high school.

Through this experience, I learned the upside of taking risks in pursuit of a passion. Having sharpened my general management skills from the Summer Institute for General Management program at the Stanford Graduate School of Business, I hope to integrate these skills with the raw knowledge of human biology from my undergraduate studies, insights from case studies in ethics, and diverse life experiences to provide ethical, efficient solutions to the many emerging roadblocks limiting quality and delivery of health care, particularly in inner-city neighborhoods.

Given what you know now, if you could redo high school, what would you do differently, and why?

Most of my learning experiences in high school and my earlier days hinged on my ability to accept failures and recognize these failures as opportunities to improve. Being unafraid of failure and learning from mistakes were pivotal in positioning myself for future success.

Entering high school, I knew I wanted to put myself in the position to help my own family as well as others experiencing struggles similar to those we faced. This became the heart of my passion, and wrestling was crucial in helping me position myself for success by my standards, as well as teaching me several life lessons through failure.

LEARNING OPPORTUNITIES

If I could do high school all over again, I would further explore some of my academic interests outside of school. In high school, my mind was set on having a positive effect on the community. I had experienced positive personal changes through my community constituents' help in raising me. I often found ways to give back through wrestling camps, clinics, and events but did not explore the same avenues in school. I was interested in biology and health care, and often yearned to explore more options such as summer programs, entrepreneurial ventures, and so on that would equip me with the tools to make change.

Fearful that these pursuits would take away from wrestling, I never explored any of these options further. Looking back, I missed out on valuable experiences. Funny enough, the years I performed best on the mat were the same years that I found myself the busiest with school. The takeaway is, even at a young age, you can have a positive influence on the community. And aspiring young leaders, particularly athletes, should remember to diversify the avenues through which you give back. The truth is, I already had the tools to make change through my experiences, but only needed to reach out and take a risk.

OPPORTUNITY TO REST

Building off of the previous point, several times I admittedly feared pursuing many opportunities to build relationships outside of wrestling. I had high aspirations that were very public, creating outside pressures to always train and try to do more. Wrestling consumed much of my free time. Looking back, I realize that at times I was overtraining, but couldn't recognize that it was causing some negative effects to my daily energy levels and overall performance in the classroom.

Taking breaks from training is essential, but a persistent tension for me was in realizing that those who are training to be the best are always looking ahead, no matter if what lies ahead is a wrestling tournament, a piano recital, the SAT, or what-have-you. I learned that I might perform even better and have my passion rekindled if I incorporated more reenergizing breaks.

OPPORTUNITY TO ACT

After graduating from high school, I returned to the largest national stage for Freestyle and Greco-Roman wrestling in Fargo, North Dakota. Having never lost at the tournament and having won four titles in two appearances, I expected to win two more and make it a perfect run. Indeed, I won the

Greco-Roman National Title in the first portion of the event and reached the final portion of the freestyle bracket unblemished. The count stood just one title shy of perfect. In order to reach the finals, I needed to beat one more opponent, who had lost to a wrestler I beat earlier in the tournament.

During the match, I was complacent and relaxed for a split second and overlooked the task at hand. I lost focus and ended up losing the match, as well as the final match of the day, unfortunately taking fourth place and seemingly letting the entire world down. Eventually, I learned to look at this as a humbling experience and a fresh start, and I used those two losses as motivation to focus on my next adventurous mission at Stanford University, keeping this event in mind among many testaments to the fragility and diversity of life.

A perfectly imperfect takeaway about Ryan:

Ryan's life has been filled with tragedies and triumphs. Upon reflecting, Ryan has found resolve in the genuine pursuit of excellence, providing both a personable perspective on life and appreciation for the learning opportunities that arise from life's challenges.

Ryan is currently a 2016 Olympic hopeful and has recently decided to move to Minneapolis, where he will be training with the Minnesota Training Center, coaching at the University of Minnesota, and looking to gain diversified work experience. In addition, Ryan plans to pursue an MBA in the future, focusing on improving the ethical and efficient delivery of health care. Although these are lofty goals, Ryan has not forgotten what got him to this point and recognizes his passion behind the goals. Ryan says: "So many people have played a role in guiding me to this point in my life, and I will never forget their influence . . . for that reason I will always be involved in the wrestling community as well as others, such as my high school, the Farm, and Omega Psi Phi."

17
Sally Zhang
Truth-Seeking Journalist

BS in Journalism, Class of 2014, Northwestern University
Medill School of Journalism

Sally Zhang set out to prove that an Asian American can excel in both the humanities and the sciences/math. In high school, she founded an activist group called Youth for Asian American Participation to encourage politically silent youth to make their voices heard in their communities. She also tested her ability to take on challenges in unfamiliar environments by participating in the Miss Sing Tao Pageant hosted by Sing Tao Daily (the world's largest Chinese newspaper) in San Francisco. And unlike many peers from the Bay Area, where she grew up, Sally chose to major in journalism at the Medill School of Journalism at Northwestern University.

Before graduating from college, Sally received several full-time offers and chose to work at NBC News, as she aspires to become a news producer who can improve the lives of her community through her storytelling. She spends her not-so-free time enjoying the outdoors and being a total foodie, especially for Asian cuisine.

A lot of people call me naïve, but I call it being optimistic. Life is too short to not be happy.

—Sally Zhang

Sally Zhang is emerging as a leader in broadcast journalism. This is her unconventional story.

I was born in China and came to the United States when I was three years old, following my parents, who came to the United States for graduate education. Both of them earned their PhDs in science. I was never bad at math or science, but I just wasn't passionate about them. Both of my parents have been extremely supportive of my decision to go into journalism, for which I am forever grateful.

In high school, Sally Zhang distinguished herself from her peers by establishing her own club based on what she saw as a social issue, rather than trying to fit her passions into any preexisting student groups. Sally founded Youth for Asian American Participation (YAAP), at which her efforts resulted in various levels of social and political change. She received a letter from State Senator Joe Simitian, who recognized her efforts in collecting thousands of signatures to petition against the California education budget cuts. In addition, Sally was a key member of the badminton team at Lynbrook High School, one of the strongest in California. She was also crowned as the 2009 Miss Sing Tao second runner-up.

Sally reflected on her experience running for the leading Chinese American beauty pageant and its effect on her via a personal essay during the college app season in her senior year. The corresponding Common Application essay prompt and her response are as follows:

Please write an essay on a topic of your choice. This personal essay helps us become acquainted with you as a person and student, apart from courses, grades, test scores, and other objective data. It will also demonstrate your ability to organize your thoughts and express yourself.

The dazzling lights that surrounded me cast an elongated shadow onto the carpet. "Three! Two! . . ." A small, red light flashed on, and my interview as Miss Singtao February at the Sina.com studio began. A month before, I would have never imagined that I would be in a beauty pageant.

Given my mom's persuasive powers, I finally decided to try something unprecedented. After I submitted the application form, I was called in for an interview with three Singtao executives in a large glass-surrounded room. With no time to enjoy the beautiful ocean view, I tried to steady my voice and maintain a confident posture. After an hour of grueling questions, I walked out the room and impatiently awaited a response. Just five minutes later, the marketing director informed me that they had made one of the fastest decisions yet, choosing me to be Miss Singtao February. This brought exhilaration to my usually placid life—catapulting me into activities such as photo shoots, newspaper interviews, and volunteer work. The talk show at Sina.com studio was the most invigorating.

As I tried to adjust to the surrounding, bulky cameras, bright lights, and large microphones, the three-hour video recording began. I gave a nervous smile said hello to all the web visitors. The two hosts exclaimed, "Wow, doesn't she look like someone fit for playing the Guzheng?" We talked about the Guzheng, a traditional Chinese instrument, rich with ancient culture, that I had been playing since I was eight years old. I proudly told them I had passed Level 8, certified by the Chinese Musician's Association. Moreover, I even taught children at YMCA centers to share my strong passion for Guzheng.

Right after I performed a serene, American song, "The Loved Ones from Homeland," the hosts quickly turned to the topic of badminton. They seemed to like the juxtaposition of the peaceful music and the hectic life of a badminton competitor. As one of the leading players on the Lynbrook badminton team since my freshman year, I had taught myself discipline and perseverance. I savored the interactive nature of teamwork, which complemented my individual accomplishments through playing Guzheng.

The comfort level became friendly as the talk show went on. The hosts wondered if my fervor in Speech and Debate had granted me this ease of conversation. Serving on the Speech and Debate team for three years taught me not only how to speak eloquently and present myself with poise but also how to think critically. I became more confident in discussing current events topics. I proceeded to teach the two hosts some French, a language I had been enthusiastically learning since middle school.

As the interview moved towards its conclusion, I realized that I had melted into the scene. I never thought I would discover another side of myself, markedly different from the person with whom I've grown accustomed. Growing up in a family with traditional Chinese parents who are dedicated scientists, my values remain conservative and humble.

Assuming the title of Miss Singtao terrified me at first. However, I adapted readily to this new identity. Rising to this challenge rewarded me with the gifts of growth and self-confidence. One month later, I found myself standing in front of a supermarket to advertise for the Singtao newspaper. While trying to persuade people to buy the newspaper, I surprised myself by approaching them confidently. I suddenly took more pleasure in attending social events, such as a fashion show to fundraise for children of the Szechuan earthquake. I walked with greater self-assurance in front of crowds of photographers and conversed with the attendees about donating to the charity. The Miss Singtao title has set me on the road to—paraphrasing Nietzsche—"becoming who I am."

A common pattern observed is that high-achieving high schoolers spend the bulk of their last two summers before graduation constructively. Sally described a memorable summer activity on her Common App:

Please briefly elaborate on one of your extracurricular activities or work experiences.

This summer, my internship brought me, and of course my camera, to Sherig Norbu Tibetan School in Qinghai, China. The endless, bumpy bus rides finally ended when I beheld the serene Yellow River passing through burgundy colored mud banks, dwarfed by the powerful mountains and mysterious Buddhist temples. The first morning at Sherig Norbu, I photographed a seven-year-old boy standing under the mountains, wearing a simple, brown sweater and pants. He looked carefree and happy, living with bare necessities that shocked me. My camera discovered him again among forty other students, ages six to twenty, all in one bare, literature classroom. Behind each distinct, facial expression, I noted the identical, enthusiastic, and appreciative look from everyone. Tibetan girls lit up my camera with their long braids, colorful traditional dresses, and sun parched faces. These students satisfied my camera's lens, but more importantly, changed my view on life.

The majority of the top-tier private colleges require applicants to write at least one "why this school is a right fit for you" type of essay. The following was Sally's "why Northwestern" essay:

What are the unique qualities of Northwestern–and of the specific under-graduate school to which you are applying–that make you want to attend the University? In what ways do you hope to take advantage of the qualities you have identified?

The mission statement for Northwestern's Communication Studies, "to prepare students to take their place as responsible leaders, engaged citizens, and pioneering problem-solvers," immediately attracted me, especially because I have already laid the groundwork for more involvement in community affairs.

The role of mass communication as a social phenomenon rather than entertainment had never drawn my attention until I started my activist group, Youth for Asian American Participation (YAAP). My idea of YAAP was born on the evening of February 19, 2008, Primary Election Day, the first time my parents were qualified to vote in the US. Until challenged by my mother, I had never perceived the limited involvement and influence of Asian Americans in social and political affairs in our community. The next day, on Facebook, I posted my idea for YAAP's first goal: encouraging more Asian Americans to vote in the 2008 general election.

To maximize YAAP's outreach, I seized a particular occasion–the Singtao Commercial Exhibition, usually attracting thousands of Asian Americans–as my first objective. Moved by our enthusiasm, the exhibition organizer granted us a booth and 500 free photocopies of our fliers. Just two weeks before the Singtao Exhibition, dire political matters–California education budget cuts–befell us. We created a petition letter outlining the negative consequences of massive budget cuts and the need for community action.

The awaited day arrived. In the large hall holding 500 booths, we mounted our "YAAP" banner at booth 472. Everyone dispersed throughout the hall, approaching and educating the visitors. A young couple, previously unaware of education budget cuts, expressed a sincere desire to petition their resistance. Many elderly visited our booth to pick up election materials. YAAP's collective efforts gleaned a total of 1,604 signatures and distributed over 1,000 flyers. A week after I mailed the petition signatures to State Senator, Joe Simitian, we received his recognition letter, applauding the objective of our organization and our accomplishment.

Writing to officials, composing petitions, and publicizing the group for recruitment opened my eyes to the role of political communication in society. I now yearn to expand my knowledge about various arenas of communications including social, political, and cultural functions by becoming a student at the School of Communication. I believe that the multidisciplinary and innovative teaching offered by the prominent faculty at the School of Communication offers a unique opportunity to discover new ideas about the impact of communication on society. In addition, the rigorous and practical preparation at the school will train me for my future career in social and political arenas.

I would relish the privilege to study under Professor James S. Ettema, whose unique research focuses on "the social organization and cultural impact of mass media and new communication technologies." Under his mentorship, I would conduct a research project on international communication and its applications in the United States, a nation composed of diverse populations, each with its own distinct ways of communication. I would like to present my work at the International Media Seminar, a rare opportunity for me to expand my network on an international level.

I would seize the opportunity to attend the Van Zelst lecture in the Communication Century Scholars program and participate in special scholarship and fellowship competitions. These activities would allow me to apply what I have learned in my courses to gain firsthand experience in the field of communication. I intend to continue my research about Tibetan debate and various forensic forms. I would also like to compare the different forms of debate, research how contrasting cultures affect the different types of debate, and analyze the application of these various types of debate in broader areas, such as education and politics.

While a lot of research revolves around science and technology, Sally had already begun research in the humanities field before entering college. She discussed a summary of her work on her Northwestern application supplement. The essay prompt and her response are as follows:

Statement on Research (optional): If you have done research or independent study outside of school, please include an abstract or summary of your work on a separate sheet.

(Research background: I was fortunate to witness Tibetan debate at Sherig Norbu Welfare School in Qinghai during my internship in China this summer. As an ardent participant in Western-style debate, I discovered more about Tibetan debate through my discussion with the school principal, Jigme Gyaltsen. I completed this research comparing the two forms and presented an overview to my school.)

Cultural differences can make the same word, "debate," the structured, competitive exchange between people, assume contrasting roles and develop different forms.

Tibetan Debate

Tibetan Debate is a unique characteristic of Tibetan Buddhism, which originated from India's scripture debate, established by an eminent Tibetan Monk nearly a thousand years ago. Understanding the concept and procedure of debate comprises an essential prerequisite in Tibetan philosophical studies.

Tibetan Buddhist Debate uses proposition, reason, and metaphor to carry on logical reasoning and the dialectics of Buddhism's religious doctrine. Through debate, one can dispel contradictions, eliminate all doubts, dig deeply into philosophical ideas, obtain wisdom, and discover true meaning. Tibetan Buddhist debate measures one's knowledge level, dialectical ability, and logical acuity.

The debate usually includes two parties, a debater who stands and asks questions and a defender who sits and answers questions. There is no judge, but there are strict rules of behavior to assure an orderly exchange of questions and answers. During debate, one can only answer "yes," "no," or "not sure," and elaborate one's answer when permitted to do so. There is no time limit for each round. The debaters switch positions when the questioner cannot find any flaws in the answers.

The systematic hand motions and gestures are important techniques used in Tibetan debate that usually take years to master. The debate starts with a high-pitched phrase and a clapping of the hands together, which represents the unity of wisdom. A robe is slung over the left shoulder, a sign of respect; and stomping, clapping of the hands, or circling around the debater with Buddhist prayer beads signifies that the debater lost.

Now, this debate technique permeates Tibetan education, not only to lead students into Buddhist philosophy, but to comprehend academic subjects. After the lectures, students debate as a means to review what they had just learned. Questioners raise incrementally tough questions as the defender proceeds, until he no longer answers without flaw. By observing the debate, the teacher assesses the progress of the entire class. The performing aspect of Tibetan debate builds enthusiasm, enabling debaters to access intellectual resources that regular classes often ignore.

Comparison of Tibetan Debate with Western-style Debate

Tibetan debate focuses more on spiritual goals, a fundamentally different approach from our Western-style debate, which is political in nature. While Western-style debate tends to emphasize disputable content and an individual's position on controversial issues, Tibetan debate aims to eliminate contradictions to reach harmony. In contrast to Western-style debate, in which persuasion according to personal opinion provides a key measurement for success and winning, Tibetan debate seeks to expand one's mind, develop analytical capability, and gain internal clarity. Winning becomes secondary.

Study through debate proves an effective way for Tibetan students to confront and then review what they have learned. This teaching method allows the students to think actively to analyze their knowledge. Such a method provides an enormous impetus to students' academic initiative.

After applying to some private and public universities, Sally was admitted to UC Berkeley, UC San Diego, UC Davis, NYU, Carnegie Mellon, and Northwestern University and was waitlisted at Washington University in St. Louis.

I knew I wanted to major in something related to mass communication and media, so after researching each school's department in this subject area, I learned that Northwestern University provided the best one, as well as being a top-ranked school. It came down to UC Berkeley and NU. I chose NU because I was enthralled by its mass communication program and because I wanted to leave California to become more independent and solve my own dilemmas and hardships while growing in college. Going to Berkeley would have made that difficult, with my parents just an hour away from school.

Sally recently graduated from Northwestern University Medill School of Journalism. I've asked her to reflect on the following:

To what extent did your college experience meet your expectations? In what ways did your experience cause you to change your perspective on your academic career, your dreams and aspirations, and your life?

I'm writing this bearing the responsibilities of being a person and professional who has entered the real world. Needless to say, college shaped me into the person I am today and hopefully (as I will soon discover) prepared me for what lies ahead. College has changed my goals and my worldview.

I entered Northwestern as a communication studies major. I was curious and wanted to learn more about the media, from a research point of view. How does the media achieve its goals? Why is it so effective? How are we influenced unconsciously? What are the future trends? I also had plans to go to law school afterward, but I wanted a solid back-up. Communication studies would teach me a wide range of skills and also allow me to find a job in another industry, such as marketing or PR.

After a few quarters of classes, I felt like I wasn't being challenged enough. I wanted something more practical than theoretical. So I got myself onto the waitlist of an intro reporting class in the Medill School of Journalism. Up to that point, I had no journalism experience at all, but every other person in Medill had been either the editor-in-chief of their high school newspaper or something of equal nature. This was both frightening and exciting. I didn't know if I would be able to catch up, but that's why I wanted to challenge myself. This decision turned out to be one of the best decisions I made in college.

Lots of back-and-forth with the registrar and several Medill classes later, I successfully transferred from the School of Communication into the Medill School of Journalism, one of the best journalism schools in the nation. Did I know I was making the right move? No, but I knew I had to take the leap in order to find out. Turns out, my journalism classes taught me so much, not just in terms of reporting, writing, and multimedia skills, but I was exposed to a wealth of knowledge and had the pleasure of telling the stories of those who were not heard.

Having gone to Lynbrook High School, a highly competitive, college-prep-oriented public school in Silicon Valley, also imbued in me a sense of overachievement. I was obsessed with spending a lot of time in the library my freshman year in college. I would sacrifice social events for more time to do homework and to study for midterms. But no one forced me to. I, myself, feared not achieving good grades. Slowly, I realized that I was missing out on more and more of those typical college experiences: parties, hanging out in friends' dorms, staying up late just for fun.

And when I finally realized it, it wasn't too late. In my later years of college, I learned how to manage my time and prioritize my work so that I could balance work and social life. This is probably the most valuable piece of practical and college/career-defining advice I can give to any college freshman. Trust me, you can do both. Four years goes by faster than you think, so treasure the time you have while you can.

My decision to become a journalist and learning how to manage my time have both changed my worldview. I feel like I have come out of a bubble and experienced more of what the world has to offer. It's easy to keep doing what you're comfortable doing, but that won't help you grow. I guarantee that taking on challenges and stepping outside your comfort zone will be rewarding, as long as you aren't afraid to try.

Given what you know now, if you could redo high school, what would you do differently, and why?

Disclosure: Even though I advise to balance your work and social life and to not spend too much time in the library, I still believe it is crucial to study hard in high school so that you *can* get the grades you need to get into the admissions ballpark of the college of your choice. So I would not have done that part differently in high school.

There are pros and cons of going to college far away from home. I was exposed to a different kind of environment and culture in the Midwest. It was something I was not used to at first, but it has taught me to be more open to different experiences and different people. It also allowed me to realize that I had taken everything I had back home in the Bay Area for granted. One thing I would have done differently if I were back in high school is appreciating more the things I had—like the weather and the food.

My first winter in Chicago welcomed me with a "snowmageddon"—one of the worst snowstorms in a very long time. At one point, the snow had covered cars on the street up to the top of their windows. I thought it was pretty cool. I could walk out and the snow would be up to my waist. We had the first snow day (even classes were canceled) in thirty years. As much as I enjoyed the novelty of a change in seasons, the long winters from October to April (and most of the time it's still cold in May) made me miss the California sun. I became noticeably paler after each winter.

It's also hard to find authentic, affordable, convenient Asian food in the Midwest. Evanston is actually pretty good, since it needs to cater to the college population, which is approximately 20 percent Asian. My friends and I usually made a few trips through the blistering cold to Chinatown in Chicago, a one-hour ride on the El train. It's always worth it after you eat that first bite of hotpot or Peking duck.

It may not be the same for you. Maybe it's not the weather or food but the people and places back home. But regardless of what it is, treasure it and don't take it for granted.

What else would you like to share with or suggest to high school students and college students, and why?

I think it's very important (especially for so many students who have not decided their majors yet) to explore new subject areas. And even if you think you *do* know what you want to major in, you should still take courses in other departments because it's so important to be well rounded nowadays. Freshman year is a great time to take classes in different departments so you can dabble and find what you don't like or do like. Many times, one class can completely change your career path.

Also for those who come from a family of doctors or engineers, I would urge you to not feel pressured to follow the paths of your parents and older generations. Of course, if you are passionate about science or math or whatever it is, then go for it. But don't feel inclined to be a biology major or pre-med *simply* because that's what your parents want you to do. And if you're thinking, Well, those are the majors that will lead me to a job that will pay the best, then rethink what you value.

You might not be able to think so far ahead or in a different kind of mind-set right now, but trust me when I say later on in life, doing what makes you happy will be worth much more than the money you make. This is something I've come to terms with myself (especially since I am a journalism major) through talking to and observing others who have more experience than I do in life.

In college it is very easy to get caught up in exams and extracurriculars. But it is important to stop every now and then, to just clear your mind of the stresses you have and think about the bigger picture. Ask yourself: Where are you in life? What outcomes are you looking for? Why are you doing what you are doing? Is this what you want or is it making you happy? Are you satisfied? Afterward, adjust your direction if needed. Otherwise, keep doing what you're doing and improve how you're doing it when needed.

Is there anything else you would want to share?

CAREER CHOICES

From the beginning of my college career, I understood the importance of internships. They're becoming even more important now, as more and more people have them, making it harder for potential employers to pick out the most competitive job candidates. With this in mind, I tackled four summer internships in three summers, with KQED, CBS News, NBC News, and ABC News, in San Francisco, Los Angeles, and Washington, DC. I wanted to explore my options at different companies and also in different cities. I know these internships are what made me one of the most competitive students in my graduating class at one of the best journalism schools in the nation.

What helped me land all these internships is this very important skill called networking. Yes, it may be "fake" in some respects, but I see networking as an opportunity to practice your people skills and step out of your comfort zone. I know I am not a natural at making small talk with strangers. The first step was forcing myself to register for and attend these events. There's no way to make it easier if these events are not cut out for you. You just have to do it. Then you'll learn to find the right balance between being aggressive and giving enough space, and most important, how to be memorable. I gathered a lot of advice and help by talking to professors, career counselors, and industry leaders themselves. Don't be afraid to ask questions.

By the end of my college career, I was grateful to have been presented with three options for post-graduation plans. One was the famous J-School, or the journalism school, at Columbia University. The other was with CBS News in Washington DC, and lastly, NBC News headquarters in New York. While several relatives and friends urged me to go to graduate school, my peers, professors, past coworkers, and supervisors told me to jump into the workforce. Both sides had their very persuasive and compelling reasons, and it was very hard to decline any of the aforementioned offers, but in the end I chose NBC News.

It is with much questioning, research, and thought that I came to this decision. In the field of journalism, employers value practical experience much more highly than graduate education. I had also spoken with the career counselor at Columbia, who told me that honestly, after the one-year program at their journalism school, they would be *trying* to get me that news associate job. The NBC News Associates Program is something I knew I wanted to be part of since my sophomore year in college. It is extremely selective (only 6 were chosen out of 2,000 applicants) and a fast track for anyone who wants to become a producer. I could not refuse this unique opportunity.

I knew I would not be where I am today without the talented faculty and staff at Northwestern, the supervisors and mentors at my summer internships, and the Northwestern News Network—the one extracurricular I devoted so much time to that was in line with what I wanted to do, which was news producing. I learned that it is more valuable to be able to do one single thing very well than to do ten different things all at a mediocre level. Take some time to explore and find where your passion lies. Then go full-force at achieving your goals and dreams.

A perfectly imperfect takeaway on Sally:

Sally's life is and always will be one of learning and exploration. She hopes to bring truth to stories while taking on her new job as a news associate at NBC News. For her, sharing the voices of those around her, and seeing the fruits of her labor affect her community in positive ways is what keeps her going. Sally believes in living life with no regrets by making the best of even the worst situations.

18

Tim Hwang

Government Innovator

AB in Public Policy, Class of 2014, Princeton University
MBA on leave, Harvard Business School

Tim Hwang caught the entrepreneurial bug early on. Right before high school, Tim founded the charity Operation Fly, Inc. for which he was subsequently given the Ernst & Young Youth Entrepreneur of the Year Award. He was one of the first field organizers for President Obama's 2008 campaign. Later, as a high school senior, he was elected as a member of the Montgomery County Public Schools Board of Education in Maryland, pushing data-based decision-making to analyze education in a large urban district with a budget of over $4 billion for 150,000 students. As part of the local government, he officiated his own high school graduation ceremony for his class.

While at Princeton, Tim founded and served as president of the 750,000-member National Youth Association (NYA), pushing the agenda of young Americans in health care, education, and energy. Continuing his entrepreneurial passion today, Tim serves as founder and CEO of Fiscal-Note, which provides online analytics solutions that help organizational clients concerned with government actions make better political predic-

235

tions and business decisions. FiscalNote is backed by over $11 million of venture capital from powerhouse investors like NEA and First Round Capital, both major VC firms, as well as Jerry Yang, Taizo Son, Mark Cuban, and Steve Case, who are all on the Forbes list of billionaires.

Entrepreneurship is a very self-directed path and it forces you to constantly challenge yourself. It may be difficult, but it beats being a cog in a larger system.

—Tim Hwang

Tim Hwang was born in Lansing, Michigan, to two immigrants from South Korea: a biophysicist and an art curator. From a very early stage, he was taught to be independent and to value continuous learning in his personal, academic, and professional life. He progressively picked up and leveraged knowledge and skills in places that his parents would not even have imagined.

Back in fourth grade as a nine-year-old, Tim became enthralled with the political process. It was the election of 2000—one of the closest elections in American history—and he was pulled into the world of pundits, candidates, and elections. This enthusiasm eventually reared its head as he delved into the election of 2008, working for presidential candidate Barack Obama.

Years later, as a high school senior, he reflected on the experience via a college app essay entitled "How Did You Get Caught?"

I stared straight into the barrel of a shotgun in the middle of *nowhere*, Virginia. He cocked it once. "Get off my property," he breathed heavily. I had been caught red-handed with forbidden items. I put my hands in the air, backed slowly off of his porch, and began running for my life as I dropped my clipboard with a list full of addresses, a script, and a handful of Obama '08 pamphlets. I had heard of people being chased by dogs and old ladies, but never had I heard of a man bringing out a shotgun.

Sprinting from the ramshackle Virginian home, I began to question the whole process. I had recruited hundreds of students to knock on a 11,000 doors, driven for five hours every weekend to campaign for a man who many thought had no chance, put countless hours into developing the plans for this weekend; and yet I found myself running from a delusional voter.

How did I ever get into this in the first place? On the car-ride back, I passed by an elementary school, and thought about what the current students must be thinking. *How would they process this historic election?*

* * *

In third grade, our Social Studies teacher handed our class a blank map of the United States. Our assignment was to color each of the states won by the Presidential candidates—Blue for Gore and Red for Bush. I desperately wanted Al Gore to win, not because I genuinely believed in him or his "lock box," but because I wanted to plaster my map with blue, my favorite color.

Eventually, November 7th stumbled its way around, and I forced my parents to the poll booth through my incessant nine-year-old nagging. Having checked off all the "blue" candidates in their sample election ballots, I made sure they voted Democrat and proudly wore an "I Voted" sticker as I, confident that I had made a difference that day, dutifully marched out of the precinct.

That night was a political firestorm. "The closest election in American history" they called it. The real nail-biter came around 11 PM. The entire West Coast was called for Al Gore, and I watched as the pundits scrutinized the election. Using my erasable red and blue colored pencils I sat comfortably in front of the television in my parents' bedroom watching the results. I colored in blue for Florida. Suddenly, I stopped—my pattern of coloring had been broken. *Was it Red?* I erased it and filled in red. *Blue?* I stayed up all night waiting for the results to be announced all the while listening to the pundits analyze the results in Florida, ending with a Supreme Court battle.

Driven by colorful maps of red and blue and the horse-race politics of the election, I was eventually sucked into a world of speeches, pundits, and pollsters. The Electoral College math game became one of my favorite pastimes every four years. Today, when I turn on the news, and hear the names of states, a number comes to mind. "California has recently..." the first thing that pops into my head is the number 55. "Pennsylvania Senator Arlen..." 21. "Ohio has recently passed..." 20. "Florida voters..." 27.

* * *

Chuckling to myself, I waited anxiously at a Marriott Hotel in Bethesda on November 4th, 2008 as I recollected that night. State Senators paced back and forth, occasionally chatting with community organizers. The local reporters had their calculators out, as they madly scribbled down notes and calculations. The state delegates' young toddlers broke the tense atmosphere by running around, oblivious of the historic election. Promptly at 11 PM, CNN announced breaking news. Every eye turned toward the projector. Wolf Blitzer came on and announced, "The polls on the West Coast have now closed and CNN is now ready to project the 44th President of the United States..."

Fast-forward several years after his initial exposure to the political process. As a fourteen-year-old high school rising freshman, Tim had already started and was relentlessly running a nonprofit organization, Operation Fly. His NGO's mission was to organize students to make positive changes in the inner city. Passionate about social-justice issues after a trip to Guatemala, he quickly gained notoriety as Operation Fly grew to service cities around the nation from DC to Los Angeles. On his college apps, he wrote about this intellectual experience that inspired him:

We were at an impasse. The Board of Directors met in a glass-enclosed room of the public library. With my hands showing more emotion than my face, I took care to control the tone of my voice as I pleaded my case: *Now is not the time to be waiting around. Now is the time for action!* Bystanders curiously looked in to see a fanatical fourteen-year-old on his feet, flailing his arms and yelping about budgets, strategic plans, and service populations. An old man in the next room even banged on the wall to remind me that my voice carried into the next room. Yet, the faces of the board members remained stoic, unmoved by my vehement argument. Cognizant of my imminent loss, I proposed that the Board take a break.

* * *

Feelings of dread and anxiousness raced through my mind as I sat frustrated in a public library the summer before freshman year. The goal was simple: organize students to make an impact in the inner city. In the past months, students had come to me asking how they could become involved in our weekly visits down to the homeless. Yet financial and legal problems stood in the way of expansion and progress.

With no money for an accountant or a lawyer, I sat in a room surrounded by books on accounting, fundraising, marketing, public relations, taxes, and project management. I saw it like a puzzle. The organization had people, it had the energy, and it had the drive, yet it was still flailing. Something was wrong. Something was missing. And the question I had to answer was: how could I make all the pieces fit together? Only through studying would that question be answered. And surprisingly, starting Operation Fly, Inc. required more studying than any class that I'd ever taken.

Unlike most founders of non-profits, I spent months in a library doing research on simply how to start and run an organization. With a laptop in hand, I poured over sample corporate governance documents as I furiously typed up bylaws, employee policies and procedures, applications, articles of incorporation, tax documents, a strategic plan, and program proposals. Interestingly, I found myself with an increasingly diversified list of books around me: books on finance, biology, history, statistics, sociology, etc. Slowly, my perspective began to broaden and I began to see the whole picture.

As I continued with my research, my quest for real social entrepreneurship was not limited to laws and numbers anymore; but it was about the whole world—about the real world of inner-city poverty meeting the academic world of books and references. And I desperately wanted to crack the puzzle to help those who needed it most. To this day, I have yet to crack it. But as Operation Fly continues to grow and change, I've learned that the value of the puzzle isn't in the solution, but in the process it takes to get there.

* * *

I snapped back from my reminiscing as Board members—unfazed—began to trickle back into the room. Once seated, I lunged again, "So, let's get down to business."

Campaigning for Obama turned out to be good practice for Tim, as he was elected to be on the Montgomery County Public Schools Board of Education while still a senior in high school. He wanted to contribute politically by representing the students' voice to the local government and help influence policy. Running in 2009 for a spot on the tenth largest school district in the country wasn't easy, given the budget challenges and hard political battles ahead. Nevertheless, he wasn't afraid to take on the hard challenges ranging from curriculum reform to pension battles. He tirelessly ran his own campaign—and won.

Students scurried around the studio looking for a place to sit as the operators shifted the cameras for the perfect angle. It would be a straight shot with no edits, no redos, and absolutely no mistakes—thirty minutes of raw footage to be broadcast to 80,000 students, 22,000 employees, and 1 million taxpayers.

All the while, my opponent and I sat in the pre-taping conference room eyeing each other in awkward silence as we waited for the moderator to enter the room. The questions for the debate had been kept under lock and key for several months, and I fidgeted with my tie as I racked my mind for known answers to unknown questions. In just three months, all secondary school students in Montgomery County would be casting a vote for their next Student Member of the Board of Education (SMOB).

My opponent and I both winced as the current SMOB entered the room. With a calm and poise that neither of us could muster, she handed us a sheet.

"Five minutes, you guys," she stated as my eyes furiously dissected the paper for places where I could inject my stump speech. To my horror, the paper contained over 100 questions. This debate would be completely spontaneous.

"Makeup!" shouted the crew. "His nose is glowing!" Slowly the lights began to rise and the room became very hot, very fast. As a bead of trepidation began making its way down my back, the crewman turned on the teleprompter and counted down.

"Three . . . two . . ."

* * *

After making some last campaign stops up-county, I drove down to the county seat. Every mile that I drove, I could feel my tired heart beating faster. With sweaty palms, I greeted the Board of Elections staffers both disgusted by the amount of perspiration I had transferred yet excited to see one of the candidates. Looking up, I stared at the gray sky—an omen, perhaps—and waited nervously outside in the drizzling rain as the votes were being tabulated by the GEMS electronic system. One by one, each of the sixty-three secondary schools came to drop off their Diebold machines and certify the election.

For months, I had campaigned my heart out, visiting close to forty different schools during the day, observing public education firsthand, and talking with tens of thousands of students, employees, parent-teacher-student associations, union leaders, administrators, and community organizers. Campaigning was grueling, it was painful, and it was stressful. I had subjected myself to constant emotional and physical stress. Nevertheless, it was fun.

But what was I signing up for? The SMOB would not only have the responsibility of representing and communicating with the students; he or she would be a full-time voting board member who had to understand the intricacies of government. Interestingly, just prior to the election, when not pressing politicians on certain bills, I was training Obama campaign volunteers on the nuances of cold calling someone and downing takeout food because Mom's cooking was a luxury. My "school day" extended to fourteen hours during Get-Out-The-Vote (GOTV) weeks. It seemed as if I had been preparing my entire life.

At 6:55 p.m., staffers ushered us into the back room, where the elections administrator was waiting for us. Folded simply in half so that the results wouldn't show, the verdict was handed to us:

Election Summary Report
Official Ballot—April 29, 2009
Summary For Jurisdiction Wide, All Counters, All Races
Tim Hwang   35654   56.49%

In high school, Tim not only excelled in the professional and extracurricular realms but also went out of his way to try to achieve as much as he could during his academic career. In his junior and senior years, he prepared for and took twenty-three AP exams, nabbing him the top slot as AP State Scholar, awarded to one male and one female each year for holding the record for the most number of AP exams taken.

I joke with Tim, "You are in trouble, young man. How could you have gotten one 4, and not all 5s in your twenty-three AP exams?" He achieved a score of 5 on twenty-two of them, and a 4 on only one. My inner voice asks me jokingly, Would someone please hack into his brain and tell me, or write me an essay, on how it works?!

It was no surprise that during Tim's college application and admissions process, he had no trouble finding acceptances into virtually every school that he applied to. Ultimately, he chose Princeton for its generous financial aid package as well as the breadth of exposure to public policy at the undergraduate level at the Woodrow Wilson School.

Tim graduated from Princeton this year. I've asked him to reflect on the following:

To what extent did your college experience meet your expectations? In what ways did your experience cause you to change your perspective on your academic career, your dreams and aspirations, and your life?

HOW CONVERSING AND INTERACTING WITH PEERS CAN INFLUENCE CAREER DIRECTION

After my intensive, immersive political experiences in high school, I went into college expecting to become a lawyer. Why? It seemed like the natural transition to study policy then go on to law school to work in government after my education. Probably halfway into my freshman year, I became more involved with the entrepreneurial community on campus, especially after my experience a few years back with Operation Fly, which I found fascinating. Through conversations with my peers, it became apparent fairly quickly that I enjoyed law, but I was disinterested in ending up practicing it. I had simply been following the same path that everyone else was on, but my true calling was entrepreneurship.

I ended up starting my first company, Articulance, which provided data analytics for small businesses, after college freshman year and from then on, I became more heavily involved in the technology space, realizing that I could potentially have a broader influence in that space. My horizons expanded out from government to opportunities that I never imagined I would be working in: artificial intelligence, data science, genomics, and so on. While I was still interested in government and policy, I began to realize that the people I most looked up to were Thomas Edison, Andrew Carnegie, and Steve Jobs more so than any politician.

Looking back, I believe that college probably provided me two things (neither of which, ironically, were linked to academics). The first thing Princeton does is to place you into an environment of incredibly high-achieving and like-minded peers. Academics, while important, are probably secondary to meeting your classmates, because most of your learning is done not in the classroom but in the everyday conversations and meetings in dining halls and clubs. These interactions do more to shape your dreams and aspirations as well as your thought process than any class. In this respect, college exceeded all expectations.

Consequently, the second thing about college is the wealth of opportunities for you to explore and then to focus down on career interest and direction. Conversations and interactions with peers and others in combination with studies in academic areas of interest absolutely help in the process of career direction decision-making.

Given what you know now, if you could redo high school, what would you do differently, and why?

242

SAY NO TO UNIMPORTANT OPPORTUNITIES, MANAGE TIME WELL, BUT EXPLORE

There are probably two lessons I wish I had learned in high school. The first runs counter to what most high school students are told. Your default should be to say no to most opportunities. Between classes, extracurricular activities, standardized tests, and family and friends, high school was an incredibly stressful time for me. I enjoy stress—the pressure of working on something under a deadline—but the stress that I took on in high school was completely unnecessary and could have been avoided by saying no to a lot of opportunities that at the end of the day added nothing to my personal development or even to college admissions.

Sleep deprivation and a lack of health consciousness eventually led to negative repercussions later, which could definitely have been avoided. High school should be an opportunity to streamline activities and find the focus you need to be successful in the future. The worst thing for finding your passion is to spread yourself so thin that it becomes too hard to reflect, develop as a person, and find your niche.

As a result, time management becomes incredibly important—not only on a day-to-day basis, but in terms of a weekly and monthly basis. As you grow older, this is probably the most important lesson that people learn: time is the one resource that you can never get back. Regardless of how much money you have or how successful you become in the future, you will never be able to turn back the clock and fit more than twenty-four hours into your day. This can serve as both a powerful motivator (Think about it! Everyone on Earth from world leaders to you have the same twenty-four hours in the day) as well as an incredibly limiting constraint. Ultimately, in this context, it doesn't make sense to continue doing activities and taking opportunities that you have no interest in.

Secondly, take some time to do things outside of your "focus" and comfort zone. I realize that this may also run fairly counter to what students are told these days in terms of finding focus in college applications, but you may be missing out on something that you could really enjoy. For me, I was so involved in policy and politics that I never explored the idea of being involved in anything else. Now, running a tech company, I wish I had done more to go outside of my comfort zone and find those potential opportunities that I may not have noticed before, such as learning to develop more of my computer science or mathematics skills that are so crucial to my work every day.

What else would you like to share with or suggest to high school students and college students, and why?

DECIDE WHAT YOU WANT, ASK THE RIGHT QUESTIONS, AND POWER THROUGH OBSTACLES

The biggest lesson I learned from a very early age was that all systems and processes are arbitrary and malleable. I found myself constantly asking people: "Why should I be doing this?" "Who decided this should be this way?"

Before I entered high school, I felt that I wasn't being challenged academically in mathematics or English, so over the summer I promptly enrolled in two semesters of relatively advanced mathematics and freshman English to accelerate my learning. In addition to enrolling in sophomore English and pre-calculus (for eventual enrollment in AP Calculus BC sophomore year) as a freshman, I decided to try out three AP courses. Consequently, during the first week of high school, my administrator flagged me to come into her office and raised skepticism about my schedule and told me to drop two of the AP courses and consider re-enrolling on the normal track. "But why?" I asked. "Who decided this system?" These practices can be fairly arbitrary and I found myself frustrated with the system.

In the end, despite fighting with my administrator, I was forced to drop two of the AP courses. But not to be defeated, I ended up self-studying for the AP exams at the end of the year. From then on, I realized that even large academic systems could be worked around given enough determination and will. I went on to take twenty-three AP exams by the end of my junior year and enrolling full-time at the local university my senior year, while, ironically, serving on the Board of Education.

Today, I think this type of don't-take-no-for-an-answer and resourceful mentality has served me fairly well. In fourth grade, I remember having to do a project where we were to present what we wanted to be when we grew up to the rest of the class. The range was astounding: astronaut, racecar driver, chef, ballerina, and so forth. But somewhere along the line, our top achievers are told to be accountants, bankers, and consultants, and I end up asking myself, "What happened?" These seemingly arbitrary standards of achievement and prestige set by society herd an entire generation of achievers into careers that have nothing to do with their dreams. This is probably why I was attracted to politics from an early age—because it was fundamentally an opportunity to change the system and allow people to achieve everything they wanted to.

Interestingly, I often get asked if I'd always thought about running a tech company at the age of twenty-one. Of course not! But then again, who decided I shouldn't be? Who decided that you have to work at Goldman Sachs or McKinsey or Google for two years and go to graduate school before you run a business? If you're passionate about something and have a deep-seated ambition or motivation to get it done, no set of arbitrary systems should get in your way (as long as it's not illegal!).

FROM POLITICAL PUBLIC SERVANT TO PROBLEM-SOLVING TECH ENTREPRENEUR

Ever since I was a child, I've had a propensity to read a large amount of science fiction. However, unlike most of my peers, I never viewed science fiction as fantasy; rather, it was a future that simply had not been realized yet. I was drawn to the sheer grandiosity and ambition in the idea that the human race could radically transform our planet through concepts like geoengineering or craft new forms of transportation such as flying cars.

As I grew older, my interest in science fiction never ceased, but it illuminated a different approach than simply becoming an engineer. I became more acutely aware of the obstacles to the advancement of these innovations and what was holding back society from turning science fiction into reality. What had started out as a fascination for science fiction evolved into a fascination with what could make it possible. I began to view my purpose in life as helping entrepreneurs transform our world by providing the skills and environment they needed for success. I realized that societal constraints such as poverty, lack of high-quality education, and access to health care were tremendously large impediments to people unlocking their dreams and perhaps we could turn government into a resource to make dreams come true.

For almost a decade, from middle school through college sophomore year, I threw myself into the world of politics. Every day, I worked with a sense of purpose, beginning with volunteering for the attorney general's campaign, working my way up to become one of the youngest field organizers in the Obama presidential campaign, serving as a school board member in one of America's largest urban school districts, and eventually leading a national policy organization. I was drawn to the idea that our work could unlock the hidden potential of millions of people around the country.

Yet as I delved deeper and deeper into the world of government, I began to realize the sheer amount of inefficiencies that were inherent in the system. While immersing myself in public service, I slowly began to get involved in entrepreneurship. In high school, my first venture, Operation Fly, implemented a more effective way to deliver social services to those in the inner city. Early in college, I started Articulance to explore data analytics for small businesses. Through both of these experiences, I was able to learn the power of entrepreneurship in influencing a social outcome.

Through my college sophomore and junior years, I was conflicted on where to commit to moving forward. Public service seemed like a natural calling, yet my limited exposure to entrepreneurship, particularly in the tech industry, had shown me that the world was moving at a faster pace and unlocking dreams faster than the government was. Ultimately, I had developed an entrepreneurial spirit with an interest in one of the most conservative industries.

By the time I reached my senior year of college, my entrepreneurial self urged me to start another company. At the time, I was commuting from Princeton to DC, serving as president of the National Youth Association (NYA), a large grassroots organization, and then I stumbled upon an idea. I was having trouble understanding what exactly was going on with governmental actions and decisions and all the complex data and interconnected reasons that had influenced them around the country. I quickly realized that there was a market for a faster and more user-friendly governance, risk, and compliance (GRC) platform that could be leveraged and used within organizations like the NYA, but also major corporations around the world.

I decided to go to Silicon Valley, which abounds in resources for technology businesses, including venture capital firms and angel groups, to start a company for this undertapped large market. Through purposeful discussions with many, I was blessed to quickly attract the attention of major investors, including elite VC firm NEA and Yahoo!'s co-founder and former CEO Jerry Yang, who decided to back the twenty-one-year-old me in my technology venture, FiscalNote. Since then, FiscalNote has grown to service everyone from Fortune 500s to national nonprofit organizations.

FiscalNote is my attempt to transform government data into actionable real-time business intelligence, essentially creating a Bloomberg terminal for Washington that shines light on the inefficiencies of government. My hope is to harness my entrepreneurial "itch" to solve a problem that I truly care about. As the company has grown, I have become more certain of the fact that my role is not as much to be an enabler of entrepreneurs and but rather to be an entrepreneur myself—that I can be the one to build the products that I have dreamed of.

A perfectly imperfect takeaway about Tim:

Determination and passion are the drivers of great entrepreneurs, politicians, and leaders. Tim indeed has an A+ combination of head, heart, spirit, and network that is already making him a beloved and creative leader and entrepreneur running a well-backed and inspired company and team, FiscalNote—the first in his serial entrepreneurship aspirations and continuum. Entrepreneurial people abound, but the reality is that only a fraction succeeds, given how difficult building a start-up is. It is clear that from an early age Tim wanted to make a splash on the world stage and hopefully he is on his way to achieve his goal. I sense that Tim, now a twenty-two-year-old, is a billionaire in the making.

19

Timothy Lee

Unconventional Engineer

BS in Mechanical Engineering, Class of 2013,
University of California, Berkeley
MS in Mechanical Engineering, Class of 2014,
University of California, Berkeley
PhD in Bioengineering, Class of 2019,
Georgia Institute of Technology

A Bay Area native, Tim started his college career as your normal aspiring engineer. During his college sophomore year, he decided to do something different and co-founded a hardware start-up, VIRES Aeronautics. The thrill of doing something innovative and new captivated him. Well versed in both the theory and pragmatics of engineering, Tim enjoys working on new and exciting projects such as developing a smart, water-consumption-monitoring showerhead or a more efficient cookstove for Third World nations. Outside of his work, Tim is an active member and leader of his student Christian organization.

Having worked in industry through various internships and externships (most recently with Boeing), Tim has decided to continue his academic career instead. In fall 2014, he has begun attending the Georgia

Institute of Technology to obtain a PhD in bioengineering. Through engineering innovation, Tim endeavors to improve the human standard of living and become an ambassador for science and technology to those around him and the world at large.

Lead your life with a passion tempered by compassion, pragmatism, and planning. Be open to new opportunities, even if they make you uncomfortable or uneasy.

—Timothy Lee

Given high expectations from parents since childhood, Timothy Lee built a habit of being methodical and meticulous in both thought and action early on.

I like to think of myself as a product of high expectations and hard work. Let's concretize what I mean by "high expectations." As an Asian American, good grades were expected. I love school, so grades weren't a problem. Rather, the high expectations I'm talking about are the subtle things in life that my middle-class parents expected and demanded perfection in.

When setting the dinner table, I had to fold the square napkins neatly into a triangle and place them under each pair of chopsticks. When washing dishes, there was a certain methodology in stacking bowls and cups on the drying rack. When eating dim sum, I had to pour tea in a certain way. The list goes on.

It's one thing to know how to use an equation that you've memorized and a completely different thing to know how to derive an equation from first principles. Know where you are "derived" from—know who you are and what drives you. Talk to your parents; hear their stories too so that you know how their stories have shaped yours.

Intellectually curious, Tim started developing a strong interest in engineering since middle school. One of his two UC application personal essays discussed this during the college app season in his high school senior year:

UC personal statement prompt #1: Describe the world you come from—for example, your family, community or school—and tell us how your world has shaped your dreams and aspirations.

"Hello class, my name is Andrew Critch. If you Google me, please click the second link unless you want to see a vulgar definition of 'critch.' Now let's move into multivariable calculus."

In the summer of 2009, I applied for a multivariable calculus course at UC Berkeley and, along with a select group of high school students, had the opportunity to participate with college undergraduates in an advanced math class. Knowing I would ultimately pursue a career in engineering, and having exhausted all possible high school math courses a year prior to graduation, I decided to challenge myself over the summer. Why not?

Studying multivariable calculus allowed me to gain a better understanding of the relation between theoretical math and concrete applications. After just a few days, implicit equations and R-3 graphs were buzzing around my head. Everywhere I went, objects became equations and movements became vector fields. Walking down Telegraph Avenue after class, for example, the simple shape of a heart painted on a gay rights sign held the following shape for me: $(x^2+y^2-1)^3-x^2y^3 = 0$. Passing a shirtless, unkempt-looking homeless man, I noticed a tattoo of planet Earth on his back. I immediately thought: "spherical change of coordinates from R3 to R2" (the mathematical translation of a 3D sphere onto a 2D surface). In short, my math intuitions were getting a little "critchy."

Taking this class not only expanded my involvement in math; it also altered my limited perception of the world. This experience has allowed me to see beyond the "bubble" that I knew as Pleasanton, an affluent mid-sized city in N. California, where I've lived my entire life. Emigrating from China during the 1980s, my parents specifically chose Pleasanton, with its outstanding school system, as the setting for my childhood. Protecting me from their life struggles, my parents felt that school should be my first priority.

Yet growing up sheltered was not a complete impediment to my growth. As a child, I was able to use my ample free time to hone my engineering passion. I tinkered with Legos, building cars, boats, airplanes, miniature cities, etc. Transitioning into my adolescence, I began making robots that could climb stairs, draw pictures, or mimic a human arm. Little did I know then that I was already applying concepts I would later become acquainted with on a much more precise and conceptual level. Now, when I invent and build things, I am consciously aware of the math that underpins my creations.

Learning about multivariable calculus has better equipped me to pursue my aspirations in high-level mechanical engineering, specifically robotics. Whether I stick with applications, or pursue more theoretical involvement, I am now ready to pursue the full range of intellectual and practical aspects of the engineering field.

Tim was especially passionate about robotics:

UC prompt #2: Tell us about a personal quality, talent, accomplishment, contribution or experience that is important to you. What about this quality or accomplishment makes you proud and how does it relate to the person you are?

This book really sucks.

Mrs. Melvin, my seventh-grade teacher, announces the title of the mysterious book she is holding, which is covered in suction cups. As it turns out, the book is really about vacuums, suction cups, and all things that "suck." Mrs. Melvin next assigns the class a month-long project. We are to create a book about something we have a passion for.

And so, as a tribute to my passion, *This Book is Really Robotic* came to be, complete with original hand-drawn sketches of humanoids replicating bartenders and house cleaners. Upon writing this book, my passion for robotics intensified. Reading about humanoids from Honda named Asimo, a robot that can mimic various human actions, or the Roomba, a vacuum-bot, really opened my eyes to new ideas. I began building my own robots independently out of Legos to sweep hardwood floors or count coins, and worked with my middle school robotics coach, Mr. Jensen, who led our team in state-level First Lego League Competitions.

Since there weren't any robotics opportunities at my high school, I competed independently in regional robotics contests. Later, I founded my own robotics team and entered the VEX Robotics league. VEX Robotics is a worldwide, cost-friendly robotics league that challenges students to compete. That year, teams were required to build a robot that would pick up three-inch cubes and place them into triangular prism goals. I soon recruited five passionate people onto the team, and we began brainstorming for the competition. At first, after bouncing ideas off one another, we did not come up with much. We were far from the world-class team we wanted to become.

My epiphany came while riding the escalator at the mall one day. *Aha! I can use an escalator to lift blocks into the goals!* Our first design derived from this idea—the concept of using a tread intake system that lifts cubes via conveyor belts. The robot we built, The Diesel, mimicked the human arm complete with elbow and wrist, mobilized by a dual tread intake system that utilized two side-by-side conveyor belts. Because of its unique design, The Diesel picked up cubes more easily and faster than other teams' robots.

Determined to go to the World Championships, we paved our way through SiaTech Regional Competition, held in San Jose, and ultimately, made it to Dallas, Texas, where we competed with teams from countries all over the world such as China, New Zealand, and Brazil. Advancing to the quarterfinals, we ranked thirtieth among 500 teams internationally. This year, I expanded my school's program to include three additional teams to compete in this year's competition, "Clean Sweep."

Had I not participated in robotics, I would not be the person I am today. Robotics has taught me to look at life holistically. For example, the concept of "gracious professionalism," or the practice of helping other teams, has taught me to see life not as a competition, but more as a cooperative, symbiotic system. And forming my own robotics team has shaped me into a leader. Exercising innovation on a daily basis, honing my problem-solving skills, taking risks, and being creative are all aspects of being a successful robotics team leader. One day, I hope to use these skills to lead people in solving world problems.

As a high school junior, Tim was taking university-level mathematics along with his other AP courses. He became the president of the Science Olympiad team and created his own robotics club—leading his robotics team to the World Championship and furthering his interest for math and science. Upon graduating high school, Tim was awarded the departmental award for mathematics.

After applying to college, Tim was admitted to a number of top universities, including Carnegie Mellon University, UC Berkeley College of Engineering, and UCLA. He chose UC Berkeley ("Cal") because of its strong reputation and high quality in engineering education. MIT, UC Berkeley, and Stanford are widely perceived worldwide as the top three research universities in engineering.

Today, Tim tells me that he continues to be passionate about robotics. He has obtained both BS and MS degrees from Cal in four years and has begun pursuing a PhD in bioengineering at Georgia Tech. I've asked him to reflect on the following question:

To what extent did your college experience—on and off campus—meet your expectations? In what ways did your experience cause you to change your perspective on your academic career, your dreams and aspirations, and your life?

When I went to college, I was under the impression that I would go to school, finish my bachelor's, maybe get a master's, and be on my way to get that perfect, high-paying job. There's nothing wrong with that aspiration, but the time I spent in college changed my aspirations. My interest from the outset was mechanical engineering; but, what I would do with that knowledge has. A few key experiences have shaped my college experience and thus have altered and molded my dreams and aspirations.

INTERNSHIPS ARE IMPORTANT

They're incredibly competitive to get, but well worth the experience if you are selected to be an intern. In the summer of 2012, I traveled to Seattle, Washington, to work at the Boeing Company. I worked as a manufacturing engineer, which, in a nutshell, meant that I wrote the instruction manual on how to build a plane. But other than the technical knowledge I gained over the course of three months, here's what I learned about *myself*:

1. I like my independence and thrive on it. I had my own projects to do and when I didn't, I just made some up for myself.

2. I love talking to people. I don't like sitting in front of a computer screen for too long. As a result, I would get up, walk around, talk to other engineers, talk to mechanics, talk to chemists, and to whomever else was willing to chat.

3. I like having my own schedule. I was working "manufacturing hours," which translates into each workday from six a.m. to three p.m. (sometimes even earlier). It was nice to have well-defined hours, but I know I like to make my own schedule.

Now, if you don't get an internship, look for research opportunities, volunteer, or do what's called an externship (which is a shorter version of an internship). All of these experiences will help shape your interests and future career goals, and will help you learn about yourself.

GET TO KNOW YOUR PROFESSORS

I'm a bit odd in that I like talking to professors—not only about their expertise but also about their life experiences, their interests, and their stories. You could say, perhaps, I'm a bit nosy. Nonetheless, get to know your professors. More than one professor has influenced my life goals—and I use the word "life" in full generality, as opposed to career goals.

One of my most vivid undergraduate memories is a casual interaction with a professor. I was sitting outside my classroom, waiting for the lecture to begin. I got there early, so the previous class had not yet exited the room. My professor had arrived a bit early as well. As he walked toward the room, he glanced at me and waved hello. Beyond that, he walked over to me and started a conversation with me. I was still a freshman at that point, so I was completely shocked. Never before (nor ever after) had a professor started a conversation with me—it has always been the opposite.

This professor would become a close mentor of mine—the go-to professor whenever I wanted advice—and the professor with whom I wanted to take all my classes. It helps that he's a brilliant instructor. Moreover, he's written two letters of recommendation for me!

I know I'm still young, and I have yet to see the world, but here's some of what I've figured out from my college experiences:

1. People are important, so invest in the people around you! Opportunities come and go, but relationships take time to build, so starting building them early.

2. If you want to do something, try it out. Go for it. If you want to work a specific job, do a test-run first to see if your expectations are in line with reality. The process of passionately pursuing something involves a sanity check: making sure that your aspirations match reality.

Given what you know now, if you could redo high school, what would you do differently, and why?

DO SOMETHING UNCOMFORTABLE

In my senior year of high school, I joined a competitive civics course known as "We the People." The format of the course revolved around formulating and presenting mock-congressional hearings based on a set list of questions, ranging from political philosophy to current events. The course required regular public speaking—something I was not very comfortable with at the time. But through the experience, I came to love it! I was able to hone my ability to speak in front of an audience; public speaking became a joy and a passion. Moreover, this skill became invaluable once I entered college. In short, students, do something uncomfortable. It'll challenge you to grow in unexpected ways.

GRADES MATTER LESS AND LESS

In high school, grades matter. As it becomes more competitive to enter universities, your GPA becomes more important. Admittedly, there are external factors taken into consideration when the Admissions Committee reads your application, but you don't want to be in the position where your application is ignored because your GPA isn't high enough.

Now, when you're in college, grades still matter—sort of. It really depends on your career goal. If your goal is to continue with higher education, then your GPA definitely matters. But if you're going into industry, your GPA may matter less. I'm not in that position—I'm going to graduate school—so grades mattered for me.

Now, once you're in graduate school, grades don't really matter. The focus is switched from academic results (in other words, what grade you get) to what you *learn*. Grad students are generally more interested in their research, so most students are awarded good grades anyway.

What else would you like to share with or suggest to high school students and college students, and why?

PRIORITIZE

At Cal, every freshman becomes inundated with flyers as he or she walks through Sproul Plaza. It takes some practice in ignoring or avoiding the persistent students who advertise their clubs. But you *will* participate in extracurricular activities; at least, I wholeheartedly encourage you to.

My freshman year, I had committed myself to the Cal Dragonboat team (a competitive canoe-esque paddling team), Model UN, Engineers with Borders, and a church group, in addition to all my coursework. It immediately became apparent that I had bitten off more than I could chew, so I had to prioritize. In the end, I stuck with the Dragonboat team and the church group.

You must prioritize among school, clubs, work, family, friends, and whatever else is in your life. College becomes a juggling act among many different activities and commitments. The earlier you learn to prioritize and multitask, the more successful you'll be during your time in university.

BE EXCEPTIONAL

Before I was even admitted to Cal, a high school teacher, Mr. Dixon, gave us a very practical homework assignment: to plan out our four years of college before we even went to college.

The early planning really helped me out: I was able to graduate in four years with a bachelor's and master's degree at a reasonable pace. But graduating early is hardly the exception today. To be an exceptional student, one needs to go far beyond what is required of them. So, here's what I did:

Graduate student instructor

During my master's program, I asked to be a graduate student instructor. It was not required of me—in fact, it wasn't allowed for my specific program—but I wanted to get some teaching experience. (I ended up loving it!) With some determination, I was able to get the position. I had to get an exception from the vice-chair of graduate studies in order to do it.

So here's the takeaway: do things that aren't required. Even if no one has done what you want to do before, there's always the exception. If someone says no, find a way around it—go to the top of the food chain until the person at the top finally turns you down.

Part-time entrepreneur

I never thought about becoming an entrepreneur, nor do I consider myself one. But the opportunity came to try it out. To see what the start-up world looked like, I went along for the ride. Now, from this experience, I learned many things that university would not teach you.

1. I learned how to pitch in front of venture capitalists. I had never done that before, and it was an invigorating experience. How to present technical information to a nontechnical audience and how to convey ideas in a very tangible and easy-to-understand way.

2. I attended networking events, the kind of events where you walk around, meet people, and exchange business cards. As a more introverted person, I learned how to compose myself throughout the night—even if I didn't want to be there. It's a soft skill but important nonetheless.

Ignoring prerequisites

You're smart. When looking at the schedule of classes, courses will have certain prerequisites. Don't let them scare you away from taking the course! If the course is being taught by an amazing professor, take it.

Now, be careful in capriciously ignoring prerequisites—they're there for a reason. But at the end of the day, you're much better off taking an interesting course with a good professor.

APPLYING TO A PHD PROGRAM

Upon finishing my master's of science at the University of California, Berkeley, I decided to go for the doctorate degree. Why did I want to go to graduate school to get a PhD? It aligns with my career goal of becoming a professor. In nearly all cases, professors hold PhDs.

I applied to four schools: UC Berkeley, Stanford, MIT, and Georgia Tech—the top four mechanical engineering schools. I applied only to schools that I would be happy to attend—no backup schools, no "reach" schools.

As I was applying, I was told many discouraging things:

"People don't like it when you finish your master's in one year."

"You don't have enough research experience."

"You *have* to go to another school now that you've done your master's at Berkeley."

Some of these statements have some truth in them, but frankly, I got tired of hearing these generalizations so often! From my experience, having a clear goal and a strong sense of implementation has allowed me to get pretty far. Don't let platitudes spoken by others define your life's direction—rather, take them with a grain of salt and make your own decisions.

Applying to PhD programs is different from applying to colleges and even master's programs. Understandably, the PhD application is much more specific. These programs typically involve you in deep and extensive research with faculty and take four to six years, so you better know what you are getting yourself into.

When you get in, it's important to visit the school before you go. The purpose of the visit is not only to gauge the school but also to find and meet the professor you want to do work with. The name of the school doesn't matter as much—it's about going to the right school to do the research you want to do with the leading expert in that field.

As a last remark, try your best to find fellowships and/or assistantships to pay for your graduate schooling. There's always a way to find money to fund your education.

UNCHARTED TERRITORY

Before I arrived in Georgia, I was inundated by e-mails from different professors, all courting me to join their lab. The e-mails came from many mechanical engineering professors, and one e-mail in particular caught my attention: "research opportunity in Precision Biosystems lab at Georgia Tech." The latter was from a bioengineering professor. The last time I had taken a course in biology was freshman year of high school—eight years ago. I knew I'd be underqualified for the position, but I interviewed with the professor anyway.

After the interview, I realized a few things:

1. I wasn't underqualified—I had important knowledge to contribute. Before the interview, I was so worried about not knowing biology that I overlooked all of my prior related experiences and studies! Admittedly, bioengineering was uncharted territory for me, but my mechanical engineering knowledge was completely applicable, if not invaluable.

2. There was always time to learn. Currently in the first semester of my doctoral studies, I am taking a "freshmen level" biology course for PhD students—the equivalent of AP Biology for high schoolers! I thought I needed to come into my PhD knowing everything—quite the opposite. You learn along the way, and frankly, I have a lot of catching up to do but am excited about the challenge.

3. I have decided to go for a PhD in bioengineering instead of mechanical engineering because of the thrill of being, learning, researching, and producing in an uncharted territory that has huge market growth potential foreseeably for decades to come.

A perfectly imperfect takeaway on Tim Lee:

As a young, aspiring engineer, Tim thought he knew the life he wanted and how to get there. But along the way he learned a thing or two. He learned from great mentors. He made uncomfortable decisions and took some time off. Most important, he didn't let convention or norms define him. Today, he has a clearer picture of his future. Tim says: "I will continue to grow and change along the way—as part of the adventure."

Act V

One to Two Years in the World and Advancing

Photo by Dan Taylor,
Heisenbergmedia.com

20

Christopher Pruijsen

Nomadic Entrepreneur

Studied toward a BA in Philosophy, Politics, and Economics,
Class of 2013 (dropout as a senior), University of Oxford

Christopher Pruijsen was the youngest-ever president of Oxford Entrepreneurs when he attended the University of Oxford, where he matriculated at age seventeen. Chris co-founded Founderbus UK in 2012 and then co-founded AMPION.org across Africa and the Middle East (formerly StartupBus Africa). AMPION organizes five-day "Venture Bus" hackathons with a focus on technology-driven social innovation, as well as a six-month fellowship program to incubate the most promising ventures by offering funding, mentorship, and access to over fifty innovation hubs.

A young serial entrepreneur, Chris currently serves as co-founder and CEO of Sterio.me, which reinforces learning with interactive and prerecorded audio lessons—accessible via any type of phone—no Internet or smartphone required. Chris is a Global Shaper of the World Economic Forum and a fellow of prestigious networks such as the Kairos Society, the Global Economic Symposium, the World Technology Network, and NEXUS.

263

Things may come to those who wait, but only things left by those who hustle. I definitely hustle.

—Christopher Pruijsen

Born in the Netherlands and raised in a very difficult family environment after his father's death, Chris Pruijsen had taught himself things one would learn from a father, and became rather resourceful, resilient, and independent early on.

When I was two and a half years old, my father was killed by another man. That single event had a huge effect on my early years, although I more recently made peace with the past.

My mother, twenty-two when I was born, was heartbroken. She struggled to keep the family afloat financially and did not have much luck with the later men in her life (until a few years ago). My father had been a truck driver, his brother a truck driver, and his father also a truck driver. My mother worked in a flower shop and later became a fitness instructor at a local gym. Not a single person in my family had attended university.

My grandfather on my mother's side was offered a scholarship to study in the 1950s but had to earn a living, as he had to take care of his family of eight siblings. Over the course of the next forty years, he worked and studied part-time until he reached a mid-level management position. He was the man I admired most in my early life, and unfortunately he passed away at the age of sixty-five before I left for university.

And it wasn't only my family background that set the odds against me from an early age. Due to a troublesome home situation, I was placed to live in a state orphanage between the ages of six and nine, and later again for half a year when I was thirteen. In the orphanages, I lived with children who came from far worse situations, including violence, abuse, and gangs.

I lived with my grandmother during my last three years of high school, which was an enormous blessing. I cannot express enough gratitude for her kindness and love.

The events that rocked my childhood made me profoundly independent as I learned early on that I could only count on myself. I was terrible at dealing with authority. I cultivated a deep sense of resilience and security. Whatever happened, I told myself that things would be all right.

In high school, Christopher was involved in Model European Parliament, Model United Nations, and European Youth Parliament sessions as both a participant and session chair on an international level. He was accepted to the European Youth Ambassadors group for his merits as a Model European Parliament chair in Rotterdam for three consecutive years. Chris was part of the leadership team of the debating society at the Erasmiaans Gymnasium, which led his school to their first national debating championship victory in years. ("Gymnasium" in the Netherlands is synonymous with the highest level of "high school" or a "classic school" for their teaching of Latin and Ancient Greek, instead of a place where one works out.)

He was also the Rotterdam ambassador for the Nederlandse Wereldwijde Studenten (NEWS), a nonprofit community of Dutch students abroad, for which he organized a citywide event to educate students about the possibilities of studying abroad in the UK, the United States, and the wider world.

When applying to UK universities, Chris submitted the following personal statement via the Universities and Colleges Admissions Service (UCAS), the British admission service for students applying to university:

Currently I am studying at the Erasmiaans Gymnasium, where I take a broad spectrum of courses. The last two years I came to realise that my interests lie in a combination of politics, history, philosophy, and economics.

My interest in debating and politics was ignited two years ago when I participated in our school's four-day European Parliament program. Since then I've participated in numerous programmes, both as a delegate and as chairman, which has helped me develop a critical mind in addition to making me think clearly about political issues.

Our school has housed several international conferences, which offered me the opportunity to discuss a lot of political issues concerning the European Union with people from different backgrounds. Additionally, I went to the 1st session of the Model United Nations of Hamburg, where I could debate world-scale issues and study the United Nations' political challenges. I would like to learn more about various political theories, their implementation, the complex workings of political institutions, and their ensuing problems.

My interest in philosophy was inspired by my teacher, whom I started taking lessons from two years ago. Since then I've been reading philosophical works in my spare time and, because I'm also apt in debating, have been participating in local philosophy debates.

The philosophers who have influenced me the most are Francis Fukuyama with his book 'The End of History and the Last Man' and Thomas More with his 'Utopia'. While Fukuyama made me see the underlying motifs and incentives of the human mind, Thomas More made me realise that even in our modern time there is a place for Utopian thinking. And additionally, his 'Utopia' is for a large part still applicable to modern society, while having been written almost five centuries ago. On the latter I am also writing my graduation essay, which is about the influence of Thomas More's 'Utopia' on Britain's 16th century politics.

And as every philosopher should be able to say; I am the end of my history of philosophy. This is because I am, and always will be, the last one to analyse and personalise philosophical theory from my perspective. I am particularly keen on learning about political, moral and ethical philosophy, as they are partially overlapping fields.

I've always had an interest in economics, originating from an early love of entrepreneurship. The last three years I've been taking Advanced Economy classes at school, as well as additional Microeconomics classes. One of the works that changed my view on economics in an almost revolutionary way was Freakonomics by Steven D. Levitt and Stephen J. Dubner. Especially the way in which they combine sociology and economics to analyse man's mind from an economic perspective intrigues me, and encourages me to use economics in altogether new ways. I am especially keen on learning how to apply complex economics on every-day life.

My proficiency in the English language stems from my foremost hobby, which is reading. About five years ago I started to read in English. My primary reason for wanting to study in the United Kingdom is that I much prefer English to my own language, and that it is becoming increasingly important in an ever-changing global market to have a profound knowledge of the English language. My secondary reasons are the culture of the United Kingdom and the experience of studying abroad.

At the moment I'm also involved in NEWS, which is an organisation for Dutch Worldwide Students. This organisation helps people from Holland to go study abroad and additionally brings Dutch students all over the world together. To this purpose meetings are held, where necessary information is supplied through workshops, and where Dutch international students can talk about their experiences. I, as an ambassador for NEWS, am active in and around Rotterdam by organising informational meetings for high school students who are interested in studying abroad.

Reflecting back, Chris tells me that the aforementioned teacher was the only philosophy teacher at school and that he was sometimes dreadfully boring, other times funny, and definitely very passionate about his subject. Chris has come to appreciate the Dutch language a lot in recent years as well. When writing his above personal essay, he was in a state of fascination about English being the global language of commerce, and he was set on moving to the UK to gain a more global perspective.

When applying to colleges and universities in the United States, recommendation letters from teachers (and if allowed by a given school, from other third parties) are one of the separate application components not included on the application form per se, and in nearly all cases is a "blind" process where the letter writers are discouraged from sharing the letter with the student requesting it. In contrast, when applying to universities in the UK, a student *must* include a recommendation letter as part of the UCAS application form. Chris's UCAS application included the following teacher recommendation letter:

Dear Sir and/or Madam,

It is with great pleasure that I recommend Christopher Pruysen, student of the Erasmiaans Gymnasium in Rotterdam. First of all because of his strong academic abilities and secondly because of his engagement in activities outside the regular school program.

Christopher's academic achievements can easily be called outstanding. He has chosen the profile "Economics and Society" (including the subjects Dutch, English, French, History, Economics, and Maths) with the three additional subjects: Ancient Greek, Philosophy and Management and Organisation. This means that Christopher has chosen two more subjects than required for an ordinary Gymnasium diploma.

In class Christopher has distinguished himself through his talent for critical questioning, his genuine interest and his overall positive attitude. He is more intelligent than average and has a particular talent for the more philosophical subjects. An example of this is that he writes his final paper (necessary for graduating) on Thomas More's Utopia and its influence on Britain's 16th century politics. Additionally, the paper will be written in English, which is also unusual and not obligatory. This indicates the English language is no problem for him.

Christopher is very active with extracurricular activities, for example debating and participating in youth parliaments. The level of his participation, both in quality and quantity, is exceptionally high and without a doubt he can be placed in the top 10 of our school (1,100 students).

Debating is something Christopher is very keen on. He showed leadership at several sessions of parliaments, MUNs and other debating sessions at which I was also present. On several occasions he was selected as chairman, a task he conducted with vigour. In his enthusiasm he can inspire his delegates to a higher level and it is of no importance to him whether the session regards a school debate, a national activity or even an international session.

To give you an impression of some of the sessions he has led or will lead as chairman:

- three times the Erasmiaans Europeesch Parlement (Erasmian European Parliament, in Dutch) -twice the Model European Parliament in Rotterdam
- twice the Erasmian European Youth Parliament (Rotterdam and Turin)

Furthermore I would also like to mention some of the sessions he participated in as a delegate:

- four times in the Model European Parliament
- three times in Model United Nations (national and international)
- once in the Erasmian European Youth Parliament

Finally I would like to point out two special activities that Christopher has taken on. He organised a conference in Rotterdam for students who are interested in studying abroad. And, to emphasize his philosophical side, he is a leading figure in regional philosophical debates.

I have known Christopher for three years now and supported him academically as his coordinator in fifth grade and as his history teacher. As I mentioned before I also accompanied him to several debating sessions and have experienced in person his extraordinary debating talents as well as his social skills regarding other students and peers. I strongly recommend him for the study Philosophy, Politics and Economics as he will be an asset to your University. Should you have any questions, please do not hesitate to contact me.

Yours sincerely,
Mr. Drs. M. van Gulik

Why did Chris choose and ask Mr. van Gulik to write a recommendation letter?

I chose Mr. Van Gulik because he was my history teacher for the latter part of my high school career, the head of the History Department, and together with one other history teacher, managed all external-facing debating events and partnerships for the school, in which I was very active in participating and contributing. I had a lot of respect for him and frequently interacted with him. He also knew me well from his history classes and the debating activities, and was well poised to make an honest recommendation. I am grateful that he did. By the way, "Pruysen," as written on Mr. Van Gulik's rec letter, is synonymous with Pruijsen in Dutch. In the past, I sometimes spelled my surname "Pruysen" instead of "Pruijsen."

In the admissions decision-making process, top UK universities tend to weigh an applicant's testing performance and interviews more heavily than top US universities do. (In addition to the academic transcript and standardized test scores, highly selective US colleges and universities weigh the quality of an applicant's extracurriculars, character, essays, and third-party recommendations as well.)

How did Chris think and work through the college/university planning, application, and admissions process? Why did he choose Oxford?

My route to the University of Oxford was relatively short. In the UK, people start to prepare for their Oxbridge (Oxford and Cambridge) applications when they begin their secondary education, if not sooner. As for me, the idea of going to Oxford came in my penultimate year in high school, when I was about fifteen years old. What led me to this idea?

I had been participating in Model European Parliament and Model United Nations conferences for over a year, at times as a chairperson or committee leader. Similarly I had been participating in philosophy debates, and with a small group of friends, I had rejuvenated the school's debating society. Soon after I became interested in studying abroad I joined the Nederlandse Wereldwijde Studenten (NEWS)—a group for Dutch citizens who study abroad. I was the youngest member, and three times a year attended events for people who were already studying at Oxford, Cambridge, the London School of Economics (LSE), and various US universities. In 2010, I organized a small conference for students who were considering studying abroad, at my school—which landed me a position as "NEWS Ambassador."

The application process is quite standard. I had to complete an English-language test (Cambridge Certificate of Proficiency in English). Then I had to sit through a two-hour exam for course entry, which functions as an initial applicant filter, after which I was required to come to Oxford (from Rotterdam) for interviews with the professors of politics, philosophy, and economics in two of its colleges (Corpus Christi and University College). A few weeks later I received a conditional offer, meaning that if I achieved high-enough grades on my final exams, I would be accepted to Oxford. The latter was the easy part. When applying to UK universities, I would advise one to tailor your personal statement to a specific course—it's your chance to demonstrate your prior interest in the field and make the professors want to teach you. So mention relevant activities, books that inspired you, and original ideas.

The debating and leadership experiences only helped me slightly in gaining the interview slots. Of course, debating had helped me articulate myself more clearly, which helped during the interviews themselves. NEWS helped me a little, as I received some advice from people who had already gained admission to Oxford. But overall Oxford puts the heaviest emphasis on academics. My test scores carried more weight than my extracurricular activities. In this regard, US and UK universities' admissions philosophies and requirements are different.

I was also admitted to the University of York to study philosophy, politics, and economics (PPE). I decided to enroll at Oxford because it offered the best PPE (triple-major) program. Oxford established the PPE program in the 1920s and other universities only followed suit from the 1980s after Oxford graduates demonstrated huge success. I chose these majors because I had been passionate about philosophy, politics, and economics. I had studied all three courses in high school and participated in a plethora of extracurricular activities in philosophy and politics, including debating competitions.

Today, at age twenty-one, Chris is a successful young entrepreneur with a heart of gold. I've asked him to reflect on the following:

To what extent did your college experience—on and off campus—meet your expectations? In what ways did your experience cause you to change your perspective on your academic career, your dreams and aspirations?

CHOOSING TO BECOME A MISSIONARY ENTREPRENEUR INSTEAD OF A WELL-PAID BANKER

My worldview today is shaped by a nomadic life in which I make positive contributions both through for-profit and nonprofit projects. The world is my canvas and my life is shaped by turning ideas into reality. That's an enormously fulfilling life—but not one I have always had. It's also not right for everyone, as the lack of structure can give you the feeling of being lost in a sea of endless possibilities. Humans are hardwired to search for patterns, structures, and guidelines, and when there are none and we have to define our own path, it can be scary.

When I was younger I was most interested in careers with predictable high returns, mainly because in my home situation I never experienced much wealth and wanted to be financially independent.

At university I received offers for internships at prestigious invest-ment-banking divisions (including Bank of America Merrill Lynch), but decided to turn them down and focus on becoming an entrepreneur. This decision was influenced by several events.

In 2011, I participated in the Global Entrepreneurship Summer School in Munich—and my team won the competition. That same year I became more involved with Oxford Entrepreneurs, the UK's largest student society for those interested in entrepreneurship. I served as the TATA Idea Idol business-pitch competition director in 2012, and later that same year I became president of the Oxford Entrepreneurs. I joined the Kairos Society in late 2011, and joined several similar networks soon after.

I realized money is a means to an end and never an end in itself, and began to dedicate myself to social change through innovation and (tech-nology driven) entrepreneurship. Solving some of the world's greatest and most endemic challenges, making a positive difference in the lives especially of those who lack a voice of their own on the global stage—these are things I am passionate about.

I then took a break from university for a year, after which, in 2013, I decided not to return. At the time I had been working on several projects, including an international conference and StartupBus Africa, so going back to university full-time would have meant losing momentum. I knew my calling was in the start-up world and that the learning and experiences I was gaining outside the classroom would prove to be invaluable. I thus became one of the few Oxford University dropout entrepreneurs.

Now, at age twenty-one, I run my own start-up Sterio.me in the mobile educational technology space. Sterio.me reinforces learning outside the classroom with prerecorded interactive voice lessons that can be accessed from any type of phone via the GSM network. The learner does not require Internet or literacy to learn, which makes learning much more accessible in the developing world. I met my co-founders Dean Rotherham and Danielle Reid on the inaugural StartupBus Africa from Harare to Cape Town, which I also co-organized. We had all been thinking about innovation in education on a personal level, and after a day of brainstorming came upon the idea that eventually became Sterio.me. Dean was an experienced self-taught entrepreneur from South Africa, having started and managed an audio-technology start-up, "Shop Beat," for seven years and having over 250 paying customers monthly. Danielle came from the international advertising industry as a creative director and had started several companies before, one of which went through the Startup Bootcamp accelerator.

I left my full-time position at a London start-up to pursue Sterio.me full-time, and it was not easy in the early days, as the telecom industry does not have a good history in working with start-ups. Also, everything takes more time on the African continent and our group was working as a distributed team mostly between Berlin, Cape Town, and London. We managed to push through the initial hurdles with sheer grit and determination—I went without a salary for eight months and we financed the development of the company as founders until our pre-seed grant of $40,000 by Startup Chile.

I am grateful that Sterio.me was honored as a finalist at the Harvard Africa Business Conference, MIT Africa Innovate, MLOVE, World Summit Award & World Summit Youth Award (Education category), World Technology Award (Education category), Mondato Summit Africa (Social Impact Award), and Mobile World Congress "4YFN." *Fast Company* named Sterio.me one of the "10 Most Innovative Companies in Africa" in 2014.

AMPION, which I co-founded after having co-founded its predecessor, StartupBus Africa in 2013, has formed a nonprofit in Germany and is organizing five Venture Bus programs across sixteen countries in Africa, with over 160 entrepreneurs. It is also providing an incubation program for the ten most promising start-ups that come out of the incubator. AMPION has partnered with such leading events as DEMO Africa and AfricaCom; institutions such as the AfDB, VC4Africa, and ALN Ventures; and received coverage from the BBC, CNN, WSJ, Deutsche Welle, Al Jazeera, and more. In 2015 AMPION will be expanding globally throughout emerging markets, with the Middle East first in line and Asia, Latin America, and Central/Eastern Europe to follow soon after.

In the years to come I will be focused on entrepreneurship in emerging markets—as my main measure of personal success is the magnitude of positive change I create for others.

And one day in the future I might move back to the Netherlands. I love going back and it never ceases to feel like home. The stability and the high standards of the health-care, education, and transport systems are a luxury, and it is true that I grew up on a bicycle—the safe riding of which I miss almost anywhere I go, including London. But it is not yet time for me to part from my nomadic ways; there are still a lot of problems to be solved which require my presence elsewhere.

Given what you know now, if you could redo high school, what would you do differently, and why?

I definitely would not change working part-time jobs such as I did since age thirteen. I worked in tomato and cucumber greenhouses, in inner-city supermarkets, as a telesales person for energy and telecom companies, and as a door-to-door and event fund raiser for charity—all while in high school.

I was working about fifteen hours a week on these part-time jobs during my last years of high school. This provided me a sense of perspective about less intellectual work, and made me a more well-rounded person— not being shy of a day's hard labor.

I would, however, have focused on learning to program and/or do web design in high school, as this would have enabled me to gain relevant experience at an early age as well as being a lot more lucrative!

I wouldn't change a thing about my habit of attending concerts and music festivals around the country with friends when I was fourteen to sixteen years old. These expanded my musical tastes and exposed me to a type of collective experience that enabled me to connect more with myself and others. I would focus more on learning to play an instrument or two myself, though, to foster an appreciation of the arts.

I wouldn't change my desire to travel, and I definitely would still go on backpacking trips through Europe. When I was fifteen, I went to eastern Europe for twelve days with one friend and at age sixteen, I traveled throughout Europe for three weeks. These travels expanded my horizons at an early age by exposing me to a wide range of people and their cultures. They also enabled me to take care of myself more, as I had to rely completely on my senses and my judgment when traveling abroad alone or with a friend. Certain experiences were quite dangerous, such as when we were in Gdansk and almost went with a local group of youngsters on a thirty-minute walk to a club along a park, which would have inevitably resulted in a robbery. We were luckily discouraged by an old lady whom we thought was crazy at the time, but who in retrospect saved our skin. Other experiences stirred our souls, such as when we visited Auschwitz to witness the horrors of World War II for ourselves, a feeling which never leaves you.

In brief, the things I *would* change, are things that (if I had time to spare), I still *could* change. This mostly includes studying more languages, engineering, and literature. Languages both for professional and personal use: French is useful, for example, in West Africa and Spanish in Latin America—both markets I am working in at the moment. Engineering because computer science is a language we will all be required to understand in the economy of the future. And books for personal growth.

What else would you like to share with or suggest to high school students and college students, and why?

My one piece of advice is to become as well-rounded a person as possible. Becoming mature in my eyes has more to do with becoming a well-rounded, self-aware, and cultured person, which most people even of adult age in society have not achieved. The earlier you grow up and become an independent person, the sooner you will be able to take your life into your own hands. So grow up, fast.

But don't confuse growing up with becoming like all the other adults in society. Don't become encumbered by the duties others impose on you. Don't feel the need to give in to societal pressures. Read books—literary pieces but also science fiction, history, and biographical pieces. Science-fiction and fantasy books especially can stimulate your creative soul (and interestingly many of the predictions science-fiction writers made about future technologies did come true, ranging from submarines and space exploration to mobile telephony, credit cards, and television).

Take risks and never be boring. No great person has ever existed who did not take risks.

Frankly, I find most people my age not so interesting to be around, as most people in their early twenties still have not defined who exactly they are—which results in their prolonged following of the general crowd. They have still not had their *own* experiences, shaped and guided by nothing but their own will and desire. They go down the beaten path of school, university, maybe also graduate school, and career. Personally, I tend to gravitate toward the unique people you can't really compare to anybody else. And that is what keeps my life interesting.

Gradually over the last six years I have come to understand what happiness means for me. I gain happiness from experiences with friends and spending time with loved ones, life's ups and downs, nature, learning, and the sense that in life I am moving forward in making a positive difference.

And to finish with a quote:

"And those who were seen dancing were thought to be insane by those who could not hear the music." The origin of this popular saying is unknown (although many people falsely attribute it to Friedrich Nietzsche), but it stands both to explain my view on those leading conventional lives and their view on my life as a nomadic entrepreneur with a focus on technology-driven social change.

A perfectly imperfect takeaway about Chris:

Chris Pruijsen came from an underprivileged background, went to one of the two most prestigious UK universities, dropped out, and subsequently co-founded several organizations of international acclaim (AMPION and Sterio.me). Against the odds, he has become successful. Currently at age twenty-one, his most successful years are still ahead. We will be hearing more from Chris in the years to come.

His path is not one for everyone to take. Dropping out of college is not always the right choice, and not everyone has the maturity level and independence he acquired at a young age. From age fifteen, he was able to travel by himself. At seventeen, he left the nest and moved to another country. Now at twenty-one, he is a leading figure in social enterprise. We can learn from Chris the meaning of grit and drive, and his focus on improving society through innovation is indeed inspiring.

21
Kemaya Lall Kidwai

Wildlife Buff and Consulting Newbie

BA in Political Science and South Asian Studies (double major), Class of 2013, Yale University

Born and raised in Mumbai, India, Kemaya Kidwai went back to her hometown after her college graduation to work for the Boston Consulting Group (BCG), a management consulting firm. Back in high school, Kemaya and some of her peers introduced to her school the Duke of Edinburgh's International Award, which recognizes teenagers and young adults for completing a youth-empowerment program; she received the Gold Medal for her efforts. Keenly interested in wildlife and the environment, she interned at Sanctuary Asia, a wildlife conservation firm, and at the Energy and Resource Institute (TERI), where she published two children's books. She also competed in varsity soccer, basketball, and track-and-field teams, and her peers lovingly recognized her as an outdoorsy tomboy.

Before landing her current full-time job, Kemaya engaged in academic research at Yale, and interned in advertising at J. Walter Thompson (JWT) and in consulting at the McKinsey & Company Knowledge Centre and

Booz & Company (now Strategy&). She also helped create the Yale year-book and spent a summer living with the Maasai in Kenya, learning about wildlife issues they faced with the Kenyan Government. Kemaya is a foodie and a movie/TV buff and loves wildlife photography and her dogs. She sees an MBA on the horizon but is open to any interesting twist.

Creating a storyline of interests and how they are linked together is important when writing college applications. It is also important when writing job applications in college. Do what you enjoy and your passion for it will always come across when discussing it with an admissions officer or potential employer!

—Kemaya Kidwai

With a Hindu mother and a Muslim father, Kemaya Kidwai grew up in a multireligious family environment that shaped her open-mindedness early on. Kemaya is especially proud of her mom, Naina Kidwai, who is a recipient of the Padma Shri, a distinguished civilian award by the government of India; Harvard Business School's first Indian woman graduate; and was ranked by *Time* and *Fortune* to be among the most powerful women in business in India. She is a role model to many.

Kemaya has always loved wildlife and the outdoors. She reflected on her purposeful actions to help protect and preserve them on a college application essay during her senior year in high school:

Yale application supplement prompt: While we leave the topic of the essay entirely up to you, try telling us something about yourself that you believe we cannot learn elsewhere in your application.

As I sat on my balcony, an eagle perched itself on a tree. It was the Great Imperial Eagle, a rarity in Mumbai! Having identified what I had seen and not calling it just another 'big bird' was satisfying. My mind wandered to the last time I had seen this eagle, which was while waiting for a tiger to cross our path in the Corbett National Park.

My family and I have been fortunate to see a tiger in the wild every year. The thrill of the experience is difficult to describe. The scent of lantana hangs in the air, as the barking deer's alarm call warns the forest of the tiger's proximity. The jungle becomes absolutely still. The faint sound of leaves being stepped on briefly breaks the silence. The mind starts seeing things. Tree stumps and shrubs assume the shape and colour of the graceful beast.

I can hear my heart thumping. Suddenly, a beautiful tigress nonchalantly ambles out into a clearing. The sunlight reflects off her fur, as she becomes an orange-red apparition and disappears into the forest.

It saddens me to think that future generations may not experience this thrill as tigers are at risk of extinction because of their disappearing habitat and poaching. When I saw this majestic beast being carried back to a forest lodge on an elephant, clawless, toothless, *dead*, I was furious at the poachers' callousness. I believe efforts to preserve our forests and these magnificent animals would be far more successful if communities living on the periphery of the parks were given incentives to conserve them. These communities need to realize that they would economically benefit from an increase in tourism that our forests and animals would attract, and it would therefore be in their best interests to join the conservation effort. The sharing of best practices between parks and communities would thus benefit wildlife reserves across the country.

Surprisingly, most of these communities have never even entered the park! Educational trips, especially for surrounding schools would help children appreciate the animals, birds, and the forest. I would love to run the "Kids for Tigers" program which I conducted in Mumbai, in these communities to involve them in the conservation movement. From my experience at Sanctuary Asia, where I participated in rallies for tiger conservation that were covered by the national media, I am convinced that children's groups can make a significant difference in spreading awareness about conservation.

After conversing with forest rangers, wildlife enthusiasts, tour guides and communities around parks, I conceived a new point system to incentivize preservation efforts. Parks would be awarded a point for every improvement or upgrade made, which would be advertised on a website. This, in turn, would encourage park officials to make better preservation efforts, improve the infrastructure, and introduce stringent certification for guides, while maintaining the authenticity of jungle camps and lodges and being environmentally friendly.

The One Horned Indian Rhino is flourishing in the Kaziranga Wildlife Sanctuary today, despite having once been on the IUCN's Critically Endangered List. Why can't we do the same for our national animal, the tiger?

Passionate about wildlife and environmental conservation, Kemaya also included the following two short essays under her Common App Additional Information:

[On interning at TERI to study and write about the impact of climate change]

My curiosity and growing interest in climate change led me to intern in the summer of 2008 for The Energy and Resource Institute (TERI), India's leading climate change institute headed by Dr. Pachauri, Chairman of the Nobel Prize winning Intergovernmental Panel on Climate Change (IPCC). I was privileged to work for him and other renowned thought leaders in the field, and am grateful for this once in a lifetime opportunity.

Contrary to my expectations, I was pleasantly surprised to be taken seriously as an intern at TERI. Within two days of joining the team, I was assigned to write two children's books and an article for *TerraGreen,* TERI's informative and educating magazine that deals with a range of issues including energy, the environment, and all issues related to sustainable development. *Each* day brought a new learning experience, and with it, greater knowledge. Typical lunchtime conversations revolved around the critical status of the Asian Gorilla or the hope that the Baiji (River Dolphin) had not become extinct. I was very impressed with TERI's Green Olympiad, an annual written examination on environment, which I introduced in my school the following term.

I was thrilled to be called "A Young Environmentalist" by the *Indian Express, one* of India's leading national dailies, for my article on their op-ed page, "Missing the neighbourhood for the trees." I still keep abreast of issues to do with climate change via articles, TV shows, and discussions to which I am invited.

[On interning at Sanctuary Asia to learn more about and contribute to conservation]

I find the inter-relationship between economics, environment, and development, and their effect on rural communities very exciting. This interest led me to work with Sanctuary Asia, India's leading wildlife and environment group. I worked for the "Sanctuary's Kids for Tigers" program, which teaches about one aspect of conservationism every year and registers schools to participate in the program. I also assisted in registering and running the "Saving India's Big Five" program. I really enjoyed marketing the programs to school principals, where they actually listened to a sixteen-year-old! I made presentations to second graders, educating them about our "Big Five" being endangered and conducting interactive games.

Sanctuary's Kids for Tigers Rally, where I campaigned for the preservation of the tiger, showed me the power of collective voice, especially when captured by national media. Children's groups can make a significant difference in spreading awareness about conservation. *Sanctuary Asia* magazine, *Maitree*, and SanctuaryAsia.com *have published* my articles on animals, conservation, and sustainable use of resources.

During the internship, I was fortunate to have interacted with some of India's leading wildlife photographers. Thanks to their stories about walking through forests for weeks in search of the "perfect shot," I now realize the effort that goes into excelling in one's profession. I continue to experiment with a camera on my trips into wildlife reserves.

In addition, Kemaya was very active and engaged as a leader in outdoor sports, including soccer, basketball, and throwball (a non-contact ball sport played across a net between two teams of seven players on a rectangular court, popular especially in the Indian subcontinent) back in high school:

Playing inter school football (that is, soccer) tournaments, I represented my school, trying to make it proud, and scoring goals not for myself but for the team. From captaining my school teams, I learned to lead without dominating, to motivate the team, to communicate and implement a strategy, and to inculcate dedication, discipline, and hard work. This also helped me to be an effective class monitor and Student Council Support Team member. Such learning is applicable to different fields—leading from the front, learning from mistakes, not giving up, and fighting to the end, having the confidence to look the opponent in the eye and playing to win but being gracious in defeat.

Football helped me hit the ground running when I switched schools by helping me forge relationships outside the classroom. It was always great to hear "Go, Kemaya!" in a new school, which encouraged me to make new friends and quickly adapt to a new environment.

In high school, Kemaya was also selected to represent her school, along with other classmates, at the Hague International Model United Nations and represented Japan in the Environment Commission. During her summers and in her free time, she volunteered at an NGO called Akanksha, which teaches English and math to underprivileged children.

281

Kemaya reflects on her college planning, applications, and admissions experience back in high school:

The thread of interest in wildlife and environment, which I've always been passionate about, was of great help in my college applications. Though I also spoke about sports and community service (two other co-curricular activities that I was involved with all through school), I maintained a focus on the outdoors and service, a theme that carried through my college application. If you have a "thing" that you are genuinely interested in and have pursued deeply, find a way to include it in your essays and make yourself stand out!

I had hedged my bets by applying to schools in both the UK and the United States. Eyeing UK universities, I applied to Cambridge, LSE, Kings College, UCL, and Warwick. Because the applications for the UK universities had to be sent out earlier, by mid-November of my senior year, I had fortunately received conditional offers from all of them, and from Cambridge by mid-December.

In the United States, I applied to Yale early. From the moment I stepped onto the Yale campus, I fell in love with it. I loved the quaint buildings, the vibe, the residential system, and was very excited by the variety of classes and activities offered. I was admitted to Yale. Because it was my top choice (and I had Cambridge as an option), I did not submit any other applications to US schools.

Today, Kemaya is happily working as a consultant at BCG back in Mumbai, India. Several rounds of interviews, practicing mock cases for hours on end, and maintaining her cool through the process was what helped her land her the job. I've asked her to reflect on the following:

To what extent did your college experience—on and off campus—meet your expectations? In what ways did your experience cause you to change your perspective on your academic career, your dreams and aspirations, and your life?

Though I grew up in India, I aspired to go to the United States for college early on. But I had no idea what to expect about (a) an American education, (b) campus life in America, and (c) living in a new country. I was very nervous about what college would be like, and if I could cope.

ACADEMIC INTERESTS

I came to college torn between majoring in environmental studies because of my love for wildlife and the environment, and economics because I thought that was the "in" thing. Choosing econ prematurely, I took the usual 101 classes and quickly realized that I was not enjoying what I was learning. Unfortunately, since I was not proactive in figuring out alternatives, I was stuck taking these classes for the whole semester. I was also dealing with some not-so-good news of my father and a friend struggling with cancer so I was not 100 percent focused. As a result, my first-semester grades were poor, which pulled down my GPA over the next three years.

The following semester, I was more careful in choosing classes. Through conversations with friends, my own research, and an understanding of the curriculum and learning styles I liked, I selected the classes that suited me best. With a new determination to find something other than economics to study, I started taking classes in environmental studies, psychology, art, and history, until I stumbled upon a political science class I absolutely loved. The professor as well as the material had an equal part to play in this—that semester, we learned about the political relationships (historical and current) between Middle Eastern countries during the "Arab Spring."

Sophomore year, I took more political science classes in different areas of study. Having attended a South Asian Studies seminar, I was intrigued by what I was learning about India, a country I thought I knew everything about but realized that I had barely scratched the surface. Learning about the nuances of India's democracy or hidden truths about the Indian independence movement was absolutely fascinating. This helped me decide that I wanted to double major. Still, I wanted to pursue a career in business.

Note to international students: While majors are not as important as grades in the United States, they could be in your home country. For certain jobs in the United States, because your employer needs to authorize and apply for a work visa for you, you may need to take some classes in the field you want to pursue if it lies outside what you are studying. For example, I was a political science and South Asian studies major, but I took some econ and math classes, as I needed to have studied some economics to allow me to pursue a career in consulting. I have been fortunate that this strategy worked out for me!

The classes I took and the way they were taught definitely helped me develop and hone the skills necessary for my job today. Having to think through a point before you raise your hand, and arguing or justifying any points made, helped me build my confidence and thought process. Yes, this was terrifying in the beginning, but once I overcame it, I felt more comfortable with the thought of having to make presentations to senior members of my organization, or voice a differing opinion from my boss's.

MY SUMMER IN KENYA

During my second semester of freshman year, I felt the need to branch out of the Yale network and usual internship choices to do something that was more unique and linked to my interests. After researching different options, I found a program in Kenya that was both academic and linked to wildlife conservation, so I sent in my résumé and essays hoping to hear back. After interviewing with the people at the School for Field Studies, I found out that I had been accepted into the program! I was extremely excited to be able study Wildlife Management via fieldwork, especially as we were going to be living in the wilderness during the course of the program.

I believe that my summer in Kenya was instrumental in putting an intense Yale education into perspective. I went into the program having received poor grades the prior semester, so I was feeling unmotivated and anxious about future semesters. However, while I was in Kenya, I was living in a shack for a month, with electricity for only five hours a day, with no phone reception, in the complete wilderness, and with electric fences to keep wild (and carnivorous) animals out. Survival training on the types of plants, insects, reptiles, and other creatures that were poisonous or dangerous, and lions roaming the perimeter of the property, were only some of the highlights that we experienced while in the field.

I was able to take a step back from Yale and from the constant over-thinking of what I needed to do next. Learning about survival in the wilderness and issues faced by the Maasai tribe helped me put my own problems in perspective. I saw that studying something I enjoyed and receiving good grades for the same were connected: I needed to choose something I really wanted to study, instead of something I thought would look good on my résumé. I believe this reshaped my Yale career, as this was what made me look into new majors and take unusual but interesting classes. And every spring break and Thanksgiving since Kenya, I traveled to a new US city (as I had been to the United States only twice before enrolling at Yale—once at age five and the other to look at colleges before applying) or to a new country, learned about a new subculture, and tried a new cuisine with earnings from my on-campus job.

INTERNSHIPS AND THEIR EFFECT ON MY CAREER DECISION

My decision to work in consulting was based more on the internships I did than what I had studied—from working on campaigns, editorials, advertisement, and research, I found my niche in the "big-picture" "analytical" space. After speaking to people about what could be a good fit for me, the word "consulting" was thrown into the mix—an industry I knew little about but wanted to explore. I was fortunate to intern at the McKinsey & Company Knowledge Centre during my sophomore summer and at Booz & Company (now Strategy&) in New York during my junior summer, both of which I enjoyed thoroughly. That was when I made up my mind about consulting, and somehow managed to get a full-time offer.

Given what you know now, if you could redo high school, what would you do differently, and why?

If I were to go through the college-selection process again, I would go through a host of different criteria before choosing—location, size of the university, percentage of international students, and proximity to a big city. I would also make sure that the core requirements suit me and that I have the ability to choose classes (if that is something you are interested in). I would research the possibility of doing more than one major or a minor, among other choices. Visiting a host of colleges on the East Coast two years before I was to enroll, helped me enormously, as I was able to think through some of these criteria.

At times, I studied for days for a test and still did not do well, or thought I had written a great essay until my teacher gave it back to me with edits all over it. I quickly learned in high school that working hard was important, but working smartly and focusing on what was required yielded better results. I also learned that approaching teachers for clarifications was helpful in showing them that I was interested in what was being taught. This helped me cement relationships with them, which in turn made me enjoy the classes more!

I realized the value of the internships I had done while in high school only when applying for internships and jobs when I was in college. Though my early internships were not linked to the career I was pursuing, the fact that I had reached out to gain work experience at a young age, along with pursuing an interest, bolstered my internship interviews in college. More important, internships in high school gave me early exposure to different professions, which helped when I was choosing what I wanted to do after college, in addition to gaining experience in interviewing.

If I could go back and do things differently, I would focus more on all the writing classes in high school. I completely underestimated the amount of work that goes into a well-structured essay. In fact, I had no idea how to correctly structure and produce a well-written essay until I got to college!

I would also work on my time-management skills. I never submitted assignments late without permission but I was definitely a "last-minute-study" type of student. While this worked fine in high school, I had difficulty coping with assignments during my first semester in college because I was relying on completing the assignment or the reading the night before it was due. Once I started planning my week, dedicating time to reading, assignments, meetings with professors, and discussion groups, work became so much easier!

What else would you like to share with or suggest to high school students and college students, and why?

COLLEGE APPLICATIONS

I think the best piece of advice I received while writing my college applications, was to keep in mind that the admissions officer reading my profile had *no* idea who I was and would spend only ten to fifteen minutes glancing through the last four years of my life. Learning that was a wake-up call: I started focusing more on how I was tying things together to try to create the most all-encompassing on-paper version of myself!

An admissions officer reads countless applications per day; that's why making your application stand out becomes so important. When I was applying to college, I created an environment portfolio that showcased my environment- and wildlife-related work as well as my interest in photography and writing. So how do you focus that person's attention on you? Talk about any leadership roles you have had, the sports you played, your extracurricular activities, work or volunteering experience, and so on. Remember not only to state what is obvious but also explain why the activity was important to you and what you learned from it.

Submission of the essays using the Common Application and school websites can take more time than you expect, so I would advise against waiting until the last minute to upload the essays. I did this for one of my college applications (luckily with one day to spare) and was directed to the next page, which had a list of five more questions to answer! Plus, servers can jam, computers can crash, Murphy's law can play out in full, so keep time on your side. I asked several people to read, edit, and even trash my essays, and give me their unhindered opinion. This helped me refine my words and also allowed me to gauge how someone else was reacting to what I had written.

Seeing a counselor to discuss my college list and essay ideas was helpful in learning things about the college that I might not have known otherwise. However, I took everything I was told with a grain of salt. The advice I was given was to stop all sports and focus on studying. I am extremely glad that I continued to play all the sports I was involved in. I believe one of the reasons I was given a chance at Yale was that I was not only studious but also participated in a plethora of other activities. Though grades are obviously important, it is not the only aspect of the application.

I think the recommendations section on a college application is more important than many people think—it is the only part in the application where someone else is vouching for you. I was very fortunate to get recommendations not only from my teachers, but also from employers at my internships. I chose professors and employers whom I got along well with and had a conversation with them about the other recommendations I was getting. I wanted to choose people who could write about different aspects of my personality or work. I also proactively offered to send in points for them to cover in cases where people were stretched for time.

In terms of choosing colleges, I pursued my dream of applying to Yale because I felt it was the right choice for me. I think that's how anyone can truly enjoy college—when your heart is fully invested in the decision! This goes back to what I was saying earlier about getting a feel for the college, be it via a college visit, research about the university, or speaking to current students or alumni (or a combination of these).

ON CREATING A STORYLINE OF INTERESTS

When in college, I was involved in the creation of the Yale yearbook and was a member of a few other clubs, which helped me meet people I would never have otherwise had the chance to meet. When I decided to major in political science, I applied to be a part of the Undergraduate Advisory Committee for Political Science. This was useful in learning more about career options. Once I got interested in consulting, I became a part of an undergraduate consulting, marketing, and creative organization called Maya. I ended up holding various leadership positions and contributing in various roles at Maya.

I believe these extracurricular experiences and contributions played a part in helping me secure an internship and full-time job in consulting. Creating a storyline of interests and how they are linked together is important when writing college applications. It is also important when writing out job applications in college. This in no way implies that you should not pursue your interests if they are diverse, or that you should pursue activities you are not interested in just for the sake of college or job applications. Do what you enjoy and your passion for it will always come across when discussing it with an admissions officer or potential employer!

FRIENDS FOR LIFE

Whenever I think of high school, a constantly busy schedule, exhaustion, and crazy amounts of fun all pop up into my head. Did I mention crazy amounts of fun? I would always take time to meet friends and hang out—who needs sleep? In my personal opinion, high school and college friends are friends for life and it is important to invest time in those relationships. My friends (college and high school) have been my support system through any roadblock or piece of bad news that has come my way. Though it seems impossible with school, extracurriculars, homework, tutorials, family time, sleeping and eating, find the time! Throughout college, whenever I wanted a piece of home, I loved knowing I had friends I could reach out to at any time of the day or night, both from home and college.

Though I am thoroughly enjoying my work in India, I get pangs of missing college, especially when I see Snapchats and Instagrams of friends hanging out together, my phone buzzing with useless Whatsapp threads and Facebook messages from all over the world, discussing "that ridiculous YouTube video" or the really stupid thing that so-and-so just did. It's great to know that even all those potential world leaders, my brilliant and talented friends, know how to have a little fun now and then.

A perfectly imperfect takeaway about Kemaya:

Having entered the real world via consulting back in India (and having survived it for the last year!), Kemaya is positively surprised by how things have worked out. She learned from her mistakes and her experiences. She had some great advisors in college and at home. And she had a rock-solid support system along the way: her friends. She decided to do what she enjoyed, including all the activities for the environment and wildlife back in high school, instead of what she thought she "should" do, and she is happy with the outcome. Though she has set goals she wants to achieve, Kemaya says: "Do what you love and have fun doing it!"

22

Patrick Ip

Digital Entrepreneur

BA in Political Science, Class of 2013, University of Chicago

Passionate in politics as a high school student, Patrick Ip assumed the role of California High School State Coordinator for Students for Barack Obama, where he rallied hundreds of local citizens and voters in support of the Obama presidential candidacy. These early high school efforts culminated in his election as Assembly District Delegate, which made Patrick one of the youngest politicians in California's history. For his commitment to local service, Patrick was also a three-time recipient of the Presidential Volunteer Award.

To begin his college career, Patrick continued his political activism by spending two years running social media at the United Nations. There he grew the United Nations Academic Impact, an initiative aimed at applying education to solve social problems, from 0 to over 700 universities in only five months. After this endeavor, Patrick founded and sold his first start-up, Kip Solutions, a social-media-based consulting firm for social causes. In 2012, Kip Solutions was recognized as one of the Kairos 50 (an annual list of the fifty most innovative student-run companies worldwide selected by the Kairos Society) and as one of *Inc.* magazine's "Coolest

College Startups." Among these accolades, Patrick was recognized as a Jefferson Award GlobeChanger, an award considered to be the Nobel Prize for community service.

Today Patrick is an assiduous Googler, working in services at Google's Small & Medium Business Department, and is also the founder and head of his own company, Kula, Inc., which is dedicated to supporting social good by globally organizing individuals through dinners.

You won't go anywhere if you don't believe you can. Start where you are. Do what you can. You'll be surprised what will happen.
—Patrick Ip

Patrick Ip grew up in a highly competitive Chinese American family environment and experienced his share of cultural stereotypes in the United States and in Hong Kong. He discussed this experience and his views via a personal essay during the college application season in his high school senior year. The corresponding Common Application prompt and his response are as follows:

Please write an essay on a topic of your choice. This personal essay helps us become acquainted with you as a person and student, apart from courses, grades, test scores, and other objective data. It will also demonstrate your ability to organize your thoughts and express yourself.

SCALING THE WALL

I cannot tell you a story of how I heroically saved children from a burning building or steadfastly found a cure to a disease. What I can tell you is the story of my life and how, despite hardships of living in a world branded by stereotypes, I managed to create a new definition of success diametrically opposed to my culture.

In Hong Kong, we are labeled as "ABCs" or American-Born Chinese. Among my family and relatives, I grew up in a fiercely competitive environment that defined success by being highly educated and then choosing a family-approved career. The first image that emerges in my head is a stereotypical Asian mother yelling at her son or daughter for not getting straight A+'s. This is tantamount to disobedience. Fortunately for me, I was the introverted, obedient child of a family who was extremely competitive. This seemed natural to me and so I didn't notice how we were used as bargaining chips. If I came to dinner among my family of aunts, uncles, and their children, the parents would be bickering about how each child was better than the other. This is the culture I lived in from early childhood until high school.

By virtue of this massive pressure, I grew up representing the ultimate "ABC" stereotype: I attended Kumon at an early age and studied incessantly. Going out with friends was a rarity. Staying home studying was the norm. I was not born gifted nor did I possess extraordinary talent, but I worked diligently because it was expected of me. The indoctrination was drilled into me . . . being truly good at something is synonymous with working hard. I upheld that creed and it became my definition of success at that time in my life.

However today, if anyone who knows me was asked, he or she would tell you without hesitation that my definition of success has changed. No longer do I view success as going into a "safe" career such as medicine or law. No longer do I measure success with the money in one's wallet. By redefining success, I created a "new" culture that is diametrically opposed to my old one. To me, success is being able to do something to the best of one's ability while feeling an enormous sense of pride.

In today's ever growing population and economy, doing something is far better than doing nothing. In my "new" culture I have come to realize I now have power to do something and feel good about it. Today's shattered society offers a decreasing middle class, a more affluent upper class, and an ineffective government to make things better. I want to counter this by informing people that there can be a better tomorrow, but it has to start today. No matter what background we come from or how we arrived at where we are today, we can make a difference. Our cultural differences can hold us back or catapult us forward to do great things. It is up to us. It should not be a world that we associate with differences, but rather a means to unite us together. This world is not divided by countries, borders, or differences in ideals. We all laugh, love, and cry...we all live together in one world united with one dream.

In addition to academics, Patrick's parents pushed him hard extracurricularly as well.

In fear of being labeled as "quiet" or "introverted" by teachers, my parents put me into high school leadership. The only way to get an "A" in leadership was to be proactive, and it was decided by my parents that I should run for freshman class president. At first, I was fearful. I hated public speaking. In addition, my opponent was a confident, popular athlete. How was I, the timid Asian nerd, supposed to win? During the election speeches, my opponent talked about how he had all the experience to be class president. When I got up to give my speech, I talked about how I wanted to help everyone achieve his or her dreams. I did not talk about myself. I won the election, and it set me on a path toward leading through consideration of others.

Patrick's college applications and admissions experience was unexpectedly difficult.

Despite my leadership success in serving as one of the youngest elected politicians in California history and leading student operations for the California Obama campaign in high school, I fought tooth and nail during the college admissions process. To try to stand out academically among most American students who took Advanced Placement (AP) courses, I took the International Baccalaureate (IB) Program instead at Modesto High. Out of the twenty universities, including Harvard, Cornell, and Dartmouth in the Ivy League, and Stanford (to which I applied single-choice early action), I received eighteen rejections. I was admitted to only George Washington University in Washington, DC, and was waitlisted at the University of Chicago, which eventually admitted me.

Having gone through colorful and challenging experiences, Patrick graduated from the University of Chicago a year ago and is doing well professionally. I've asked him to reflect on the following:

To what extent did your college experience—on and off campus—meet your expectations? In what ways did your experience cause you to change your perspective on your academic career, your dreams and aspirations, and your life?

REDEFINING SUCCESS AND SHARPENING PERSPECTIVE

College redefined success for me. In high school, success is often measured by your academic standing, extracurriculars, and college admissions. However, what I found in college is the focus shifts toward your summer internships and ultimately the job you undertake post-college. The competition is especially fierce in the most elite colleges and universities. Scores of the most ambitious students hope to join the ranks of elite banking and consulting firms like Goldman Sachs and McKinsey. These positions were often the most selective.

In my first year at the University of Chicago, I applied to many of most sought-after internships at top firms. Unfortunately, I was unable to land anything. While at the time it seemed like a failure, I sent a cold e-mail to a foundation in Melbourne, Australia, that was working in education (a field I was passionate about). The cold e-mail turned into an internship opportunity, where they paid for my accommodation and provided a stipend for me to work for them for ten weeks in Melbourne. Additionally, while in Australia, I was appointed to join the United Nations as the co-chair of the UN Youth Committee of Australia and subsequently spent two years working at the United Nations before starting my first company.

The definition of success in high school and earlier days, to me and many of my peers, hinged on college acceptances. In retrospect, I find that past definition was too narrow. Since I was young, my mom tried to help me prepare to improve chances for elite college admissions and to strengthen my mind-set, including critical-thinking skills, as well. In fifth grade, my mother drilled me on college-essay prompts. One of the prompts from Harvard was "What do you see outside the window?" As a fifth-grader, I naïvely answered trees, the street, and people walking by. My mom gave me a disapproving look and explained that the correct answer was to talk about how you see opportunity—whether in creating new products or a company, or in improving the lives of others. It isn't about what you actually see outside, but about what you envision being there.

In college, my mom's depth of perspective became clear to me. Success should not be what school you get into but should be what you envision doing beyond attending college. As an entrepreneur, I believe that I see the world differently from many of my peers. I often imagine achieving success not within existing markets and offers, but within new market segments or innovations I will help create.

A year out of college, I now work at Google and have run three businesses (one of which was acquired) in the time since Project Yes We Can, my first organization as a senior in high school. I never could have predicted my success or the hardships that I faced.

CHOOSING FRIENDS WISELY

"You are the average of the five people you spend the most time with," said the late motivational speaker Jim Rohn. If you know that finance or consulting is the field you want to go into, then spend time with individuals who share that vision. If you're undecided, then be sure to seek others who have it figured out. When my start-up was in an accelerator, I was surrounded by the ten most promising start-ups in Chicago. However, I realized midway that the worst thing a start-up could do was to be surrounded by other start-ups that didn't understand how to become a company. Instead, we shifted gears and our team began hanging out with the companies we admired and the people we wanted to help consult. Be with the people you want to learn from and emulate.

TRUE INTERESTS ARE MORE IMPORTANT THAN COLLEGE MAJORS

I also thought that majors were extremely important before applying to college. However, while in college, I found the major selection to be negligible, as college for many is a process of self-discovery. This was true at the University of Chicago, and many liberal-arts schools, where rigorous common core classes exist that you must take in order to graduate. You should really select a major in which you are truly fascinated by the course material, but give yourself room to explore other fields as well. I majored in political science, but after attending classes in several different fields, I found that I really enjoyed sociology and then had the flexibility to write my senior paper in this field. Your interests should mature as you progress through college, so give yourself the room to grow. If you've truly learned anything in college, the way you think should change by the time you finish your college years.

Given what you know now, if you could redo high school, what would you do differently, and why?

I think the key to my high school success was focus and developing my passions. In my junior year, I joined Obama for America as a precinct captain (the smallest position you can have in a campaign). Over the course of hosting fund-raisers and growing Students for Barack Obama in high school to over 150+ universities, I was promoted to California High School State Director. The opportunity to serve at the statewide level led to several national and global leadership opportunities, such as using the Students for Barack Obama network to launch Project Yes We Can, which paired high school students with local politicians to reform education.

I have had the opportunity to interview prospective students now for my alma mater and I have found that the students who most impress me are those who have been able to find their passion early on and really develop them. One of the three criteria University of Chicago looks for in individuals is how well an applicant knows him or herself. It is a deeply difficult question to answer as a mid-to-late teen, but it's this level of introspection that really stands out. As an interviewer, I can tell immediately when students really own their own passions or follow those of others.

In some regards, I think outsiders would point out that I should have studied harder in order to get better SAT scores and higher grades, and to get accepted to more universities. But at the end of the day, it is a trade-off. I had a hard time studying when my only goal was getting into university. My wholehearted priority was in working on the campaign and Project Yes We Can, which opened up opportunities for everyone and which I thought was a more important cause.

Everyone who had written my college recommendations thought I'd be a shoo-in because of all my extracurricular success. My failure to get into the universities I thought I was qualified for was a learning experience. It really set the precedent that failure was no big deal; all that mattered was what you did with what you had. When I was wait-listed at the University of Chicago, I wrote an unusual but successful response letter (see the appendix at the end of this chapter). If you can turn each "failure" into an opportunity, you'll do amazing things.

What else would you like to share with or suggest to high school students and college students, and why?

FINDING GENUINE INTERESTS

High school students, to help find your interests, if not passions, here are three things I would do:

1. **Participate in extracurriculars in and outside of school.** A lot of individuals only do school clubs. I would recommend seeking involvement in organizations outside of school, whether it be community organizations or local and state government (in my case, it was a district within the California State Assembly). It's a great opportunity to find things that a lot of high school students aren't involved in, and a lot of organizations would benefit from your involvement.

2. **Attend quality summer programs.** One of the life-changing moments for me was attending Stanford's Educational Program for Gifted Youth (EPGY). Prior to attending, as an Asian American and first-generation American I found it much easier to adapt to the ambitions and dreams of my parents as opposed to understanding my own passions. When I attended EPGY, I met students who genuinely had passions and ambitions of their own. That was a pivotal period for me. Those three weeks taught me to have my own dreams and really own them (in my case, campaigning for Obama).

3. **Aim as high as possible.** I tend to think that society and elite colleges have a bias when it comes to people who can think big-picture. While not everyone may be looking to make a global change, I think it's important to think in terms of how your local and individual work can be tied to something much larger. Once you've spent some time thinking about it, make it happen. One resource that would be good to check out is Project Rocket at the Jefferson Awards Foundation website, where you can learn how to "scale" your ideas. Go as far and high as you can.

Whether you are a high schooler or a university student, whatever you decide to do, love what you do. It is a bit of a cliché, but I believe you'll find more success when you don't feel drained or tired from your day-to-day activities. I found a lot of solace in doing sports in addition to my other activities. I ran cross-country during the fall and played golf in the spring. They were both nice breaks from the grind, and I enjoy the feeling of being on the starting line in running or at the beginning of a match for golf. It is just another way to keep your energy high.

People often ask me how I manage to run a real business and attend university at the same time. As a freshman at UChicago, I was part of the crew team. We had practice at four a.m. six days a week. It conditioned me to be an early riser and opened up more hours in a day to being focused. There's no secret to success. It's mostly dedicated hard work.

WHAT PROPELLED ME INTO PUBLIC SERVICE IN HIGH SCHOOL

In May 2008, tragedy rocked my community. A drive-by shooting took place across from my public high school. A bullet lodged in the kidney of Joshua, a twenty-two-month-old baby. The entire community was in shock and unable to move forward. My principal and I decided to act, and within a week we were able to raise nearly $1,500 to help the family.

This incident propelled me into public service because I did not want our high school and the Modesto community to feel unsafe. I began attending local board meetings, met with gang-prevention police officers, and spoke out against gang violence through the support of the mayor and other local public officials. In 2009, just after my eighteenth birthday, I ran for Assembly District (AD) delegate and earned enough votes to be elected one of the youngest AD delegates in California. My community work propelled me to become a three-time recipient of the Presidential Service Volunteer Award.

A perfectly imperfect takeaway about Patrick:

A year out of college, Patrick has run three businesses (one of which was acquired) since high school and now works at Google. His high school and college journey was filled with more ups and downs than the story he would get if he only studied and got great grades. His path has allowed him to improve the lives of those around him and do things that are unheard-of for people his age. He suggests, "As a high school student, find mentors. The earlier you can find mentors, the quicker you can learn from the mistakes and success of those around you. But it's not enough to learn from mentors. It's only enough when you can personally succeed, fail sometimes, and learn from those failures."

APPENDIX:

The following was Patrick's letter to the University of Chicago's Admissions Office, in response to his being waitlisted for admission. A lighthearted and popular phrase among students and alumni of cerebrally intense UChicago is "(the place) where fun comes to die," which doesn't mean that *per se*. Even UChicago t-shirts proudly display this phrase as a design. Patrick astutely included this on his letter. Though the writing quality could be better, his genuine passion was undeniable. Coupled with a very strong recommendation from his high school principal, Patrick's unusual approach turned out to be successful.

Dear University of Chicago,

William Allin once said, "Education is not the answer to the question. Education is the means to answer all questions." It is my passion to find the answers of interest, and participation in politics has caused me to think about the knowledge I find most important—the types of issues and question I hope to someday help to solve and answer. I believe that peace comes from understanding, and understanding comes from knowing.

After spending the last two years leading Barack Obama's Student Campaign in California, I understand the ideas that created one of the largest grass-roots movements in history. But now, at one of the most decisive turning points in my life, I am not looking for a life in running the campaigns of the political elite, though I have been personally asked by both California Lieutenant Governor John Garamendi and San Francisco Mayor Gavin Newsom to run their student branch. Instead I am looking for the basis of the transformative ideas that sustain our country and world. Why, after political gridlock and corruption, does the country still move forward? What was the conviction that brought our founding fathers together? Why is it that we still have the ability to act civilized in a world of turmoil? The questions I hold can no longer be answered by political campaigns, but only by turning to the environs of academia. Although University of Chicago is known as "the place where fun comes to die," my "fun" and passion come from searching out these questions I have about the world.

Having traveled across California on the campaign trail, and having attended both the Democratic National Convention and Inauguration, I have asked many people one question throughout my entire term in my State Position: "What is Change to you?" The answers varied; some said simply they wanted to put Barack Obama into the presidency, while others suggested how radically we must change our viewpoint on the issues . . . it all boiled down to one thing: transformative ideas. We—as a nation and as a world—need to have more and need to implement more transformative ideas.

In 1776, it was transformative ideas that founded the United States of America. In 1890, it was transformative ideas that founded the University of Chicago. In 2007, it was transformative ideas that founded the campaign of Barack Obama. And it is now, through the power of transformative ideas that our lives continue to move forward and brings us together.

It is with these transformative ideas that I want to be challenged. While I was a Full-Diploma International Baccalaureate Candidate, I helped to run one of the most politically active campaigns in history; this shows that if my full concentration were put into academics, I could strive to break the same barriers in education just as Students for Barack Obama did in America. Being previously exposed to a core curriculum through the International Baccalaureate Program, I respect the different facets of academia and value the discourse that leads to knowledge. University of Chicago would allow me to continue this discourse with more depth. It would allow me access to great thinkers and exposure to ideas and inquiry that would help me answer those transformative questions.

I want to know.

Sincerely,
Patrick Ip
Executive Director
Project Yes We Can
Patrick@projectyeswecan.com

23

Sonia Agarwal

The Gandhian Innovator

BS in Strategic Management and Marketing, Class of 2012,
Babson College

Sonia Agarwal, twenty-three, is a vivacious young woman from India. Prompted by her love for social entrepreneurship, fashion, and conservation, she aspired to become a serial entrepreneur. Sonia is the founder and CEO of Whitenife, a global luxury fashion brand that uses innovative, animal-friendly materials to cater to fashion and art connoisseurs. A scion of the textile giant Donear Industries Ltd. in India, she holds formal duties there as president of marketing and communications.

Sonia is often invited by reputed institutions such as WIPRO (a global IT, consulting, and outsourcing company serving clients across six continents), the National Institute of Fashion Technology, and the Indian School of Business to deliver speeches to their students on innovation and social entrepreneurship. Additionally, she is global head of marketing for Indiapreneurship, a platform that globally connects entrepreneurs in India, and is also founder and president of SOCH, a nonprofit organization that connects NGOs to volunteers.

303

In 2013, the Kairos Society honored Sonia as one of the top fifty most innovative student entrepreneurs in the world. She also won the "India's Hottest Startup" award for Freshmentors Inc., an educational technology company, from which she exited in early 2014. In addition, she is a Dhirubhai Ambani International School alumna and has studied fashion management at Istituto Marangoni (Paris) and Università Bocconi (Milan). In her spare time, Sonia teaches underprivileged children near her house every Saturday, plays Monopoly, writes poetry, and rides horses.

Happiness and growth do not come from ordinary success. They come from sincere madness, compassion, and a deep desire to always learn.
—Sonia Agarwal

Sonia Agarwal was born and raised in a Marwari family in India. Many in India recognize that the Marwari community has long been astute and influential in both society and in industry.

I grew up in a huge family of entrepreneurs—one that is too big to fit in one room or one photo frame. The elders proudly told fascinating stories about their struggle to build their business empires from next to nothing. I enjoyed dinner-table conversations that revolved around evaluating business strategies and playing our own version of Monopoly that accounted for asset depreciation, complex negotiations, and hedging of risks.

One time, at the Mumbai Airport, my father walked up to me and laid a book on my lap. Given that he is neither much of a reader nor someone who makes such gestures frequently, I was truly amazed and intrigued. The cover read *Think Big, Act Small*, by Jason Jennings. What was the book about? Why had he gifted me this book? Had he even read it? I raced through the book the next day. Although it was a wonderful and insightful book, I knew my father had given me the book because it summarizes the advice that every great entrepreneur should abide by: Think big, take small steps in the direction of achieving big goals, and focus on "getting it done."

When Sonia was a high school student, she constantly challenged her own limits and was always hungry to learn. She not only emphasized the pursuit of academic success but also actively participated in many community projects—for example, supporting AIDS/HIV-infected orphans and organizing events to make her classmates more considerate about the environment. She has also been a state-level gold-medalist figure skater, and has passed six grades of Trinity London Examinations in Speech and Drama with distinctions. In addition, she represented her school in playing chess and soccer and learned pottery and how to play golf.

Sonia insisted on getting work experience early on, and was just fifteen when she secured her first internship. She worked with CNN-IBN as perhaps the youngest journalist to get two national bylines. The subsequent summer, she worked with the Nielsen Group of companies as a junior market researcher conducting qualitative market research for high-profile clients such as L'Oréal, Hershey's, and VIP (a renowned luggage brand in Asia). She reminisces:

I looked forward to my internships every summer and truly enjoyed my experiences. I then carried my energy and diligence to Babson College, where I enjoyed contributing to the community by taking on several leadership positions in various campus organizations and clubs. These included serving as the youngest member of the executive Campus Activities Board and participating in many Habitat for Humanity Projects, as well as other activities organized by the Luxury Fashion Association.

One summer, I studied Luxury Fashion Management at Istituto Marangoni (Paris), where I first confirmed my love for the fashion business. Another summer, I worked as a marketing associate at Planet Retail Pvt. Ltd., a company that holds distribution rights in India for Accessorize, Nautica, Guess, Debenhams, and Next. The experience at Planet Retail introduced me to the retail industry in India.

Planet Retail applauded Sonia for her contributions. Then she spent a semester abroad in Milan to further her knowledge of the fashion field. While in college, she also self-published her first work of fiction entitled *My Mom Is Driving Me Mad*, an entertaining book about the mother-daughter relationship. Her book was recognized as a bestseller in Boston and was recommended by several relationship counselors.

Since graduating from Babson, Sonia has been passionately pursuing her entrepreneurial career. She returned to India the morning after she graduated to become the founder and CEO of Whitenife. I've asked her to reflect on the following:

To what extent did your college experience meet your expectations? In what ways did your experience cause you to change your perspective on your academic career, your dreams and aspirations, and your life?

Most of us assume that college is an institution where we will "figure out life," yet I neither expected that from college nor did I embark on such a journey. I arrived as a freshman at Babson College driven to learn, perform, and thrive. Babson allowed me not only to nurture my love for entrepreneurship but also to acquaint myself with other subjects. When I graduated, I knew that I didn't know everything, but I did know that I was prepared and perhaps a little too eager and excited to take on the "real world." And I learned how to learn, fast. These are some of the things I've come to realize:

NEVER GO TO A BUSINESS SCHOOL JUST TO STUDY BUSINESS

I am a strong believer that a good business degree is inadequate without a proper understanding of other fields. I embraced my opportunity at Babson to take a large range of classes, such as in art history, biotechnology, political economics, psychology, philosophy, media culture, and environment studies, along with essential business classes and other electives such as business law, consumer behavior, operation research, managerial accounting, strategy building, and marketing management. As a personal rule of thumb, if a course had interesting books in its reading list, would contribute significantly to my pool of knowledge, could nudge me to think differently, and/or might lead to worthy and interesting dinner-table conversations, it was a good course.

During my first few years, college introduced me to many new concepts, frameworks, ideologies, and methods that contributed to my steep learning curve; however, such learning was not limited to academics, and I found myself actively participating in organizations and clubs on campus.

In the second half of my freshman year, I was selected (as the youngest student in Babson history) to be a part of the six-member team to lead the Campus Activities Board—a group that was responsible for organizing and hosting all activities on campus. In my role as vice president of marketing, I was responsible for creating, coordinating, and promoting every event that took place on Babson's campus. These events included the president's ball, spring concerts featuring renowned artists and bands such as Ke$ha and the Dropkick Murphys, weekly coffees with the dean, organization fairs, and all official campus parties. I participated in several Habitat for Humanity projects and in other activities that the Luxury Fashion Association organized.

While these individual activities may seem less relevant in the larger scheme of things, they were great opportunities for me to hone my planning, organizational, and people skills. In order to rightly juggle these leadership roles, my classes, and my social life, I soon came to understand the importance of planning and time management. It was during college that I found friends (whom I now call family) my sense of fashion, my first company, and largely myself.

Although I had never had any real exposure to the fashion business, I felt strongly drawn to the field. In order to better understand my intuition, I decided to spend a summer exploring "luxury fashion management" at one of the finest fashion institutes in the world, Istituto Marongani, located in the heart of a significant fashion hub—Paris. At the end of the summer, I knew my calling was true, and I decided to pursue it more aggressively. The following summer, I worked as a marketing associate with a firm that holds retailing rights in India for big fashion brands such as Guess, Accessorize, Nautica, Debenhams, and Next. I acquired a practical understanding of methods for facilitating interactions among media publications, stylists, and celebrities in order to achieve the goals that the brand heads and their merchandizing team set.

Given the intensity of my experience with those brands, I was much tempted to drop out of college and get right to work, but I decided to continue pursuing a formal degree. Instead of going back to Boston that semester, however, I chose a study-abroad semester in Milan—another fashion hub of the world—at Università Bocconi. I wanted to better my understanding of fashion and took classes in international economics, product innovation, and global fashion management. While I was in Milan, I enrolled at Burgo di Moda, a design institute, for its evening program to explore my sketching skills, only to find them shockingly poor.

By the end of my junior year, I had worked out only one quarter of the puzzle. I knew I was passionate about entrepreneurship and luxury fashion, yet I recognized my family wished for me to return to India after graduation so that I could live nearby. During my senior year, most of my friends rushed toward job interviews, studied for GMATs, and tried hard to have as many options for themselves as possible, but I knew I was headed home. I used that year to identify and explore business models and opportunities that I felt would be exciting and feasible to pursue back in India.

On returning home, I discovered that I felt rather unprepared to be there. I had not only spent four years living an independent life away from home, but those years had been vital and had greatly transformed and contributed to my belief system. While it was hard for me to readjust back in my hometown, it was equally difficult for my family to see me so unsettled. The business plan I'd brought with me back to India was immediately dismissed by my parents. I had not invested time in developing a sound contingency plan, and they had not been aware that I wanted to come back and pursue a serious career as an entrepreneur. In retrospect, I regret not having discussed my own entrepreneurial career goals with them prior to my graduation.

STARTING MY OWN COMPANY

Shortly after graduating from college and returning home, I founded Whitenife, a luxury fashion house, headquartered in India, that understands design, appreciates craftsmanship, and uses only innovative, animal-friendly materials. Currently, the company uses Elfh—a patented, mineral- based composite that is 89 percent identical to genuine elephant ivory—and the company will soon be introducing other products that use high-quality, exotic faux leather. Whitenife offers a spectrum of products. Sculptural jewelry, exquisite home artifacts, couture apparel, and so forth. The company is certified by People for the Ethical Treatment of Animals (PETA), a global animal-welfare organization followed by millions around the world. Whitenife works under the auspices of the Ministry of Environment and Forestry in India.

Establishing Whitenife was serendipitous, for it is the perfect combination of luxury, fashion, conservation, and entrepreneurship. I had conceived the idea of Whitenife in high school: I was seventeen, in love with biotechnology, passionate about fashion, and eager to change the world. I first shared my idea with my father while walking on the beach. It sounded like science fiction to him, as he had never heard of such technology or imagined how this could change the fashion business.

But I knew I wanted to actualize it someday—a day when I thought I'd be ready and experienced. Five years later, a week before my college graduation, I described this idea out loud for the second time to a friend, whose response changed my life. He said, "Go big or go home." And so I did go home—and hoped to make it big, too.

Initially, many challenged my capacity and practicality to found Whitenife as a twenty-one-year-old Marwari girl who carried a heavy opportunity cost of not contributing all her time and skills toward growing her family business.

As CEO, I feel my strength is in brand development, design direction, model and system creation, marketing strategy, and communication. Since Whitenife was completely unrelated to my family business, I became my own mentor for the most part. I had little understanding, let alone experience, in signing up a R&D facility to commission research, register a proprietorship, comply with import-export formalities, work with artisans to ensure timely and quality workmanship, organize brand launches, generate leads, form strategic alliances, draft legal documents, direct design, and engage in media activities. Some of these are basic managerial responsibilities that can take someone years to master, but instead I took the sink-or-swim approach.

Within a few months of establishing Whitenife, I was overjoyed when the Kairos Society honored my venture on the NYSE as one of the top fifty most innovative companies in the world. Leading publications, such as *India Today*, *Times of India*, *Entrepreneur*, *Verve*, and *Society Interiors* have given my company great credit. In 2014, Whitenife was chosen to design the crown for Miss World Australia, making it the first Indian company to design a crown for an international pageant.

I've asked Sonia: Given what you know now, if you could redo high school, what would you do differently, and why?

To me, a good school, a good curriculum, and parental support that stimulate learning and personal development are the most obvious, less available, and most vital contributors to one's development. I pursued my entire pre-college education in India, where I had all of these advantages.

While working on a semester project for a Babson class, "Solving Big Problems," taught by Professor Gaurab Bhardwaj, I learned of a few eye-opening statistics about the education system in India: 45 percent of children discontinue school because it is too expensive; one-quarter of the teachers are absent from school at unannounced visits by government authorities; and only 7 percent of students graduate from high school.

The moment I read through these statistics, I knew I was fortunate and blessed to have received an education of such fine quality. I not only had the rare luxury of receiving a quality education, but I was also fortunate to be born to parents who invested their time and energy in helping me get the most I could from what I had. Unlike most parents, they evaluated my performance not on grades but on my effort and approach.

The educational system in India requires children and their parents to make important choices at a very early age regarding what one chooses to study. Different schools and curriculums share different cultures, teaching techniques, and have different end goals. After switching schools three times and being exposed to three curriculums; I found myself most compatible with one of the most selective, high-achieving, and reputable schools in Asia, Dhirubhai Ambani International School (DAIS), where I pursued International General Certificate of Secondary Education (IGCSE), followed by the IB program. This school provided me with an intimate and stimulating environment, where people were as determined, motivated, and quirky as I was.

Some lessons I learned:

1. **Choose the right school/curriculum.** DAIS provided me with a wonderful environment to explore, grow, and learn. I feel it not only built my knowledge base but also allowed me to develop fundamental skills and helped shape my value system. No regrets there!

2. **Work smart, not just hard.** I would continue to give a lot of attention to the key assignments but would do a better job in organizing my efforts more strategically. My mother understood the concept of value and worth and helped ensure that I put the right amount of emphasis on the right things.

3. **Give a fair shot to everything.** I would be more experimental and not rush to conclusions about whether I had a liking or an aptitude for a certain subject. Today, I regret not having a better understanding of physics simply because I never took any interest in the subject. I also criticize myself for using SparkNotes to work through Shakespeare instead of embracing great works of literature. I repent of my fearfulness to run a hundred-meter race on my school's Sports Day simply because I never thought of myself as a "runner." I now have two of my own books published and have successfully completed in half-marathons and three full marathons. While I regret not exploring everything, I know that for the subjects that mattered, I left no stone unturned. I don't regret asking teachers, other adults, and peers the multitude of questions I did. Ask them all, even the stupid ones, and learn to build a thick(er) skin. Doing so will ensure that your fundamentals are in place.

4. **Be yourself.** I do recollect playing "Hermione" for many of my classes and participating in a large range of activities around me. I am happy

that, unlike many classmates, I was very comfortable being myself and sharing the views I held. I fondly look back at my naïve but sincere attempt to clean up the overly polluted Mithi River near my school.

5. **Look beyond your grades.** My high school and my parents both pushed me to do better and emphasized participating in extracurricular activities. Even though I no longer pursue any of them, they largely contributed to my personal growth. I am glad I took the time to know my peers who were juniors and seniors. We have tried to stay in touch ever since.

Although most advisors would tell students to focus on building their CV, I gladly focused on building myself. I wanted to explore the world, learn every hour, and grow every day—just like what Walt Disney said: "I don't like to repeat successes. I like to go on to other things."

What else would you like to share with or suggest to high school students and college students, and why?

COLLEGE CHOICES AND APPLICATIONS, AND BABSON COLLEGE

Fortunately, we live in an era of technology so we have access to more information and opportunities than we can even process or utilize. The global marketplace connects scientists, designers, and engineers to investors and managers in an increasingly global and nonexclusive manner. Some of the most prestigious universities around the world today offer their course material for free online. Reputable R&D divisions have started relying on open innovation models for problem-solving and product innovation. Notable search engines share a spectrum of opinions on every possible subject conceived by humans. So the natural question is, why does one need to go to college?

When I was applying to my list of dream colleges, targets, and backups, I did not ask myself this question. I wish I had. Although many college essay questions prompted me to do so, and even to go a step further and question my reasons for wanting to attend that particular college, I mistook them as opportunities to simply highlight some of my academic and nonacademic accomplishments and pack in words of praise for the university I was writing the essay for.

Because I was the eldest child, my parents had little understanding of how to guide me with my applications. I was certainly directed to some of the finest counselors in the city, but finding myself at Babson College was a completely unplanned but fortunate affair.

My high school was a school of overachievers, many aspiring to go to an Ivy League college. My classmates undoubtedly had exceptional intellect, dedication, and compassion in common. While each may have sounded strikingly confident and certain of his or her ground, in retrospect I believe only a few of them really understood their decisions.

While I spent numerous hours putting together my applications, studying for my SATs, and juggling my project deadlines for school assignments, I had spent only a few hours thinking about what I wanted to study and why. While I shared equal love for business and biotechnology, I opted to study business "for now," which is one of my biggest regrets so far. I wish I had better understood what career I might have had if I'd opted to pursue biotechnology in college instead. I wonder sometimes: Where would I be in five to ten years if I chose a different degree than business? What path would take me there?

After an hour spent with a guidance counselor and my parents, I walked out of the room having written down what I wanted to study, the country in which I wanted to study (a country I had never visited before), and the universities that would be most appropriate. Little did I know how rushed that exercise had been.

My list did take into consideration college rankings, as well as my academic and nonacademic interests, but it had not differentiated between private and public universities, nor the cultural influences of studying and socializing in a certain country or city. I had not thought much about what I wanted to do after I graduated college, but I had enough faith in myself to know that I would make the best of every opportunity in college or I would transfer to another one if I felt the need to.

Despite this long list of missteps, I am very proud that I allowed all my applications to truly represent who I was and what I had done, rather than presenting a fabricated profile. While I felt that I was not equipped to choose a direction for my life, I allowed the admissions officers to decide whether the school was a good fit for me.

Accepting the offer from Babson College was one of the luckiest bets I ever made, for Babson was a breeding ground of entrepreneurs and new ideas. It had a diverse set of people with opportunity-seeking minds who shared a warm and intimate relationship with one another.

Even today, I feel a proud and profound relationship with Babson College, as well as a strong relationship with Boston as a city. Babson College has defined a core part of who I have become.

It is not about which college chooses you, it is about which college you choose. In the times we live in, we don't need to go to college merely to acquire knowledge: we need to go to college to explore, interact, make mistakes, achieve, read, and discover ourselves.

IS THERE ANYTHING ELSE YOU WOULD LIKE TO SHARE?

It is important to know what you want, how to add value, and (if you are entrepreneurial) be (extremely) hands-on. My father believes that one must aim to specialize and focus, but I believe that one must specialize and be versatile. While it is impossible to know everything, it is nevertheless important to ask lots of questions, observe, and care to know enough about each division. I am blessed to have been born into a family who have chosen a simple and modest personal life but are passionate about business life. We share concerns and love for one another and make room for each other's dreams.

CAREER CHOICES: A RISKIER ENTREPRENEUR'S LIFE OR THE ESTABLISHED FAMILY BUSINESS?

I do not have to give up a dream in order to pursue another one. I have always dreamed of having a strong career and of sharing strong family ties. An entrepreneur's life is thrilling but demanding.

When I first returned to India after college, I was uncertain about what I wanted to do and how I wanted to proceed. It took patience and sincere effort for me to accept and adapt to my new life in India. Given that my family business, Donear Industries Ltd., is the third largest textile-manufacturing company in India with over 100,000 retailers and exports to forty countries around the world, it was only natural for my family to think that I would wish to join them. Although my family felt that I would add much value to the business, they allowed me to make my own decisions.

I had many options: I could have taken up a job at a fashion consulting firm, adopted formal responsibilities in my family's business, accepted my offer letter from Parsons School of Design (NYC), or even decided to stay at home to pursue nonprofessional leisure activities (something many of my female friends had decided to do). But I am very happy that I became an entrepreneur and had the courage to pursue building a start-up.

I remember pitching my family close to twenty business ideas before they agreed to funding Whitenife. They had wanted me to identify a low-risk, low-investment opportunity with high returns (don't we all?). Although I found this period of my life rather unsettling, in retrospect, it allowed me to refine my business goals and problem-solving skills and develop the ability to conceive innovative and efficient business models.

JOINING MY FAMILY BUSINESS (FINALLY) WHILE RUNNING MY OWN VENTURE

Today, while my family has accepted my calling and made it possible for Whitenife, my own venture, to exist, and celebrates with me as Whitenife accomplishes notable milestones, I have also taken up formal and demanding responsibilities as president of marketing and communications at Donear Industries Ltd. in order to contribute to the family business's growth and learn from the business challenges facing larger entities.

Within a few months of taking up these responsibilities, I have been able to consolidate and structure Donear's brand architecture and define a clear positioning and communication for each brand. I am happy to contribute to my family's business while pursuing my own and to know that my contribution has a sizeable influence.

MAKING SPACE AND LOOKING AHEAD

There are still very few women entrepreneurs who serve as good examples in the Indian community, and I wish to be one. It is arguably much harder for women to rise to important, high-level roles in the corporate world in India than it is for men. Even significant discussion panels in India often have no women on them. I wish to be an inspiring example for young women in South Asia and worldwide who wish to pursue their entrepreneurial dreams.

I see a promising future for Whitenife and work toward it each day. Within just a year of founding the company, I have been honored with the opportunity to design the crown for Miss World Australia, have secured shelf space in luxury retail locations, and have secured national award-winning artisans to work for Whitenife. I have licensed my brand in Australia to two very enterprising individuals and have business development associates working to establish us in Dubai.

Whitenife started out being nothing but a big dream, but today it has taken small, necessary steps to carve out its niche. It is truly rewarding to know that my efforts toward growing Whitenife are helping to raise awareness about and sensitivity toward animals poached for fashion. I envision Whitenife allowing its supporters to express their concern over animal poaching and share their love for design and craftsmanship, all with taste and true elegance.

A perfectly imperfect takeaway about Sonia:

Sonia is a wonderful example of a young businesswoman who has used her compassion to create ventures that will make a positive difference in the world and in her family. She has not compromised her dreams or the beautiful vision she has for Whitenife. Inspired, she spearheads her own efforts to be the change she wants to see, as Gandhi would say.

Epilogue

Success Patterns Seen and Concluding Advice

In life, school, or work, you must resourcefully act with purpose,
curiosity, and wisdom toward positive outcomes, if not a vision.
Passionately develop a positive and pragmatic psychology; a fine
skill set; strategic thinking; and execution effectiveness. Continuously
practice, strengthen, and expand this repertoire in you. Doing so will
help you go a long way.

—Jason L. Ma

Congratulations on nearly completing your journey through *Young Leaders 3.0: Stories, Insights, and Tips for Next-Generation Achievers!* I hope that you have enjoyed the learning adventure and found the contributors' stories and perspectives meaningful and helpful. You may not have read each chapter, and as I said in the beginning, that's OK! But it is interesting to note that there are threads of commonality among high achievers, so I would like to take some time to explore with you some of the success patterns that can be drawn from their examples and to provide some additional advice as well.

I would encourage you to go back and reread favorite chapters or other parts of the book to your heart's content. Purposeful repetition is key to successful learning and skill building. I myself read and listen to three to four books or audiobooks per month on average and exercise this habit consistently.

SUCCESS PATTERNS SEEN

Family support

Loving parents and close families help shape the values and some core skills of teens and young adults. Cherish family support if you have it. Oftentimes parents mean well but sometimes don't come across that way because of a generation gap or mistaken assumptions on both sides about beliefs or values, which leads to misunderstanding. Bridge miscommunications by talking to parents, hearing their stories, and learning how they've shaped yours. Family-oriented faith, trust, and alliance are important. Embrace high expectations from "demanding" parents if what they are demanding is your positive growth and learning.

Make the most of your circumstances and optimize your abilities to the best of your potential. If you find yourself in a dysfunctional situation with parents or immediate family, seek a positive external support system (grandparents, teachers, mentors, family friends). If you don't have a father, seek out father figures; if your mother is out of the picture, seek mother figures. Try to make the most of underprivileged circumstances to learn to become resourceful and independent early on.

High school life

Start early (hopefully, even before high school) with focus and passion. The more you learn and contribute early on, the more you will learn and accomplish later—this is what I often refer to as the "positive stacking effect." The earlier you find quality mentors, the quicker you can learn, grow, and succeed.

Participate in purposeful activities that you love or at least genuinely like. Your corresponding accomplishments, the relationships you build, and the know-how you gain will influence who you are and what you choose to do in the future. Decide what you want, ask questions, and power through obstacles. Challenge yourself, prioritize, and find ways to be exceptional. Establish your own club based on genuine interests. Contribute to your local community as well as school organizations. Work hard but take reenergizing breaks. Spark your fire. Be human. Learn to speak and listen well; these skills can move people and organizations, and can also help you make friends. Learn to write well (especially essays!).

Be relentless in your pursuit of knowledge and the truth. Set a high bar for yourself and use that bar as a springboard to leave your own legacy. Find a path you like and leave a trail for the next generation to follow. Despite tragedies or hardships, find resolve in the genuine quest for excellence, convert problems to opportunities, and gain fulfillment by helping others, creating smiles, and delivering happiness.

Reading books other than textbooks can make you a more intriguing and magnetic person. Reading is fundamental! Take your classes seriously even during senior year so you will be prepared for the rigor of the college curriculum; you can't coast through college.

Procrastinate (much) less. Focus on priorities. Reduce the wasted time and opportunity costs that accompany an addiction to video games. To hone your computer science skills, program games instead of playing them. Learn to recognize unimportant opportunities and say no to them, making time instead for what's truly important. Manage time well, but don't just focus on the requirements; explore outside your comfort zone as well. Learn to study efficiently, thereby decreasing net time spent studying and increasing time for socializing.

Don't overcommit your time to a romantic relationship in high school, especially if you see it taking away a lot of your time and energy, bringing you down at times, and disrupting your balance and more important priorities that affect your future. Form quality relationships with people who will support your passions and goals, and evaluate if you want to devote your time and energies to people who will hold you back.

Surround yourself with a strong community, especially doers and people smarter or more accomplished than you, and learn from their best qualities. Don't be afraid to reach high and fail, because one day you will reach high and make it. Being the dumbest person in the room is a surefire way to accelerate learning. Get out more.

Spend the bulk of the last two summers before graduation constructively. Go for established summer internships or programs but don't be afraid to create unconventional activities. While contributing in internships, you can learn a great deal about yourself. Embrace diverse cultures.

On failure: One strengthens character by learning more from mistakes than successes (but fail fast and learn quickly). If you can turn each "failure" into opportunity, you'll do amazing things. Try something different, give it 100 percent dedication, and don't fear failure. Every time you work hard and fail, you will be another step closer to success. Failure can provide inspiration and strength.

On success: Be relentless and resourceful. Success may be traditionally measured by the quality of academic standing, extracurricular activity, and college admissions, but true success encompasses genuine personal fulfillment and direction. Compare yourself to yourself and your yet-to-be-realized capabilities, not to others; don't hinder your own growth. If a future career track (doctor, lawyer, etc.) pleases only parents and not you, say no early. Avoid the trap of résumé building. Embrace your inner goofball, if you have one.

College admissions

Start college planning early in high school, visit colleges before your senior year, and start the college applications process in your junior year. A common mistake many people make is that they (vastly) underestimate the total *elapsed* time and focused effort necessary to plan, research, execute, and produce realistically competitive and strong applications to upper-tier colleges. Building a genuinely interesting story and likable character takes years, not months. Don't procrastinate, and never submit applications late.

Regarding the college application process, the next three paragraphs are excerpted from my own daughter Sabrina's chapter and provide words of wisdom.

Sabrina says, "In your essays, explaining *why* something is important to you is often more important than *what* you actually did and *how* you did it because the "why" reveals more about your values, beliefs, character, or motivations. Write reflectively about what matters to you. Allocate lots of time for brainstorming, drafting, and revising dozens of long and short personal essays (plus short-takes), and your résumé. Without devoting sufficient time to these tasks, your essays will not be of high quality and you will regret it. Ask for input from friends, teachers, mentors, and parents (but remember to keep your authentic 'voice' intact)! You will learn a lot about yourself and maybe even improve your reflective thinking and writing skills with this feedback.

Budget numerous additional hours for the following purposes: Research colleges; prepare for the SAT or ACT with Writing and SAT Subject Tests ("SAT IIs"), if these are not yet done by junior year; work with teachers, your school counselor, and any other non-school recommenders; attend college-related events; prepare for interviews; and take care of whatever else may be necessary to ensure you are submitting high-quality applications on time—on top of your busy schoolwork and extracurricular activities.

Try not to take rejections personally. Acceptances or rejections—in regards to college admissions and life as a whole—should not and do not define you or your self-worth. Just try your absolute best and be yourself. If colleges can't see how awesome you are, they don't deserve you anyway."

NOTE: While it's very easy to find other people's college application essays, and there are many examples even in this book, you must avoid any temptation to plagiarize or even paraphrase, or you may find yourself in a very awkward situation and face college rejections, if not blacklisting.

Get to know the schools that you applied to and that have admitted you by visiting them, talking with people there, asking questions, and assessing the degree of a mutual fit. A good fit encompasses school culture, academics, social dynamics, extracurricular opportunities, internship/job opportunities, geography, financial aid, and any other criteria profoundly important to you. Choose the school based on true fit, not on just brand name.

College life

Frankly, most of the success habits that were key in high school still apply in college, so there's no need to repeat them in this section. What defines a successful time in in college, however, is commonly judged in terms of your summer internships and ultimately the job you undertake post-college.

Be careful in choosing your classes . . . or you'll be stuck in sucky classes! Through conversations with friends, your own research, and an understanding of the teaching and learning styles that work for you, select the classes that suit you best. If you are interested in a particular field in which you don't have any connections, do not be afraid to reach out. Research the people in that field before approaching them and make sure you ask intelligent questions that will help you decide if you want to pursue further study.

Non-academic pursuits in college can be just as important or even more important than classes and grades. College grades matter less than high school grades (except when applying to highly competitive graduate and medical schools). Don't try to plan your entire college career in advance, because some of the most pivotal moments can be completely unexpected. Be sure to do something you like outside of class, but don't spread yourself too thin. Travel far and wide. Studying, living, or working abroad can immensely widen your perspective of the world. Keep your focus on the big picture. Learn soft skills (people skills) as well as hard skills (technical skills).

Socializing and collaborating sincerely can enrich and reward you more than comparing and competing obsessively. Connect, share, listen, discuss, learn, and work together open-mindedly with purpose and some humility. Conversing and interacting with peers can influence your career direction. Get to know professors, who can become mentors and friends. Build relationships and leverage them when needed. Knowing someone within a target company may dramatically increase your chances of getting an interview for an internship or a job. Express your gratitude to the people who have guided, supported, or encouraged you.

For international students applying for certain jobs in the United States: because your employer needs to authorize and apply for a work visa for you, you may need to take some classes in the field you want to pursue if it lies outside what you are studying as your major.

In order to have a healthy mind, you need a healthy body (and vice versa). Find quiet time by yourself to prioritize, reflect, reorganize, and plan. In college it is very easy to get caught up in exams and extracurriculars. But it is important to stop every now and then, to just clear your mind of the stresses you have and think about the bigger picture. Ask yourself purposeful questions about your goals. Talking to others is important as well. In order to cope with the stresses of college life, you have to have a support system. Some of the best moments among college friends arise when people genuinely share their thoughts, without actively trying to impress each other.

While it is perfectly normal to shift focus (and change majors) in college to account for newfound interests, even graduate students can venture into uncharted territory. Students can sometimes achieve a sharper focus of academic interests and career goals while discovering postgraduate options.

Internships, jobs, and careers

Creating a "storyline" of your interests and how they are linked together can be a great tool when writing out job applications in college. Demonstrate your knowledge of how you fit into the role you're seeking. Be prepared for a rigorous job application process: spending hours preparing for interviews, going through several rounds of interviews, and remaining calm under pressure were what helped someone land a coveted consulting job.

In some fields, employers value practical experience much more than graduate education, so if it comes down to choosing between graduate school and an entry-level job, weigh your decision carefully.

Determination and passion are the drivers of great entrepreneurs, politicians, and leaders. An A+ combination of head, heart, spirit, and network can make you a beloved and creative leader and entrepreneur running a well-backed and inspired company and team. An entrepreneur's life is thrilling but very demanding. If you are of an entrepreneurial spirit, you need that little extra bit of gumption to succeed. Remember to keep your support system strong: you can have a thriving career and still maintain strong family ties.

Not every hobby or passion has the ability to turn into a professional career. Think deeply about how you feel when doing what you love and how it aligns with your goals and aspirations. Ask yourself: Will I be able to achieve my vision for the future if I continue on this path? What sacrifices will I need to make to achieve my dream? When you take a deep look into your goals, make sure they align with your values, and act according to your inner compass.

CONCLUDING ADVICE

A core piece of wisdom I want to impart to teenagers and young adults is this: In life, school, or work, you must resourcefully act with purpose, curiosity, and wisdom toward positive outcomes, if not a vision. Passionately develop a positive and pragmatic psychology; a fine skill set; strategic thinking; and execution effectiveness. Continuously practice, strengthen, and expand this repertoire in you. Doing so will help you go a long way. You will become even more successful, more effective in powering through obstacles, fear, and failures, and more fulfilled in life, school, or work.

Managing failures and mistakes made—including bouncing back from miscalculations, learning quickly, and moving on is much easier with a strong mind-set to begin with. Failures often help make emotionally healthy people even better and stronger. With a strong mind, you may even make a breakthrough after a crisis or failure. You can learn to condition your mind and body and enhance your EQ. I will explain why and how in this section.

But first, here is an analogy that helps distill and define above components, given that your generation is far more technically astute in our increasingly interconnected, sophisticated, and inundated digital age:

- Your **pragmatic psychology** in your brain and nervous system is equivalent to an operating system (OS), such as iOS or Android. I am sure you want a quality OS and see it periodically upgraded and increasingly become more powerful and useful.
- Your **skill set** is equivalent to the useful apps that you can use on your devices. Likewise, I am certain you want your apps to be frequently updated, including bug fixes, reliability improvements, and feature enhancements—and that you add apps as needed or desired.
- Your **strategic thinking** is equivalent to the intelligence in your OS and apps (working together) that define the outcomes or results you want to achieve, the compelling (emotional and logical) reasons the achievements will be important to you, and the consistent methods you employ to get there. This intelligence encompasses what, why,

for whom, with whom, when, where, and how you use your apps (skills) and other resources. It is wise to craft and execute a strategy for any given type of vision or outcome you want to achieve.

- Your **execution** is equivalent to your entire "system" actively working to purposefully, resourcefully, and effectively get things done, preferably with high signal-to-noise ratio. If your execution is poor, nothing matters. A combination of strong, positive, and pragmatic psychology, skill set, strategy, and execution may just make you hard to beat!

The commonly touted 80-20 rule in business states that roughly 80 percent of effects (outcomes) result from 20 percent of the causes. I prefer to think of it in the sense that about 80 percent of our results can come from 20 percent of our activities. I also believe that people should focus 80 percent of their time on (thinking about, planning, and implementing) the solution and not on (bickering and complaining endlessly about the people or the issues around) the problem, and that success stems from roughly 80 percent psychology and 20 percent mechanics.

That being said, I coach my own mentees to focus their time and energy on the causes (for example, replacing a limiting belief with an empowering one or sharpening practical relationship building and oratory skills), not on the effects (for example, spending time and energy worrying or feeling sorry for yourself or being consumed with negative self-talk about not getting a desired role at a target organization). In addition to nourishing their mind and spirit, I teach them on how to fish and fly better so they can soar, adding to their arsenal of confidence-enhancing achievements and skills. With sound causes, positive effects will typically take care of themselves. It's wise to track both causes and effects. Doing so will help you learn valuable patterns of success that can be reapplied over and over again.

Planning, organizing, and executing based on (strategic) priorities are key to success, and your priorities should stem from your positive values, not on habitual superficial gratification or pain avoidance (for example, spending lots of time aimlessly surfing the Internet). Most people unfortunately tend to act first and think later, which is the opposite of how it should be. Saying yes is easy and saying no may be hard but will make you a lot more successful over time.

To me, time is the most precious resource in life. Even billionaires share with us mortals exactly this same resource and cannot buy more than 168 hours per week and 24 hours per day of their own time. I attempt to conscientiously use time well weekly and daily, and am always learning to enhance my own skills of time management and resource allocation. So should you. Without a positive and strong mind, time and energy will be wasted, and rarely anything will work well. (Among the plethora of productivity-enhancement and time-management tools and programs I have come across, I think Tony Robbins's Rapid Planning Method (RPM) is by far the best and most effective.)

Most successful people tend to start with the end in mind. They are clear on what outcomes or results they want and why achieving them is important. If they weren't clear yet, they would work toward developing clarity of goals because clarity is a must. Unclear or unnecessary complexity is an enemy to accomplishment. Winners apply and align both EQ and logic with *purpose*. Their empowering and positive beliefs and emotions radiate within themselves and onto others. They are purposefully and persistently action-oriented because without astute and effective execution, nothing matters.

Strong leaders, especially successful and creative entrepreneurs, also have a compelling *vision*. I believe that a great way to predict the future is to create it (in my case, a vision of the future in which writing and publishing this book has positive and helpful effects on you and the society as a whole!). True leaders teenage to middle-age—are committed and act in ways that take into consideration purposeful outcomes or a vision, with focus, passion, and resilience. They develop and then follow a clear road map to get from where they are to where they desire to be.

What does pragmatic psychology mean to you, specifically?

Allow me to expand a bit on what I mean when I talk about pragmatic psychology, if it hasn't yet begun to crystallize for you. Your psychology comprises (1) your belief system, which projects your character and narrative about yourself and is the glue between your mind and soul, and (2) your range of states of mind, which is your set of emotions and facets of your personality.

Your beliefs comprise essentially general rules and principles and if-then statements in your brain. Your core values are the strongest beliefs and desired emotional outcomes in your belief system. Beliefs can be changed, but only if processed through the subconscious mind, which has accumulated vast experiences in life and is subtly more powerful than the conscious mind.

At any given moment, what you mentally focus on derives from both your beliefs and your self-talk (aka your inner voice) and, if you are presently with people, the language you use to communicate with others. Your mental focus and your physiology together instantly put you into a particular state or emotion. Physiology absolutely matters. Exercising, or better yet, implementing a complete fitness program (in other words a regimen that safely works both your cardio and muscles—even yoga!) increases the effective use of oxygen and gets rid of waste throughout your brain and body, and helps soothe your soul.

Emotional states of mind, which range from the worst (a suicidal state) to the best (a peak or flow state), are powerful. Your state drives actions, decisions, and even indecision, and is the direct predictor of results somewhere between the lowest to highest in quality. Your results subsequently affect your beliefs, and at times, even change those beliefs, if not your own story in your head.

The lesson here, if not a critical success factor, is to consciously and continuously strengthen the *quality* of your belief system, inner voice, and physiology, empowering your mind and body and stretching their thresholds and tolerance for obstacles and making way for creative thoughts. Doing so means you will spend and enjoy a lot more time in productive and positive states, and increasingly more time in high-performance or flow states, producing more positive outcomes. The best state is a peak or flow state. Have you noticed how easy it is for champion athletes and other incredibly accomplished individuals to trigger themselves into peak performance states? Imagine how satisfying it will be for you to spend the bulk of your time in positive and highly productive and flow states!

Some more tips on how to build a positive and pragmatic psychology

The good news is that you neither need to be perfect nor become a saint! In most cases, aim for high quality but avoid the trap of absolute perfectionism that is unnecessary and consumes much more time and energy than called for; use your best judgment. (Notable exceptions to whether perfectionism is called for would be rare events such as brain or heart surgery, which would necessitate well-timed, perfect precision in execution.)

Grow by purposefully contributing, connecting, and learning, with doses of compassion. Give your time and add real value in good causes. Communicate empathetically and clearly, and keep learning to do so. Inspire others. You will very likely end up getting more by giving. Over time, your good deeds will translate subconsciously to solid success habits. Keep at it, and you will find your identity and confidence enhanced. Without contribution and growth, you will not be fulfilled. Without fulfillment, you may not feel truly successful.

Your biggest competitor should only ever be yourself. Avoid the trap of comparing yourself with others. Measure your success only against what you are capable of achieving. If you are in college, the college you attend does not define you; it is what you make of it. Nothing beats hard work with focus and passion. Stretch yourself. Be resourceful, creative, and open-minded in all sorts of situations. Plan ahead and act with purpose, but allow room to explore, experiment, and discover. Be multifaceted. Build your emotional and mental muscles in tenacity, resilience, and perseverance. Don't be surprised if a breakthrough emerges from a well-managed crisis. Don't be afraid to be an influential and innovative change-maker. Don't accept the status quo if you know things must be improved and you have the power to change it.

To me, learning is adventurous and enjoyable and must be never-ending. Be intellectually curious always. Learn by osmosis. Learn by doing as well as by studying, by yourself and with other people. Learn how to learn. Ask intelligent questions. Your thoughts are essentially internal conversations or a series of questions and answers by your inner voice. How can you ask good questions and be able to come up with sound answers if you haven't learned? Leaders are readers and listeners. Read good books, especially nonfiction ones to help nourish your mind, heart, and soul. Listening to audiobooks (which is a huge growing trend) is often just as effective as reading ebooks and print books, and is incredibly convenient (it can be done while driving, walking, or making coffee). Many of the most effective people learned to become world-class learners.

Apply the power of proximity. Find role models. Befriend and learn from mentors. Make friends with people smarter than you and more successful in fields you are interested in. Build not just networks but genuine relationships; when you collaborate with these key people, you can lean on them when a need arises. Break away from consistent groupthink. Talk with and learn from people different from you. Be open to dialogue with acquaintances and even select strangers, as you may uncover interesting opportunities.

Make sure that you are connecting with good people and for the right reasons—not wasting a disproportionately huge amount of time by yourself or with your so-called buddies on lost causes, aimlessness, or addictive habits of the wrong kind like video games or watching brain-dead stuff on the Internet and TV. Going down that path only results in opportunity costs, and it malnourishes your neurons, which then end up making poor synaptic connections in your brain, leaving you numb. A little bit of gaming, occasional web surfing, and TV is fine, but not too often.

Lack of integrity and laziness are your enemies—at home, in school, in your community, and at work. Avoid these enemies at all costs, and permit yourself to destroy them. Rest assured that reputable colleges, universities, and employers can detect, and rightly despise, cheating and laziness, which are reflective of poor character. Focus instead on sound values and hard work. These will both pay off for you in the end.

Smile genuinely, everywhere, or learn to do so; this radiates outward and affects people positively!

If you want to be an entrepreneur, then please heed this advice: Entrepreneurship is hard. In no particular order, you need to

- attract and work with only A-game players who share your vision, values, mission, goals, and chemistry but with complementary skills and know-how for the core team (absolutely the founders)
- make certain to climb the ladder on the appropriate wall as you're starting out—that is, identifying and targeting the right growing market
- add lots of value to your clients/customers through your product and services
- differentiate clearly what you do in comparison to your competitors, all the while remembering whom you and your team serve
- keep innovating

Furthermore, if you are entrepreneurial, you need to craft and implement a strong marketing and distribution strategy, be a good storyteller, build good relationships internally and externally with key ecosystem constituents, take calculated risks, be quickly adaptable and flexible, communicate humbly but firmly, recruit all the time, implement sound business processes, and execute-execute-execute pragmatically within your ecosystem with purpose! If not, success will be just a pipe dream or fleeting experience, as building a start-up successfully is quite difficult. And great ideas don't just come to you. You must pursue them.

Regardless of what your vision for the future is, find ways to keep strengthening your pragmatic combination of mind-set, skill set, direction, strategies, know-how, and execution! If the featured young leaders in this book have achieved successes from their purposeful strategies and actions, as well as trials and tribulations, so can you. Apply at least some of what you have learned in this book. Be outcome-focused, purpose-driven, and action-oriented. Your resolve truly tests who you are and who you want to be!

Finally, my own professional core values, which are similar to my personal core values, are as follows. I challenge you to think through and write out your own!

- Contribute profoundly to my clients toward a vision
- Build trusting and genuine working relationships
- Be passionate, creative, and open-minded always

- Inspire and empower my mentees/students, clients, and teammates
- Learn and grow continuously, and innovate often
- Execute pragmatically and with integrity
- Have some fun and don't hold back on humor

What is next for Young Leaders 3.0?

My mission forward is to enhance and perhaps even transform the minds of teenagers and young adults and to influence parents and business executives around the world. My vision includes an exciting world in which a dynamic global network of my mentees, students, and book readers will shine as value-added, good-hearted leaders and citizens of the world.

Related to the *Young Leaders 3.0* theme, I plan to conduct purposeful seminars and conferences tailored to high schoolers, college and university students, young adults just recently launched into the world, parents, and business executives in phases. I will also be actively contributing and hopefully inspiring on the speaking circuit. In addition, I may consider planning and offering new, value-added programs and services both at home and abroad. I hope that along the way, one or more of these events, programs, or services will add significant value to you and your family, friends, and peers.

Please visit www.YoungLeaders3.com, the book's website, or www. JasonLMa.com, my personal website, to view events, news, and additional resources, or subscribe to my simple, occasional newsletter from either of these websites. You are also welcome to submit your success stories and any great ideas via either of my websites.

My *Forbes* site, www.forbes.com/sites/jasonma/, where the theme is Mentoring Young Leaders, may also be helpful to you. As a *Forbes* contributor, I write about preparing for elite college/university admissions and a lifetime of leadership, including entrepreneurship.

I believe that the secret to success is within your grasp. May your personal and/or professional journey moving forward be (even more) exciting and meaningful!

Cheers and Godspeed,

JASON L. MA
Author and Founder
YOUNG LEADERS 3.0
www.YoungLeaders3.com

Acknowledgments

I am very grateful and blessed that so many wonderful friends and supporters have helped me realize and sharpen the vision of this book project. I want to thank wholeheartedly each one of them. This book project is not only deeply meaningful and fulfilling but also highly interdependent and complex. It is like building a company, in addition to authoring.

Now that the book is published, I somewhat miss working closely with my team on putting together all the chapters with shared focus and passion. It was during that period of late nights and days at my home office, at hotel rooms (very productive with only me, myself, and I) during my business travels worldwide, at cafés (I enjoy the cappuccinos, though often with earplugs on), and at libraries when I felt like I had virtually entered the temples of the minds and souls of these wonderful twenty-three individual contributors and young leaders. It is an interesting state of mind, similar to when I am deeply guiding and taking care of my mentees/students . . . and losing myself a little during the process.

The team time put into this book project was a few thousand hours (mostly yours truly's!)—from the book project's inception in 2012 to publication more than two years later—encompassing my research, planning, and brainstorming process; decision-making on the book content and publishing whats, whys, and hows; building a high-quality team of dozens, including support cast; orchestrating the team and relevant ecosystem constituents; working with, coaching, and guiding teammates; brainstorming again, reflecting, and asking for help; writing and rewriting individually and together; driving the publishing process; working and getting things done with my team and external supporters and partners; and finally launching the book and moving toward my longer-term vision of a world to be increasingly led by next-generation leaders and achievers.

That said, first and foremost, words cannot describe my love and gratitude for my parents, who retired as blue-collar workers. My dad, now 90, was a custodian and my mom, now 82, was a seamstress. From the Guangdong Province in China, my dad had nearly zilch education and my mom only finished her middle-school education in her early twenties, around the time of the Cultural Revolution. There was a little bit of "Tiger Mom" in her, and though my dad did not have the faculty to teach me anything, their incredible work ethic taught me a lot.

To my late third uncle—Without you, we would not be here in the United States. My mom looked up to you as a father figure since she was little. I thank you most deeply for your constant and incredible kindness, generosity, and positivity.

My better half. Hon, I deeply appreciate you for supporting your visionary, entrepreneurial, and nutty hubby through the years. And sweetie, the older we get as middle-aged "senior youth," the more I realize that I am in love with you. Our greatest gift and my greatest joy are our daughters.

And Lydia, I love you MTTBNITWWUAMTT, multiplied by infinity. I am so proud of you, my feisty li'l one! Thanks for being such a sensitive and visually sharp confidante and sounding board for yo' dada. I totally treasure your advice.

Sabrina, you feel next to me though you're 3,000 miles away wreaking havoc in DC. Flatten the Hilltop (as a sport) for me, would ya?! Kidding aside, as Big Girl of the "MAfia," you will go places . . . My friends all love your killer chapter in this book!

To my twenty-three awesome contributors (in alphabetical order by first name)—Angela Wang, Christopher Pruijsen, Danny Levy, Enrico Bonatti, Erica Ma, Felipe da Paz, Jeremy Fiance, Ivy Xing, Kemaya Kidwai, Kimberly Han, Leila Pirbay, Max Song, Ngan Pham, Patrick Ip, Ryan Mango, Sabrina Ma, Sally Zhang, Shreya Indukuri, Sonia Agarwal, Sophie Mann, Tim Hwang, Timothy Lee, and Youyang Gu—I cannot thank you enough for giving and sharing your stories, successes, failures, lessons learned, and considered advice through your chapters. Great work! Your futures are so bright; I need to wear shades! I would also dearly like to thank your parents, siblings, and friends who have helped and supported you through this profound, challenging, and adventurous book creation and publication journey.

To my copyeditor, thank you for an outstanding job editing my monster-size manuscript. (Because of a surge in popularity, my copyeditor has to turn down many more projects than she can take and needs to scale back on how often she is name-checked. How's that for preferring to remain anonymous?!) Also a nice thanks to content editors Lisa Pedersen, Leila Pirbay, and Daniel Chung, as well as contributor Youyang Gu for volunteering to edit a few rough chapter drafts in their early forms. Nothing beats authenticity. Fine work, all!

My eyes have enjoyed feasting on the stunning work by front and back cover designer, website designer, and graphics extraordinaire Irving Torres. I am so happy to have brought on board Stephanie Zhou as my passionate online happiness specialist, Howard VanEs as my publication support guru, and his Let's Write Books, Inc., as my interior designer. And a very special thank-you to my support staff, ambassadors, and volunteers for helping behind the scenes!

This book project would not have whipped itself into such a quality and voicy shape without the collective fervent suggestions, support, and encouragement from my friends (and mostly fellow parents) Guy Kawasaki, Don Levy, Paul Bradley, Tony Palmucci, Martin Roll, Dr. Tan Chin Nam, Clark Kepler, Dr. Rod Berger, Rick Giarrusso, Prof. Lou Marinoff, Derrick Sweet, and Cynthia Maxey—thank you so much. To Steve Piersanti, thank you for helping me deepen my understanding of the book business. Timely words of wisdom from fellow seasoned gray-haired folks really helped.

More young leaders to thank! To Sachin Sadana, Jiaze Li, Christopher Lau, Steeve Simbert, Carolyn Yang, Marissa Teitelman, Ravi Patel, Lexi Antunez, Krish Ramineni, Emily Hsia, Aritro Mukherjee, Kongping Han, Tony Ho, Zach Hamed, Madison Maxey, Kevin Wang, John Meyer, Celia Wong, Ian Alas, Greg Nance, Jennifer Chen, Brandon Liu, Rebecca Hu, Matt Bilotti, Nikhil Desai, Heather Chu, Sanjay Rajpoot, Justin Pinn, Ali Hamed, Thaddeus Talbot, Alex He, Morgan Beller, Will Poff-Webster, Tara Raghuveer, David Neustadt, Chris Ling, Crystal Lee, Harshil Goel, Michael Medved, Carl Shan, Daniel Li, Victoria Huang, and Tiffany Zhou. I thank you for your creative, networking, or otherwise high-EQ support and encouragement. Stay awesome!

To the folks at Forbes; the insanely awesome K50s, Fellows, and champions at Kairos Society, including Alex Fiance, Vince Fong, Karolina Stawinska, Daniel Gross, Jonathan Ofir, Sarah Tulin, and many others; the folks at Silicon Valley Education Foundation (SVEF), including Muhammed Chaudhry and Connie Skipitares; and Cathy Meng, Tony Li, Sumit and Smita Sadana, Catherine Shen, Henry Wong, Paul Rogers, Lani Yap, Narayana Murthy, Paul Tagliabue, Elizabeth Jordan, Ambassador Melanne Verveer, Mary Poland, Charles Skuba, Patricia Grant, Celia Ly, Heidi Roizen, Jonathan Rosenberg, Peter Liu, Andrew Ishibashi, Grettel Castro-Stanley, Dipty and Sohag Desai, Rebecca Cheuk, Naina Kidwai, Beth Fiance, Raju Indukuri, Drs. Frank and Nadja Richter, Steve Sargent, Richard Goyder, Robert Milliner, Ivan Cook, Wilfred Wong, Deborah Biber, Tan Sri Michael Yeoh, Ng Yeen Seen, Janet How, John Riady, Stephanie Riady, Sachin Gopalan, Lin Neumann, Patrick Daniel, Ryan O'Connor,

Abbe Wright, Anurag Chandra, Garth Robertson, and Raj Dey—thank you for your kind (past) support, ideas, or encouragement.

And to Vikrom Kromadit, Tan Sri Dato' Lee Shin Cheng, Goh Peng Ooi, Dr. William F. Miller, Eric Yuan, Jim Miller, Richard Dasher, Leslie Yuen, Curtis Mo, Stephanie Xu, Victor Wang, Scott Humphrey, Jordanne Brenkwitz, Kerri Ramgren, Abhishek Sharma, Raj Abhyanker, Dalia van den Boogaard, Stan Newsome, Harumi Supit, Hon Mun Yip, Praveen Raju, Amit Chatterjee, Kyoungmoo Kwon, Guy Sivan, Chris Boehner, Nicki Fung. Angela Sun, David McCauley, David Wang, Bruce Hammond, Travis Coverdell, Ted Corbould, Dr. William Wan, Sarah Lam, Raj Kumar, Myk Rambus, Tara Loader Wilkinson, Lee George Lam, Oliver Weisberg, David Berger, Derek Lau, Robyn Meredith, Philip Leung, Cheuk Fei Man, Steve Tight, Catherine Shiang, Victor Ngo, Kwing Ng, Norris Lam, Phil Anderson, Virginia Cha, Suguna Madhavan, Mike Barclay, Rajiv Kochhar, Finian Tan, Kuo-Yi Lim, Prof. Shoucheng Zhang, Ben Ng, Bill Li, Hong Chen, Hanson Li, Min Guo, Alfred Chuang, Michael Moe, Kayvan Baroumand, Li Jiang, Michael Horn, Tony Perkins, Robert Levin, Prof. Stanley Kwong, Prof. Xiaohua Yang, Bruce Pickering, Judy Crawford, Raul Villacis, James Hahn, Kai Chen, Dr. William Moore, Herb Chi, Bob Lin, Qiming Huang, Rajesh Setty, Chuck Ng, Ken Singer, Mitch Gordon, Shirish Patel, Sonja Markova, Blake Masters, Danielle Strachman, Nick Arnett, Terry Abad, Cameron Teitelman, Alexa Lee, Dave Wong, Travis Darrow, Rebecca Fannin, Roy Ng, Eric Gonzales, Sheridan Tatsuno, Mark Minevich, and John Stringfellow, thank you for your gracious (past) support, ideas, or encouragement.

Last but absolutely not least, I am deeply grateful to have learned personally from or via the programs or books by masters Tony Robbins, Rabbi Daniel Lapin, Jay Abraham, Keith Ferrazzi, Tony Hsieh, Brian Tracy, Stephen Covey, Tom Peters, and others. Your teachings are profoundly helpful and life-changing.

And finally, I am deeply grateful that God has blessed me with a higher purpose. It is my highest honor and privilege to serve Him.

If I have left out anyone well deserving of acknowledgment for your kind support, please forgive me for my oversight and e-mail me at JMa@YoungLeaders3.com and we'll get it fixed in reprint or ebook update.

About the Contributors

A short biography of each of the contributors is located in the beginning of his or her chapter. You can also learn more about the contributors at the *Young Leaders 3.0* website, www.YoungLeaders3.com. Please feel free to contact us via this website and we can facilitate the communication.

Photo credit: Erin Ashford

About the Author

Jason L. Ma is author and founder of *Young Leaders* 3.0 and serves as founder, CEO, and chief mentor at ThreeEQ, a premier private mentoring program and global business consulting firm. An international speaker, he addresses CEO summits and business and education events worldwide. Jason is a *Forbes* contributor, APEC CEO Summit delegate, Kairos Society mentor, Thiel Fellowship mentor, B20 Human Capital Taskforce member, Pacific Basin Economic Council member, and Anthony Robbins Platinum Partner. He has also been a Forbes Global CEO Conference delegate for eight years. He holds a BS degree in Industrial Engineering and Operations Research from UC Berkeley College of Engineering and attended graduate school at Santa Clara University Leavey School of Business.

Jason's commitment to contributing to his clients, communities, and book audience is surpassed only by his love for family as a father of two vivacious teenage daughters and husband to his kind and lovely wife. In his leisure, he enjoys celebrating with family and friends, reading, listening to audiobooks, diving into great food, tasting fine wine, staying fit, watching good films and musicals, vacationing with family in exotic places, and blasting hip hop with his teenage kids while driving on Saturday nights!

You can reach or learn more about Jason at:
- Website: www.JasonLMa.com
- Facebook: www.facebook.com/JasonLMa
- Google+: plus.google.com/+JasonLMa
- Twitter: www.twitter.com/JasonLMa

Resource List
for *Young Leaders 3.0*

- **Website for this book:**
  http://www.youngleaders3.com
- **Follow *Young Leaders 3.0* on social media:**
  Facebook: https://www.facebook.com/YLeaders3
  Twitter: https://twitter.com/YLeaders3
  Google+: https://plus.google.com/+YLeaders3
- **Follow author Jason L. Ma on social media:**
  Facebook: https://www.facebook.com/JasonLMa
  Twitter: https://twitter.com/JasonLMa
  Google+: https://plus.google.com/+JasonLMa
- **Newsletter, events, offers, additional stories, and other goodies:**
  http://www.youngleaders3.com
- **Press kit:**
  http://www.youngleaders3.com/#press
- **Internship and job opportunities:**
  http://www.youngleaders3.com/#internships
- **Book Jason L. Ma to speak:**
  http://www.jasonlma.com/#speaking
- **Jason L. Ma's premier private mentoring and global business consulting firm, ThreeEQ:**
  http://threeeq.com
- **Contact us:**
  http://www.youngleaders3.com/#contact
  Email: author@youngleaders3.com
  Snail mail: Mr. Jason L. Ma
  Young Leaders 3.0
  555 Bryant Street #330
  Palo Alto, California 94301, USA

Valuable Information for Readers of *Young Leaders 3.0*

Get exclusive tips, tricks, and resources to up your game as a leader or supporter. Whether you are a high school student, a university student, a young professional, a young entrepreneur, a parent, an educator, or a senior executive, stay up-to-date on our upcoming events, special offers, additional stories, and other goodies by signing up for our newsletter at http://www.youngleaders3.com.

Made in the USA
Las Vegas, NV
29 July 2021